Books by Mortimer J. Adler

THE CONDITIONS
OF PHILOSOPHY

*Its Checkered Past, Its Present Disorder,
and Its Future Promise*

THE CONDITIONS
OF PHILOSOPHY

Its Checkered Past,
Its Present Disorder,
and Its Future Promise

MORTIMER J. ADLER

Based on the Encyclopaedia Britannica Lectures
delivered at the University of Chicago, 1964

ATHENEUM

New York

1965

T O

CAROLINE

primae inter causas secundas

Preface

THIS BOOK is based on the Encyclopaedia Britannica
Lectures delivered at the University of Chicago during the winter and spring of 1964. The audience included citizens of Chicago as well as students and faculty
from various divisions of the University. It was not an audience of professional philosophers. Like the lectures, the
book is addressed to anyone troubled, as I am, by the present state of philosophy, and concerned with its place in
liberal education, in our universities, and in our culture.

John Dewey, in his last public appearance before the students at Columbia University, "gave it as his parting mes-
sage," Professor Randall reports, "that the most important
question in philosophy today is, What is philosophy itself?
What is the nature and function of the philosophical enterprise?" The consideration of these questions leads to questions about the relation of philosophy to other disciplines,
especially science, mathematics, and religion; and questions
about the past and future of the philosophical enterprise as
well as about its condition today. Such questions spell out
the query that people raise when the subject of philosophy
is broached: What is it about? What is it up to?

The present book attempts to answer these questions in
a way that makes sense in the middle years of the twentieth
century. The answers here proposed have been maturing

in my mind since I began the study of philosophy at Columbia more than forty years ago. At various times in my intellectual career, I have answered them in ways that no longer seem tenable to me. It would be presumptuous to say that the answers at which I have now arrived (through the correction of earlier errors and the amendment of earlier formulations) are the final answers; but I am persuaded that they come much closer to being the right answers than any which I have hitherto entertained.

I am aware that most professional philosophers today are committed to views of philosophy which, in one way or another, run counter to the view of it here espoused. I would, of course, be gratified if my efforts at persuasion were to effect some change in their minds, but that is not my principal aim, and so I have not engaged in the polemics necessary to achieve that result. So far as possible, I have tried to avoid technical jargon and to state analyses and arguments in ordinary language and in skeletal form—without the adornments of imagery or eloquence. The charm of colorful style often diverts attention from the argument, and it is on the argument itself that I have relied chiefly for persuasiveness. In addition, I have tried to call the reader's attention to the steps I was taking in order to persuade him to move toward the conclusions that I hoped he would adopt, accompanying this by a statement of the alternatives he had to face in making up his own mind for or against the point of view submitted for his consideration.

Few concrete examples or illustrations are offered—too few, perhaps, for the reader's comfort in grappling with abstract distinctions and analyses. Their absence is not due to neglect on my part; it is necessitated by the peculiar nature of the task I set myself: to present a view *of* philosophy which would be intelligible and acceptable to those who hold quite diverse views *in* philosophy itself. To do this perfectly would require one to discuss the nature of philosophical thought and knowledge without committing oneself to any positions whatsoever about the nature of thought and knowledge or the nature of the world thought about and known. This is, of course, impossible to accomplish; but I have tried to approximate it by keeping my underlying philosophical commitments to the two mentioned in Chapter 4. With these two major exceptions (and perhaps a few other minor ones), I think I have succeeded in discussing philosophy with an eye largely on its procedures and without getting involved in its substance. In order to avoid substantive commitments, I have had to be chary of concrete examples and illustrations because these tend to reflect some particular philosophical view of the matter being illustrated or exemplified. The few examples and illustrations that I have used are, I hope, sufficiently neutral to be unembarrassing to this effort to treat philosophy from a procedural point of view.

I said earlier that the conception of philosophy expounded in this book emerges from a lifetime's consideration of questions about its character and worth—its respectability —as an intellectual enterprise. I should add that the immediate occasion which called forth the view of philosophy here presented was a session of the Board of Editors of *Encyclopaedia Britannica*, at which searching questions were raised about the proper manner of treating philosophy in a truly twentieth-century encyclopedia. Having, in response, outlined for a committee of the Board a view of philosophy which, in my opinion, illuminated its twentieth-century condition in the light of its checkered past, and which also held out some hope for its future, it seemed to me appropriate to devote the first series of Encyclopaedia Britannica Lectures at the University of Chicago to this subject—the conditions of philosophy, past, present, and future.

In closing this Preface, I wish to express my gratitude to Encyclopaedia Britannica, Inc., for the grant to the University of Chicago which made the lectures and this book possible; and to the Chairman of its Board of Directors, Senator William Benton, and the President of the company, Mr. Maurice B. Mitchell. I also wish to express my pleasure in returning, after an absence of twelve years, to the university where I enjoyed what were for me twenty-two extremely fruitful years of teaching and learning.

Mortimer J. Adler

Aspen, Colorado
December 28, 1964

Contents

Part One
Proposals and Promises

Part Two
Efforts at Persuasion

Part Three
Applications and Confirmations

Part One

Proposals and Promises

CHAPTER I

Introduction

THE PLAY ON WORDS in the title of this book calls attention to two related concerns. One looks to the condition of philosophy—its present state. The other asks about the conditions of philosophy—the requirements to be met if philosophy is to recover from its present state or to improve its condition.

I naturally hope that I can solicit a wide interest in both of these concerns, though I am well aware that many, acquainted with the literature of philosophy, may recoil from another—still another—exercise in self-examination. I can readily sympathize with such a reaction. This type of undertaking has been repeated so often in the recent history of philosophy that it has become tiresome. If there is any intellectual excitement left in philosophy, it certainly lies in the consideration of genuine philosophical problems, or even in the clarification of philosophical puzzles, rather than in questions about philosophy itself—what philosophy is, what philosophers should be doing, how philosophy stands in relation to other disciplines.

Have I any apology for still another undertaking of this sort? I think so. In any statement of genuine philosophical problems or of the methods for solving them, a conception of philosophy is implicit; there is always some virtue in making that explicit. Doing so, however, may still be tiresome unless some things can be said which change the picture and put philosophy in a new light. If that could be done, the effort would be fruitful and, perhaps, exciting. I should not engage in this undertaking if I did not hope to achieve that result. I hope to do so by laying down a set of conditions—reasonable in themselves and not impossible to meet—which, if satisfied, would lead to the improvement of philosophy's condition.

(1)

Science, in our society and culture, is generally respected, and there is little doubt among us that it deserves the respect it is accorded. In earlier epochs of our Western civilization, philosophy enjoyed a similar standing. I will not raise for the moment the question of whether the respect that it then received was deserved; it may have been, under the cultural circumstances then prevalent and by standards then current.

What of philosophy today? Is it now accorded the respect that is given science, either by men in general or by the learned world in particular? And, if not, should it be? My answer to both questions is negative: negative to the first, in spite of some indications to the contrary; and negative to the second, because of the present state of philosophy as a profession and as an intellectual enterprise.

One explanation of this situation, which I do not share, is offered by those who are convinced that philosophy is now bankrupt—that it has reached the end of the road. In their

4

view, philosophy is now barren because it has at last fully discharged its procreative function—its mothering of all the special sciences, both natural and social, which, one by one, have split off from the parent stem. At an earlier time, when philosophy represented the whole, or at least the major, effort to know the nature of things, to understand the human situation, and to solve the practical problems confronting men and societies, it deserved, and received, the respect now accorded science. Now that all the special sciences have come into existence and grown to maturity, that no longer is or should be the case.

If this view were correct, the present condition of philosophy would be irremediable. There would be no conditions which, if satisfied, might justify regarding philosophy in the way we regard science. And the project with which this book is concerned would be in vain.

I do not deny the fact that there is a widely prevalent sense of philosophy's bankruptcy in the twentieth century. But I would offer a different explanation of it—not that philosophy is at the end of the road, but that it is on the wrong road, that it is not dealing with the right problems in the right way. The appearance philosophy gives of being bankrupt does not mean that it is really barren, but only that it is temporarily insolvent. That is a remediable condition.

What is the remedy? Under what conditions would philosophy be intellectually respectable, both in its own right and as compared with science? I shall try to answer that question in Chapter 2; and the subsequent chapters of Part One will, I hope, further elucidate the conditions there set forth.

There are, of course, further questions to answer. Can

philosophy satisfy the stipulated conditions? Can it be shown that there are no insuperable obstacles to philosophy's satisfying them? I am going to try to show just that in Part Two of this book. Should I succeed, the reader will, I think, be interested in the details of my answers to the two questions with which Part Three is concerned: Have these conditions ever been fully satisfied in the whole of philosophy's historic past? If they have not been, as I shall try to show, what is the prospect of their being satisfied in the future?

(2)

The answers to all these questions should be of some moment to young men facing the choice of an intellectual career.

As things stand now, I would not urge a young man to go into philosophy, to adopt it as a special vocation, as an intellectual profession—an enterprise which has professors, and students who aspire to become professors. Assuming that he is interested in something other than worldly success—something other than money, fame, and power—I do not think that philosophy in its present state offers him intrinsic rewards as an intellectual pursuit comparable to those offered by other professions—science, mathematics, engineering, historical research, law, or medicine. I do not think that it is a career he should adopt if he wishes to use his mind to the fullest and most fruitfully. I do not think that it is an enterprise he can look forward to engaging in without misgivings, without apologies, and with complete self-respect and satisfaction.

If, however, this book succeeds in persuading young men

concerned with their intellectual careers that philosophy can become as respectable an enterprise as science and as rewarding a profession as any other (perhaps more so), then they may be challenged by the opportunity of contributing to philosophy's future, making it better than its past. The number of young men for whom this may be an option worth considering is, of course, small—too small to justify the effort of this book. However, I do not conceive of this book as being addressed exclusively to them. I address it to everyone who is interested in thinking about the world in which he lives, the direction of his own life, and the problems of the society in which he lives.

When I was a very young man, barely fifteen, the first philosophical book that I read was *Pragmatism*, based on the lectures William James delivered to popular audiences at the Lowell Institute in Boston in 1906 and at Columbia University in New York in 1907. The opening pages of that book made a lasting impression on me; they did more than that, I should add, for together with my reading of a dialogue by Plato at about the same time, they determined my choice of a career. That, however, is not my reason for referring to them here; it is rather that they eloquently state the striking fact that philosophy is the business of every man, as other intellectual callings are not—at least not in a comparable sense.

William James begins by quoting from an essay by Chesterton, who had written: "There are some people— and I am one of them—who think that the most practical and important thing about a man is still his view of the universe. We think that for a landlady considering a lodger it is important to know his income, but still more important to know his philosophy. We think that for a general about

7

to fight an enemy it is important to know the enemy's numbers, but still more important to know the enemy's philosophy." Saying that he agreed with Mr. Chesterton in this matter, James then addressed his lecture audience as follows:

I know that you, ladies and gentlemen, have a philosophy, each and all of you, and that the most interesting and important thing about you is the way in which it determines the perspective in your several worlds. You know the same of me. And yet I confess to a certain tremor at the audacity of the enterprise which I am about to begin. For the philosophy which is so important in each of us is not a technical matter; it is our more or less dumb sense of what life honestly and deeply means. It is only partly got from books; it is our individual way of just seeing and feeling the total push and pressure of the cosmos. I have no right to assume that many of you are students of the cosmos in the classroom sense, yet here I stand desirous of interesting you in a philosophy which to no small extent has to be technically treated. I wish to fill you with sympathy with a contemporaneous tendency in which I profoundly believe, and yet I have to talk like a professor to you who are not students. . . .

Believing in philosophy myself devoutly, and believing also that a kind of new dawn is breaking upon us philosophers, I feel impelled, *per fas aut nefas,* to try to impart to you some news of the situation.

Philosophy is at once the most sublime and the most trivial of human pursuits. It works in the minutest crannies and it opens out the widest vistas. It "bakes no bread," as has been said, but it can inspire our souls with courage; and repugnant as its manners, its doubting and challenging, its quibbling and dialectics, often are to common people, no one of us can get along without the far-flashing beams of light it sends over the world's perspectives. These illuminations at least, and the contrast-effects of darkness and mystery that accompany them, give to what it says an interest that is much more than professional.

But for one point that needs elucidation, I would gladly let the foregoing statement stand without comment, passing it on to the nonprofessional philosophers who have read thus far as their motivation for reading further. The point which I think needs comment is the distinction, adverted to by William James, between the philosophizing done by the man in the street and the philosophizing that is done in classrooms or in books by men who regard themselves and are regarded as engaged in a special professional task for which they have a special technical competence. Since it is my feeling, as it was William James's when he introduced his lectures on pragmatism, that what follows should be of concern to the layman as well as to the professional, I think it may be useful to say how I see the interests of the one in relation to the interests of the other.

There is a continuum, as I see it, between the novice in any sport and the champion player of the game. They are both engaged in playing tennis, golf, or baseball, though the one does it with little and the other with consummate skill. The vast difference in degree of competence which separates them does not prevent us from acknowledging that both are playing the same game. On the contrary, precisely

9

because it is the same game, we also recognize that the inexpert at it can learn from the more expert, acquiring through imitation and practice higher degrees of skill and satisfaction. The same holds true of every art. The child who begins to draw pictures or the man who begins to paint stands at one end of a continuum which has Leonardo or Michelangelo at the other. The woman who plans and cooks meals may never become Escoffier, but she improves by acquiring in some degree the understanding and techniques of culinary matters which lesser cooks, who are her preceptors, pass on to her.

Thus it is with the philosophizing done by the layman and the professional. Both are engaged in the same intellectual activity. The difference between Socrates and the ordinary man, each thinking about the nature of things, the choices that life presents, and the values which bear on them, is one of degree, not of kind, as is the difference between the champion at a particular sport and the tyro, or the difference between Leonardo or Escoffier in their particular arts and the novice. But there is one very important distinction to be made between these others and Socrates (here taken as the symbol of a high degree of skill in philosophical inquiry).

To realize their humanity, all men need not—and, in fact, they do not—engage in every particular sport, nor try to acquire skill in every art, just as they need not try to acquire the techniques of law, medicine, or engineering, or the technical knowledge of a physicist or a biologist. Hence, while Leonardo may represent the acme for those who want to draw or paint, and Escoffier for those who want to cook, they do not represent a competence or expertness which all men should try to approach to whatever degree their native capacities make possible. Not so Socrates: as the symbol of consummate skill in philosophizing, he does represent an ideal which every man should try to approximate in the highest degree possible; precisely because philosophizing, as William James declared, is everybody's business, or because, as Socrates before him said, "the unexamined life is not worth living" (and, might one add, the unexamined world and the unquestioned society or culture are not worth living in).

It may, nevertheless, be the case that most men, as regards philosophizing, are like children in kindergarten drawing their first pictures rather than like those who take up tennis or golf with the serious intention of learning how to play the game as well as possible. The latter are inclined to read books about the game, take coaching lessons, go to exhibition matches, and study, as well as admire, the technique of the champions at their particular game. The champion for them is the master from whom they can learn—not directly, of course, but through intermediary lesser lights. They usually know his name and regard themselves as starting at the bottom of a ladder to the top of which he has risen. This is not true of kindergarten children beginning to draw; they are not conscious that they are engaged in the practice of an art which has superior practitioners or, for that matter, that they have anything to learn. They draw almost in the same way that their elders doodle—without premeditation, plan, or purpose. In the same sense in which it can be said that they draw without knowing that they are doing it or what is involved in doing it, so it can be said that most men philosophize.

Since philosophizing is everybody's business, as drawing is not, this common defect should be remedied by schooling.

Everyone should receive training in philosophy in the course of his education. Everyone should be made conscious of the fact that he, if he is going to be fully human, cannot avoid thinking about certain types of problems; he should come to understand the special character of these problems, which have traditionally been called "philosophical"; he should recognize that he is a novice at thinking about them and that other men have displayed great skill or expertness in doing so; he should try to improve his own skill within the limits of his capacity, getting what help he can from books or teachers more proximate to his station than the very great; yet he should be inspired by those sources of his tutelage to study and to imitate the masters; in short, he should see himself at the bottom of a ladder which has Socrates at the top.

To say that some training in philosophy and some study of philosophy should be an essential part of everyone's liberal education can be defended only if what I am now going to call academic or technical philosophy—the philosophy that is taught and studied in courses or read in books which bear the official label—has a certain character. The essential requirement here is that it should be, both in its problems and in its techniques, continuous with the philosophizing of the man in the street or the child, as was and is the philosophizing of Socrates (and a relatively small number of others). With few exceptions, academic philosophy, as it is now taught and studied or written in books, does not meet this requirement. Since the seventeenth century, it has progressively lost the character it should have in order to justify its playing an essential part in everyone's liberal education. It has more and more lost touch with the thinking of the ordinary man.

I said earlier that it was the central purpose of this book to set forth and discuss the conditions which academic or technical philosophy must satisfy if it is to deserve the respect that is accorded science as an intellectual enterprise. Let me now add that it must satisfy the very same conditions if it is to perform the educational service it should perform in the cultivation of the human mind generally, not just exercise and perfect the talents of those who have special gifts or propensities for what goes on at present in our colleges and universities under the name of philosophy. And I would add one thing more: only if these conditions can be satisfied, and only if they are satisfied at some future date, will philosophy discharge the special function that no other academic discipline is able to discharge.

In our universities and in our culture, oriented as they are toward science and technology, philosophy is more and more needed, not just to bolster up the humanities, but to shed a light on science and technology that would enable them to be viewed in their proper perspective as parts of the whole human enterprise. Understanding the human enterprise as a whole—in which science and technology, as well as history, religion, the various arts, and the institutions of the state and of the church are component parts—is a task that calls for philosophizing of a high order, yet philosophizing of a kind that everyone engages in to some degree. It is a task that no other discipline, no other part of our culture, is able to discharge. It is a task that academic philosophy, as currently constituted and practiced, either turns away from or fails to measure up to.

The importance of reconstituting philosophy for the performance of this task, as well as the importance of making academic philosophy serve, as it should, to guide and perfect everyone's natural human tendency to philosophize, may overshadow the importance of philosophy's becoming as respectable as science or other intellectual disciplines that are now accorded more respect than philosophy, certainly in learned or academic circles and by the public generally, or at least by the well-informed public. Nevertheless, it is the third of these three points of importance which seems to me basic; for, in my judgment, unless philosophy as an intellectual enterprise can and does become as worthy of respect as science and other disciplines, it cannot discharge the cultural and educational functions for which it, and it alone, is specially suited.

(3)

Ancient and mediaeval philosophers never asked themselves whether philosophy was worthy of respect. I do not mean that they never had to defend philosophy against detractors. Plato did, against the sophists and businessmen of his day. Scholastic philosophers did, against contempt for the vanity of all worldly learning and against a certain type of dogmatic theologian who treated philosophy as theology's handmaiden in a wholly servile sense of that term. But prior to the seventeenth century, philosophers themselves never doubted the respectability of their calling and its role or value in education and in society. There is not the slightest evidence of such concern to be found in their writings.

That concern begins in the seventeenth century. Starting with Descartes, most of the eminent figures in modern philosophy manifest worry about the state of philosophy, its achievements, its progress, its relation to other disciplines. The evidence of this concern is their intense preoccupation with new methods, new organons, new points of departure for philosophy; or their therapeutic recommendations, reforms, reconstructions to cure whatever it is they think is ailing philosophy and to improve its condition.

We find such manifestations in Leibniz and Spinoza as well as in Descartes, in Francis Bacon and Thomas Hobbes, and most poignantly in that extraordinary triumvirate— Locke, Berkeley, and Hume—who are responsible with Descartes for most of what has happened and is still happening in philosophy. In consequence, we have the Kantian attempt to lay down a new ground plan with safe and secure foundations for all valid knowledge; and this is followed in the nineteenth century by the various post-Kantian constructions that override Kant's cautions and transgress his critical restrictions on the philosophical enterprise. Finally, in reaction to these excesses, the pendulum swings back in the twentieth century, and we have all the varieties of philosophical reformation, reconstruction, new departures, and therapeutic programs that are associated with American pragmatism, logical positivism (both Viennese and British), analytic and linguistic philosophy (both British and American), and phenomenology and existentialism (mainly European).

If there is any one thing that all these philosophical movements have in common, it is their anxiety about the blind alleys into which philosophy has stumbled, their concern with its validity and its significance, and their effort to remedy its condition and set it off on a new path toward prosperity and progress. There is, perhaps, one other thing that these modern considerations of philosophy's condition have in common. The modern thinkers who ask themselves, in effect, whether philosophy is quite respectable or how to make it so do not themselves hold philosophy prior to the seventeenth century in high esteem. We are thus confronted with the fact that the earlier philosophers, who never doubted the intellectual respectability of what they were engaged in, do not have the respect of modern and contemporary thinkers, least of all from those who are most concerned about the respectability of philosophy itself.

(4)

Among my readers there may be those who would be willing to stop right here. The problem of philosophy's intellectual respectability does not interest them. I have not yet persuaded them that it makes a great deal of difference whether philosophy is as worthy an intellectual profession as science, law, medicine, or engineering; or that, since everyone philosophizes and should, everyone should also try to philosophize better and should be helped to do so, in school and by books, by those who are technically more expert; or that academic philosophy has an important function to perform in relation to all the other disciplines that constitute a university and all the other elements that constitute our culture. I want to ask such readers to perform an intellectual experiment, which may open their minds to the importance of the problems dealt with in the remaining chapters of this book.

Some years ago I gave a lecture on love in which I was concerned with the difference between love and desire. I asked my audience to perform the experiment of imagining a world without sex—a world in which everything else was exactly the same, but from which sex was totally absent. Some of them, I must confess, found this difficult to do. Some were even reluctant to try. Those who tried, however, learned something about love, or at least understood the full import of the question about the relation of love to sexual desire.

The experiment I am now going to propose is no less difficult but, I hope, just as illuminating. Try to imagine a world in which everything else is exactly the same, but from which philosophy is totally absent. I do not mean just academic philosophy; I mean philosophizing in every degree—that done almost unconsciously by ordinary men or inexpertly by scientists, historians, poets, and novelists, as well as that done with technical competence by professional philosophers.

Since philosophizing is an ingrained and inveterate human tendency, I know that it is hard to imagine a world without philosophy in which everything else is the same, including human nature; yet it is certainly no harder than imagining a world without sex as one in which everything else is the same. In each case, of course, we are required to excise one element from human nature and leave the rest unaffected by the surgery. That can be done. It has been done before, for example, when we imagine men, who are by nature social, living anarchically in a state of nature, totally bereft of civil society and government—a useful hypothesis, as Rousseau pointed out, even though it involves a supposition contrary to fact.

In the world I have asked you to imagine, all the other arts and sciences remain continuing enterprises; history and science are taught in colleges and universities; and it is assumed without question that everyone's education should include some acquaintance with them. But philosophy is completely expunged. No one asks any philosophical questions; no one philosophizes; no one has any philosophical knowledge, insight, or understanding; philosophy is not taught or learned; and no philosophical books exist.

Would this make any difference to you? Would you be completely satisfied to live in such a world? Or would you come to the conclusion that it lacked something of importance?

You would realize—would you not?—that even though education involved acquiring historical and scientific knowledge, it could not include any understanding of either science or history, since questions about history and science (other than questions of fact) are not historical or scientific but philosophical questions. You would also realize that a great many of your opinions or beliefs, shared with most of your fellow men, would have to go unquestioned, because to question them would be to philosophize; they would remain unenlightened opinions or beliefs, because any enlightenment on these matters would have to come from philosophizing about them. You would be debarred from asking questions about yourself and your life, questions about the shape of the world and your place in it, questions about what you should be doing and what you should be seeking—all questions which, in one form or another, you do in fact often ask and would find it difficult to desist from asking.

There may be some whose only response to all this is a shrug of indifference. To them I have nothing more to say. The rest, I am sure, would find a world devoid of philosophy and philosophizing sorely lacking an important ingredient, one they would feel deprived of if they did not have it as part of their education and their intellectual life.

This experiment does not solve the problems with which this book is concerned. It merely justifies the effort, by writer and reader, of considering the conditions that academic or technical philosophy must satisfy in order to provide the guidance it should give to everyone in his efforts to philosophize; and in order to supply the enlightenment which we know, or should know, to be unobtainable from history and science and which, therefore, would be lacking in a world bereft of philosophy.

CHAPTER 2

The Five Conditions

BEFORE STATING the five conditions to be fulfilled by philosophy if it is to be worthy of respect, I would like to call attention to certain features of this undertaking. In the first place, I propose to state the conditions in minimal terms; that is, I propose to make demands which are within reach of fulfillment rather than hold up unattainable ideals. In the second place, the conditions stipulated will, in every case, be conditions applicable to other comparable intellectual enterprises, such as historical scholarship and scientific research, about the respectability of which there is little or no doubt. None of the conditions is peculiar to philosophy. In the third place, though they are common to science, historical scholarship, and philosophy, these conditions are, or can be, satisfied in quite different ways in each of these disciplines. Hence, to say that philosophy should be able to satisfy them is not to say that philosophy should be scientific, in either method or spirit.

It is important to avoid that mistake. It has been made in other connections. We are so given to using the word "scientific" as if it were equivalent in meaning to "intellectually respectable" that we speak of "scientific history" when all we mean is that historical scholarship, without being scientific, satisfies the same general conditions of intellectual respectability that science satisfies. It may, therefore, be thought that I have looked for the characteristics which make science respectable in our culture and then turned them into conditions for philosophy to satisfy—that, in other words, I am asking philosophy to ape science in order to become as respectable. That is hardly the case. The conditions I am about to state are requirements which any mode of inquiry must satisfy to be respectable. They are generic conditions, applicable to all specific branches of knowledge, among which science is only one.

The fact that most of us believe that these conditions are satisfied by science does not alter the picture. Nor does it affect our effort to answer the following questions: Are these conditions now met by philosophical thought? If not, can they be met in the future? Can they be met in a way that is different from the way in which they are met by scientific research and historical scholarship?

With these preliminary remarks, I turn to the five conditions. The brief statement of each condition contains critical terms that need elucidation. I will call attention to these and try to explain the meanings that I attach to them.

(1)

FIRST CONDITION. To be intellectually respectable, as history and science are generally recognized to be, philosophy must be *a branch of knowledge*. It must be a mode of inquiry that aims at, and results in, the acquisition of *knowledge* which is characteristically different from the knowledge that is aimed at and achieved by historical scholarship and scientific research.

In this statement, the critical term which needs clarification is, of course, the word "knowledge." But the reader will note that the phrase "a branch of knowledge" is also italicized. This is intended to call attention to two things which are spelled out in the remainder of the statement: that whatever meaning is attached to the word "knowledge" applies to each and every branch of knowledge; and that each distinguishable branch of knowledge differs from every other in certain characteristic ways, without such differences affecting their common or generic character as knowledge.

What is involved in distinguishing branches of knowledge will be discussed later. The fourth condition, as we shall see, requires philosophy to be not only a distinct branch of knowledge, but also a relatively autonomous branch of knowledge. For the present, let our whole concern be with understanding what it means to say that philosophy must be a mode of inquiry that aims at and succeeds in acquiring knowledge in the same sense that one would say this of historical scholarship or of scientific research—or, one might add, of mathematics.

There is a sense of the word "knowledge" which sets too high a standard of achievement for it to be applicable to either historical scholarship or scientific research. At times in the past, it was thought that mathematics could measure up to this high standard. At times, philosophy also was thought to be knowledge in this high or strong sense. But in the centuries which have seen the greatest development of scientific research and historical scholarship, it has seldom, if ever, been thought that either scientific or historical knowledge was knowledge in this sense.

To impose this sense of "knowledge" upon philosophy

not only makes an unreasonable demand upon it by asking it to pursue an unattainable ideal, but it also falsifies the statement of the first condition which philosophy must satisfy in order to be intellectually respectable in the same way that science and history are.[1] All that is required by the first condition is that philosophy should aim at and acquire knowledge *in the same sense* that science and history do, *not in a loftier sense of that term.*

Before I attempt to explain the moderate sense of the word "knowledge" (in which history, science, mathematics, and philosophy can or should all equally claim to be knowledge), let me explicate the too high or too strong sense of the term which I wish to exclude as inapplicable to all the disciplines just mentioned.

The attributes of knowledge in the high or strong sense are: (1) certitude beyond the challenge of skeptical doubts, (2) finality beyond the possibility of revision in the course of time.[2] Such knowledge consists entirely of (3) necessary

[1] For brevity of reference, I shall from time to time use the word "history" as short for "historical scholarship," "historical research," or "historical inquiry." Unless otherwise explicitly indicated, I shall *never* use the word "history" for historical narratives of the kind exemplified in the works of Herodotus, Thucydides, Polybius, Tacitus, Gibbon, Mommsen, Froude, Beard, and the like; or for speculations about the pattern or meaning of the historical development of human life and society, of the kind to be found in the writings of Vico, Spengler, Toynbee, and others. Hence, when I speak of history as a branch of knowledge, the knowledge I am referring to is the type of knowledge acquired by historical inquiry or research. The distinguishing characteristics of this type of knowledge will be discussed later.

[2] We sometimes say that we are certain of something when all that we mean is that we have *at the time* no reason to doubt it. But when the attribute of finality is added to certitude, our meaning when we say that we are certain must be that we *cannot* doubt, that reason makes it *impossible* to doubt. This is the unchallengeable certainty of necessary truths.

truths, which have either the status of (4) self-evident principles, that is, axioms, or of (5) conclusions rigorously demonstrated therefrom.

The Greeks used two words as names for such knowledge. They used *nous* for our knowledge of self-evident principles—expressed in axioms which are not merely undemonstrated but intrinsically undemonstrable, and which are the ultimate premises employed in the demonstration of any conclusion that is strictly demonstrable. They used *epistēmē* for the knowledge that is comprised in all conclusions which can be rigorously demonstrated, having their ultimate grounds in self-evident principles. The Latin equivalents of the Greek words, especially as used in mediaeval commentaries on Greek thought, were *intellectus* and *scientia*.

For the purpose of this book, I propose to use the Greek word *epistēmē* for knowledge in the sense specified by the five points mentioned above.[3] I am aware that, in doing so, I am extending the meaning of *epistēmē* to cover self-evident principles as well as demonstrated conclusions; but this seems to me justified by the fact that if there were any demonstrated conclusions of the sort which the Greeks called *epistēmē*, their truth could not be known apart from knowledge of the self-evident principles which the Greeks called *nous*. This whole set of propositions would then constitute an organized body of knowledge.

I propose, therefore, to use the word *epistēmē* for, *and only for*, an organized body of knowledge which involves a

[3] My choice of the word *epistēmē* rather than *scientia* is dictated by the fact that the latter, by reason of its look and sound, might get confused with the English word "science." No one will be troubled by the statement that science is not *epistēmē*. They might be by the statement that science is not *scientia*.

number of indubitable and incorrigible propositions that serve as premises for other propositions that have the status of conclusions. An organized body of knowledge is always a set of compendent propositions—propositions that hang together through one or another type of relationship—but it is not always one in which the type of relationship is deductive; it does not always consist of propositions some of which are self-evident premises from which the rest are derived as demonstrated conclusions. That would be the case *only if* the body of knowledge had the characteristics of *epistēmē*. But, I submit, no existent body of knowledge meets those exacting requirements; neither history, nor science, nor mathematics, nor philosophy are bodies of knowledge that have the properties of *epistēmē* in the sense indicated.

To say that no recognized body of knowledge has the characteristics of *epistēmē* does not require us to deny that there may be any number of propositions which have the two properties of indubitability and incorrigibility. (These characteristics, it will be remembered, are but two of the five points mentioned above, all of which would characterize a body of knowledge if it conformed to the requirements of *epistēmē*.) A single proposition may be indubitable and incorrigible, but standing by itself it does not constitute a body of knowledge, nor does a whole collection of such propositions constitute a body of knowledge if the members of the collection lack the compendency or logical relationship required.

One school of thought adopts the Greek view of such propositions and calls them "self-evident principles," "indemonstrable axioms," "*propositiones per se nota*" or "propositions known through themselves." It regards such propositions as necessary truths and also as informative or instructive. Another school of thought takes a contrary view; it calls such propositions "analytic" or "tautological." It regards them as nothing more than explications of our conceptual or linguistic conventions or habits. They do not give us any information about the world, nor do they state necessary truths about the nature of things.[4]

For present purposes, it is unnecessary to dwell further on the disputes which have arisen over the precise character of these isolated propositions that have the twin properties of certitude and finality or—what is the same—of indubitability and incorrigibility. It makes no difference in what follows whether such propositions are self-evident, indemonstrable, necessary truths about reality or merely analytic and tautological statements about our own meanings. In the one case, they would be the kind of knowledge which the Greeks called *nous;* in the other case, they would not be. But in either case, what I want to say remains unaffected; namely, that there are no demonstrated conclusions of the kind which the Greeks called *epistēmē,* and hence there is no body of knowledge of the kind for which I am appropriating that Greek word.

Even if there are axioms—self-evident and indemonstrable necessary truths—it is my contention that they are always isolated propositions, never the principles from which compendent conclusions are demonstrated to constitute a body of knowledge. If what are thought to be

[4] There is another class of statements which are indubitable and incorrigible: the statements each of us makes from time to time about his own subjective experience, such as "I feel pain" or "My vision is blurred." If the speaker is not prevaricating, such biographical statements have certitude and finality for those who make them, but they can hardly claim to be communicable knowledge.

axioms turn out to be nothing but analytic statements or tautologies, my contention remains unchanged. One might devise a set of tautologies that would serve as premises from which compendent conclusions could be demonstrated. Such a set would look like an *organized body* of propositions, but it would not be an organized body of *knowledge* in the sense of *epistēmē*. Therefore, the existence of isolated propositions which are indubitable and incorrigible—no matter how their being indubitable and incorrigible is interpreted—does not require us to modify or qualify the statement that *epistēmē*, as defined, sets before us an unrealized and, I think, unrealizable ideal.

Was this ideal ever taken seriously and regarded as attainable—more than that, as actually attained? Mathematics, and more particularly Euclidean geometry, was for centuries thought to be *epistēmē*—by Aristotle, Descartes, Leibniz, Spinoza, and Kant. It is now generally acknowledged, since the work of Kurt Gödel, that neither Euclidean geometry nor any other department of mathematics realizes the ideal of *epistēmē* or ever can.[5]

In addition, both Plato and Aristotle, together with their mediaeval followers, appeared to demand of philosophy that it be knowledge in this high sense. In the seventeenth century, Descartes, Spinoza, and Leibniz, idealizing mathematics as *epistēmē*, tried to force philosophy to conform to or approximate the model it afforded by constructing their own philosophical thought in the mathematical manner, *in ordine geometrico*. In the next century, Kant invented his

[5] See B. Meltzer's translation of Gödel's monograph, *On Formally Undecidable Propositions of Principia Mathematica and Related Systems*, New York, 1962. The book contains a readable Introduction by R. B. Braithwaite.

extraordinary apparatus of synthetic propositions *a priori* in order to defend physics (that is, pure, not empirical, physics) as well as mathematics from skeptical doubts; but the result, on the positive side of the picture, was represented by his claim to have shown how there can be *epistēmē* in several, though not all, fields of inquiry. This includes his showing that certain departments of philosophical thought, though not metaphysics as Kant understood it, can be bodies of knowledge having the character of *epistēmē*. In our own day, there still persists, in the tradition of scholastic philosophy, the mediaeval use of the word *scientia* (equivalent in meaning to *epistēmē*); and the conception of a body of knowledge which this word expresses is applied by the scholastics to metaphysics as well as to other departments of philosophy, such as the philosophy of nature or even ethics.[6]

In what sense of knowledge, then, are history, science, mathematics, and philosophy branches of knowledge? If *epistēmē* sets too high a standard, what is the moderate or weaker sense of the word "knowledge" in which it is applicable—and equally applicable—to the disciplines just mentioned?

The properties of knowledge in this moderate sense are that it consists of propositions which are (1) testable by reference to evidence, (2) subject to rational criticism, and either (3) corrigible and rectifiable or (4) falsifiable. The Greeks had another word which I propose to use for "knowledge" in this sense. That word is *doxa*, and it is

[6] This brief historical review is by no means exhaustive. It is offered merely as a citation of exemplary and eminent instances, to show the vitality of *epistēmē* as an ideal.

usually rendered in English by the word "opinion." As the properties enumerated above indicate, what is being referred to is responsible, reliable, well-founded, reasonable opinion. When the English word "opinion" is used to signify the opposite of knowledge, what is being referred to usually lacks these very properties. It is irresponsible, unreliable, unfounded, unreasonable; it is mere opinion, sheer opinion, irrational prejudice.

We have here, then, the following threefold distinction: (1) knowledge in the sense of *epistēmē*, (2) knowledge in the sense of *doxa*, and (3) sheer or mere opinion. I propose to use the English word "opinion" whenever I wish to refer to something which is not knowledge in either of its two senses. This, I believe, conforms to ordinary usage. No one, I think, would call the conclusions of scientific or historical research "opinion" rather than "knowledge." But when they are called "knowledge"—at least in learned circles today—that word is used in the sense of *doxa*, not *epistēmē*.[7] On the other hand, when certain critics of philosophy—or, more specifically, of the type of philosophy which they call "metaphysics"—wish to exclude it from the group of disciplines that are entitled to be regarded as knowledge (in the sense of *doxa*), they dismiss metaphysics as mere opinion. They deny that it can satisfy the first condition of being as worthy of respect as history or science—namely,

[7] Consider the following statement by Professor Karl Popper: "The realization that natural science is not indubitable *epistēmē* (*scientia*) has led to the view that it is *technē* (technique, art, technology); but the proper view, I believe, is that it consists of *doxai* (opinions, conjectures), controlled by critical discussion as well as by experimental *technē*" (*Conjectures and Refutations*, New York, 1962, p. 103, fn. 12).

that it deserves to be regarded as a branch of knowledge in the sense of *doxa*, not *epistēmē*.[8]

Before turning to the second of the five conditions, I should like to comment briefly on the significance of relinquishing—for philosophy in particular—the claim that it can achieve knowledge in the sense of *epistēmē*.

Epistēmē represents an illusory ideal that has bemused man's understanding of his efforts and his achievements in the pursuit of knowledge. It has led philosophers to misconceive philosophy and to make unsupportable claims for their theories or conclusions. In that branch of philosophy which is called epistemology (especially in the form that it takes in contemporary Anglo-American thought), the abandonment of *epistēmē* would eliminate three problems with which it is obsessed—the problem of our knowledge of material objects, of other minds, and of the past. These are baffling, perhaps insoluble, problems only when the claim is made that we can have knowledge of material objects, other minds, and the past—knowledge which has the certitude and finality of *epistēmē*. Retract that false claim, substitute the sense of *doxa* for *epistēmē*, and the problems cease to be problems, or at least to be baffling. A large portion of epistemology—at least that part of it which has contem-

---

[8] Just as I shall try consistently to use the word "opinion" to name the opposite of knowledge in either of its two senses, so I shall try to make the following consistent use of the word "knowledge." I shall never use it in the sense of *epistēmē* without explicitly indicating that that is the sense in which I am using it. If I use the word without any qualifiers, its meaning will always be that of *doxa*, as defined by the properties enumerated in the text above. If I wish to make sure that the reader does not forget that this is the sense in which the word is being used, I shall say "knowledge in the sense of *doxa*." And I shall never use the word *doxa* to signify mere or sheer opinion.

porary prominence—would simply wither away if "know" and "knowledge" were never used in the sense of *epistēmē*.

Abandoning *epistēmē* as an illusory ideal would not only shrink epistemology to its proper size, but it would also starve, if not silence, the skeptic who feeds on the claim to achieve *epistēmē* in any department of human inquiry. Claim no more for philosophy, or science, or history, than the achievement of knowledge in the sense of testable, corrigible, falsifiable *doxa,* and the skeptic will either be out of work or find the task he sets himself less to his liking.

(2)

SECOND CONDITION. The second condition follows closely on the first. For philosophy to be respectable as a branch of knowledge, philosophical theories or conclusions must be capable of being judged by appropriate criteria of *goodness;* or, in other words, they must be capable of being judged by reference to an appropriately formulated standard of *truth.*

The two words that require comment are the italicized ones—"goodness" and "truth." The criteria of goodness appropriate to anything that claims to be knowledge are criteria of truth. To say, in connection with historical scholarship, scientific research, or philosophical thought, that one conclusion is better than another is to say that it is sounder or truer.

There are other criteria of goodness in human works or products—aesthetic and utilitarian criteria. One musical composition or piece of sculpture may be judged better than another by relevant aesthetic criteria; one implement or machine can be judged better than another by standards of utility. But while scientific theories may also be evaluated by reference to aesthetic or utilitarian criteria, they are, in addition, subject to the criteria of truth, which are not applicable to musical compositions or machines.

When I lay down the requirement that philosophical theories or conclusions must be capable of being judged for their relative truth—one truer or sounder than another—I am saying that if philosophy is a branch of knowledge, in the same sense that history or science is, then it can never suffice merely to find one philosophical theory more to our liking than another; or to regard one as better than another simply because it is more pleasing to consider, more harmonious to contemplate, or more useful for whatever purpose we have in mind. We must be able to say that it is truer than another, or at least to hope that we can find some theory which is truer than others. And when we say this, we must use the word "truer" in the same sense in which we apply it in making judgments about scientific theories or historical conclusions, relative to one another.

What is that sense? Since we are not here concerned with *epistēmē*, but only with knowledge in the sense of *doxa*, we can eliminate at once the standard of indubitable and incorrigible truth that is set by self-evident propositions and demonstrated conclusions. We can also eliminate, I think, the standard of truth which would be set by statements that are *completely verified* by empirical data, if complete verification were possible, as many now realize it is not.

Those who supposed that complete empirical verification was possible were, in effect, still looking for knowledge in the sense of *epistēmē*, even though they renounced self-evident principles and conclusions demonstrated therefrom; for if a statement could be *completely verified* by empirical

data, it would have the certitude and the finality—the indubitability and the incorrigibility—that sets knowledge in
the sense of *epistēmē* far above knowledge in the sense of
doxa. The only standard of truth that is consistent with
knowledge in the sense of *doxa* must eschew certitude and
finality; it must allow for the judgment that one theory or
conclusion is *truer* than another, or for the judgment that
it is false, but never for the judgment that one theory or
conclusion is *absolutely true*, rendering all other theories of
the same matter necessarily false.

Professor Popper, having asked us to renounce the illusory ideal of *epistēmē* and to regard scientific knowledge
as knowledge only in the sense of *doxa*, quite consistently
substitutes *falsifiability* for *verifiability* in the appraisal of
scientific theories. In his view, a scientific theory can be
falsified by empirical data, but its falsification does not make
competing theories true. If they were put to the same test
and escaped falsification, they would simply be truer than
the falsified theory, but not true in any final or absolute
sense; for the next time they were put to the test, they too
might be falsified. The more times that a theory which is
being tested in different ways escapes falsification, the more
assured we are of its truth, or the more its being true is
confirmed; but such successive steps of confirmation simply
increase the degree of its approximation to truth in a
gradation of degrees which never reaches the limiting point
of final and incorrigible truth.

At any point in this series, the next test might result in the
falsification of the theory. Hence, the truth that is attributed
to a theory which has been tested a number of times and not
yet falsified is not the grade of truth which makes all other
competing theories false. It only makes the theory in

question truer for the time being than other theories which have been less amply tested or, as tested, have been falsified. Therefore, when we speak of a theory as "true" or as "having truth," we should always understand this in a relative, not in an absolute, sense; in other words, we should understand that it is only *truer* than some other theory, but not that it is *true* in and by itself.[9]

Professor Popper's standard of truth is as applicable to the conclusions of historical research as it is to scientific theories and conclusions. Since I hold that philosophy can be regarded as knowledge in the same sense that history and science are esteemed as knowledge (that is, *doxa*), I also maintain that the same standard of relative truth which is applicable to them is applicable to philosophical theories and conclusions.

Professor Popper denies this. He thinks that the property of being falsifiable by reference to experience draws a sharp line of demarcation between scientific and philosophical theories. If that were so, philosophy and science could not

---

[9] See Karl Popper's *The Logic of Scientific Discovery*, New York, 1959; and also *Conjectures and Refutations*, especially pp. 33–65, 97–119, 215–250. Cf. *The Open Society and Its Enemies*, Princeton, 1962, Addendum, pp. 369–381. It should be pointed out that whereas a theory may be judged *truer* when, put to the test, it escapes falsification, it must be judged false when it is empirically falsified—that is, simply false, not just *falser* than some other theory. There are degrees of confirmation in the direction of truth, but no degrees of falsification. Of course, the formal contradictory of an empirically falsified proposition must also be judged true, not truer than some other proposition. But this does not require any amendment or qualification of Popper's position. What has been learned from experience is exactly the same whether it is expressed by saying that a particular theory or conclusion is false or that its formal contradictory is true.

be knowledge in the same sense, and one philosophical theory could not be judged truer than another in the same sense that one scientific theory can be judged truer than another.[10]

When I say that philosophical theories are, like scientific theories, falsifiable by reference to experience, I do not mean that they are falsifiable in the same way or by the same kind of experience; this will become clearer later.[11] Furthermore, to say that philosophical theories are subject to an empirical test which may result in their falsification is not to say that this is the only way in which they can be tested; there are at least three other tests or criteria, as we shall see.[12] Of these four criteria, two—the empirical and the logical tests—are applicable to scientific as well as philosophical theories; but two, which shall go unnamed for the moment, are peculiar to philosophy.

These four tests provide us with a basis for regarding one philosophical theory as truer than another—or even, perhaps, for rejecting a theory as untenable—but never for maintaining that a particular theory is finally established as true, the one and only right theory of the matter. In addition, the application of these tests may enable us to discover various ways to rectify or otherwise improve a particular theory, thus making it truer, more nearly true, but never absolutely true. Nothing more than this need be, and nothing less than this should be, claimed for philosophy if it is to be intellectually respectable as a branch of knowledge.

[10] See *Conjectures and Refutations*, pp. 66–96; cf. pp. 184–200.
[11] See Chapters 7 and 8.
[12] See Chapters 9, 11, and 12.

(3)

THIRD CONDITION. The first two conditions stipulated that philosophical work should achieve a certain kind of result—that is, knowledge that has relative truth. The third condition stipulates that philosophical work should be carried on in a certain way. It is procedural rather than substantive; like the first two conditions, it is one that history and science are generally thought to satisfy. As modes of inquiry, they are conducted as public enterprises, not as private affairs. To be worthy of respect as a mode of inquiry aiming at knowledge and developing theories capable of being tested for their relative truth and capable of being falsified, rectified, or improved, philosophy too should be conducted as a *public* enterprise.[13]

The operative word here is "public." We have come to see that any human work is personal in some sense and to some degree—a scientific theory, a historical interpretation, as well as a poem or a painting.[14] But the inescapable personal character of any human work does not necessarily make it exclusively personal in the sense of being wholly private. It can have a public as well as a private aspect. There may be some things which are exclusively private, such as certain emotional experiences, the mystic's vision, the voice of conscience, and the like. The exclusively private is, of course, also incommunicable. Hence, insofar as knowledge in general, and any branch of knowledge in

[13] Implicit in this is the assumption that work which aims at knowledge and which is capable of being judged by standards of truth *should* have the character of a public enterprise.

[14] See Michael Polanyi, *Personal Knowledge*, Chicago, 1958.

particular, is communicable, it cannot be exclusively private.

The distinction between public and private is a matter of degree. What we are concerned with here is the degree to which a type of human work—scientific research, historical scholarship, or philosophical thought—assumes a public character. I am, therefore, going to try to specify the conditions under which human work takes on the character of a public enterprise.

A mode of inquiry aiming at knowledge has a public character

(i) if the participants in the enterprise are willing and able to answer the same questions; [15]

(ii) if the questions or problems to be faced by the participants in the enterprise can be attacked piecemeal, one by one, so that it is not necessary to answer all the questions involved in order to answer any one or some of them;

(iii) if it is possible for the participants to disagree as well as to agree about the answers to be given to the questions that direct the inquiry;

(iv) if disagreements among the participants, when they arise, are adjudicable by reference to standards commonly accepted by participants in the enterprise; [16]

(v) and if cooperation is possible among the participants; that is, if it is possible for a number of men

[15] It is not necessary that all participants do in fact answer the same questions, but there should be evidence that some do, and it should be possible for all to do so. Philosophy is a private affair, not a public enterprise, if each philosopher answers his own questions —questions whose significance is determined by his own "system of thought," so that they are not genuine questions for anyone standing outside his system.

[16] This is another way of saying that philosophical work has the character of a public enterprise only if it is somehow policeable.

37

working on the same problem or question to make partial contributions which are cumulative and which add up to a better solution than any one of them proposes.

The possibility of progress is not itself one of the requirements of a public enterprise, but rather a consequence of conducting an enterprise in a public manner. If a cognitive enterprise—whether it is history, science, or philosophy—has a public character, according to the requirements stated above, then it will also be an enterprise in which the state of the discipline can be more advanced at a later time because of the cumulative effect of the work done by contributors who add to or correct the work of others. In the temporal picture of the enterprise as a whole, there can, in short, be an increase in knowledge, in the approximation to truth, in the degree or extent of understanding achieved.

(4)

FOURTH CONDITION. The fourth condition makes explicit what was implied by the earlier statement that philosophy must be a branch of knowledge. To be such, it must be clearly distinct from other branches of knowledge. In addition, it must have *relative autonomy*—that is, some degree of independence of other branches of knowledge.

A branch of knowledge, as the words indicate, is a distinguishable substantive part of the totality of human knowledge. Similarly, a mode of inquiry is a distinguishable procedural part of the whole human effort to know. A discipline which is, substantively or procedurally, only a part of the whole picture cannot be completely autonomous—that is, in every way independent of all the rest. Yet it must have some measure of autonomy if it is to claim the status of a separate and distinct branch of knowledge, or to claim the possession of a separate and distinct mode of inquiry.

I am saying that philosophy should be able to make these claims. What is the basis of making them—for philosophy or for any other discipline? On the substantive side, a discipline has the requisite measure of autonomy if it has some questions of its own to answer—questions which can be answered by it and by no other discipline, and questions which it can answer without reference to results obtained by any other discipline. And on the procedural side, it must have a method of its own for answering whatever questions are proper to it.

This does not preclude the possibility of questions which the particular discipline shares with other disciplines; that is, questions two or more disciplines must cooperate to answer, or questions which can be answered by one discipline only by taking into account the results obtained in some other discipline or by some other mode of inquiry.

Let us now apply these considerations to philosophy. To have the requisite autonomy, it must have certain questions of its own. I propose to call these "philosophical questions," purely and simply. These are the questions which it and it alone can answer; these it can answer without reference to what is known in other disciplines; and these it can answer by a mode of inquiry distinctively its own. There may also be what I propose to call "mixed questions," questions the answers to which involve both philosophy and science, or both philosophy and history. Whatever contribution philosophers can make to the solution of mixed questions depends on the answers they give to questions that belong to philosophy alone.[17]

The existence of mixed questions is widely acknowledged. Scientists and historians recognize that they frequently consider questions that go beyond science and history—questions which cannot be answered solely by means of the knowledge that has been acquired by scientific or historical research. Similarly, lawyers, physicians, engineers, poets, novelists, musicians, painters, architects, or educators often face questions that call for thinking on their part which requires them to go beyond or outside the sphere of their special professional competence. To answer such questions they need knowledge of a kind that is not to be found in their own special field of learning.

Not all such mixed questions involve philosophy as the additional kind of knowledge or special competence that is required for their solution; there may be mixed questions which call for a combination of scientific and legal knowledge, of medical and historical knowledge, of architectural and engineering knowledge, and so forth. But some of them—and by far the most important ones, in the view of the professional in one or another special field of learning—are questions that require him to philosophize—that is, to have recourse to philosophical knowledge or philosophical thought, in addition to the knowledge supplied by his own branch of learning or field of technical competence.

Unfortunately, the specialist seldom recognizes that philosophy is also a special branch of learning, having questions

[17] Philosophical progress is independent of progress in other fields of inquiry so far as the pure questions are concerned, but that is obviously not the case with regard to the mixed questions. On the distinction between pure and mixed questions in philosophy, see C. I. Lewis, *Mind and the World-Order*, New York, 1929, pp. 4–8.

of its own (just as his own special field has questions of its own), questions that require a special technical competence (just as do the questions in his special field). As a consequence, when he deals with mixed questions involving philosophy, he too often is content to philosophize without the requisite knowledge or competence. His philosophizing is on about the same level as that of the uninstructed but intelligent layman who thinks about problems which are purely philosophical.

The critical point here is that the mixed questions which require the addition of philosophy to some other special field of learning are exactly like the mixed questions which require the combination of any two distinguishable branches of knowledge—for example, science and law, medicine and history, architecture and engineering. In all instances of the latter sort, the specialist in one field usually recognizes that he must call upon the specialist in some other field to help him deal with the mixed question; or he must himself acquire the requisite special knowledge which belongs to that other field. He must proceed in the same way, I am contending, when the mixed question involves science and philosophy, history and philosophy, law and philosophy, medicine and philosophy, education and philosophy, and the like.

The procedure recommended is right only if philosophy is itself a special field of learning, a distinct branch of knowledge, with questions of its own (that is, questions which are purely philosophical) and with a special technical competence of its own for answering them. Were that not so, it would be perfectly all right for the specialist to philosophize with no more competence than the intelligent layman exhibits when he does so. But then it would also be the case that philosophy could not possibly satisfy the first condition of its being a respectable academic discipline; namely, that it be a distinguishable branch of learning or knowledge.

The fourth condition, with which we are here concerned, adds an important corollary to the first: that, as a distinct branch of knowledge, philosophy must have a measure of autonomy, or independence of all other special fields of learning. It must have questions of its own— questions which are purely philosophical and involve no other field of learning and no other special competence than that possessed by the philosopher.

This entails a further corollary: when a philosopher, or anyone else, faces a mixed question that involves philosophy and some other special field of learning, a competent solution of the problem must draw upon philosophical knowledge as well as upon the knowledge to be found in the other special field of learning, whatever it may be. This confirms a point that was made earlier: the character of the philosopher's contribution to answering mixed questions which involve philosophy and some other branch of knowledge is determined by the philosopher's answers to questions which are purely philosophical—questions which can be answered competently only by those who have the special competence of philosophy as a distinct and relatively autonomous branch of knowledge or mode of inquiry.

(5)

FIFTH CONDITION. This last condition concerns the subject matter of those questions which are purely philosophical—that is, which belong to philosophy, and to

42

philosophy alone, as a special field of learning or mode of inquiry. Such questions, the fifth condition stipulates, must be primarily questions about that which is and happens in the world or about what men should do and seek, and only secondarily questions about how we know, think, or speak about that which is and happens or about what men do and seek.

Philosophical questions about that which is and happens in the world deal, for example, with such matters as: the nature of being and existence; the properties of anything which is; the modes of being and the types of existence; change and permanence in being or mutability and immutability; the existence of that which changes; change itself and the types of change; causation and the types of causes; necessity and contingency; the material and the immaterial; the physical and the non-physical; freedom and indeterminacy; the powers of the human mind; the nature and extent of human knowledge; the freedom of the will. (In addition to such purely philosophical questions, there is a host of mixed questions—questions about the nature of man, about society, and about history—the answers to which depend in part upon scientific and historical knowledge.)

Questions about what men should do and seek are concerned with human conduct and the organization of society. They deal, for example, with such matters as: good and evil; right and wrong; the order of goods; duties and obligations; virtues and vices; happiness, life's purpose or goal; justice and rights in the sphere of human relations and social interaction; the state and its relation to the individual; the good society, the just polity, and the just economy; war and peace.

For brevity of reference in all that follows, I propose to call questions about that which is and happens or about what men should do and seek "first-order questions" and the knowledge that is contained in tenable answers to such questions, "first-order philosophical knowledge." In contrast, "second-order questions" are questions about our first-order knowledge, questions about the content of our thinking when we try to answer first-order questions, or questions about the ways in which we express such thought in language. The tenable answers to such questions constitute "second-order philosophical knowledge."

As second-order knowledge, philosophy may be reflexive; that is, it may be analytical and critical of its own concepts or of its own language; it may examine its own knowledge and try to give an account of it. But it may also deal with other branches of knowledge or other modes of inquiry; and, by doing so, provide us with an account of scientific knowledge, historical knowledge, mathematical knowledge, or the kind of knowledge that is to be found in the deposit of common-sense beliefs. Furthermore, on the plane of its second-order questions, philosophy may achieve clarification of concepts and language, not only in its own field of discourse, but in that of any other special discipline; and it may also perform what has come to be called the therapeutic function of curing the intellectual defects that arise from conceptual unclarity or the misuse of language, on the part of philosophers or any other specialists.

If we use the words "critical" or "analytic" for all these aspects of philosophy as second-order knowledge or as a mode of inquiry on the plane of second-order questions, then what the fifth condition stipulates is that philosophy *must be more than critical or analytic*. And if we use the words "constructive" or "synthetic" for philosophy as first-order knowledge or as a mode of inquiry on the plane of first-order questions, then the other face of this same stipulation is that philosophy *must be constructive or synthetic*.[18]

I said earlier, in connection with the fourth condition, that philosophy's contribution to the solution of mixed questions depends on the answers it gives to questions that are purely philosophical. Hence the latter have an obvious priority. Now I want to add that, while second-order questions in philosophy may all be purely philosophical, not mixed, whereas only some first-order questions are of this sort, it is nevertheless the case that the answers philosophers give to second-order questions are determined or affected by their answers to first-order questions, either as explicitly given or as assumed and unacknowledged, as is too often the case. This means that first-order questions, pure or mixed, have primacy in philosophical inquiry; and that, of these, the pure questions take priority over the mixed.[19]

This fifth condition imposes a demand upon philosophy which in certain circles of contemporary thought would be

[18] For a contemporary discussion of the distinction between philosophy as critical or analytic and philosophy as constructive or synthetic, see C. D. Broad, "Two Lectures on the Nature of Philosophy," in *Clarity Is Not Enough*, ed. by H. D. Lewis, London, 1963, especially pp. 56–75. Philosophy as first-order knowledge or as dealing with first-order questions is also sometimes called "speculative"; and sometimes it is identified with "metaphysics" as that word is currently used. Cf. Manley Thompson, in *Philosophy*, Englewood Cliffs, 1965, pp. 133ff.

[19] If I allow myself to misuse once more that much misused word "metaphysics," in order to refer to that part of the philosophical inquiry which is concerned with first-order questions, then I can rephrase what is said above by saying that metaphysics, as constructive philosophy, is prior to epistemology and to conceptual or linguistic clarification, all of which constitutes critical philosophy.

45

deemed excessive or even impossible to meet.[20] The uninstructed layman who has done some thinking about
philosophy might never suspect that an influential, professionally esteemed, and highly skilled group of philosophers
have restricted their own inquiries to second-order questions and have seriously questioned the possibility of dealing
with first-order questions by any method at philosophy's
disposal which would result in the achievement of knowledge, even when that is cut down from *epistēmē* to *doxa*.
Those who are acquainted with the literature of British and
American thought in the last forty or fifty years will
recognize at once what I hasten explicitly to acknowledge:
that, in laying down this fifth condition for philosophy to
meet, I am taking sharp issue with positions taken by the
positivists, the analysts, and the linguistic philosophers.

They have said, or they have appeared to think, that, if
not all, then at least the main problems of philosophy are
epistemological.

They have argued, and even tried to prove, the impossibility of metaphysics, by which they mean any attempt to
answer first-order questions in philosophy.

---

[20] The reader may not see why this fifth condition need be added
to the other four. If philosophy were to satisfy the other four, and
yet restricted itself to being critical or analytic, would it not deserve, as a special discipline having a technical competence of its
own, the kind of respect that is accorded to historical scholarship
and scientific research? It would; but conceding this must not lead
us to overlook two things: that the solution of second-order problems in philosophy presupposes the solution of first-order problems;
and that, to perform its function as an essential ingredient in everyone's liberal education, academic philosophy must stay in touch with
and be instructive to the philosophizing of the layman, which is almost exclusively concerned with first-order questions about that
which is and happens in the world or about what men should do and
seek.

They have said that philosophy does not and cannot add to our information about the world. They have said that philosophy gives us no new knowledge; it serves only to clarify what we already know. It cannot give us knowledge of new facts, but only a better understanding of the facts already known by other disciplines.

They have said that since mathematics answers all formal questions, and since science together with history answers all questions of fact, all that is left for philosophy is to clarify the answers and the language of science and mathematics.

They have said that the philosopher does not add to the sum-total of human knowledge in the way in which the scientist and the historian do.[21]

This last statement contains, in my judgment, a kernel of truth; for if philosophy is first-order knowledge, it is not first-order knowledge of the same sort as science and history: it is not knowledge of the same subject matter nor is it achieved by the same method. The point at issue here is, therefore, not whether philosophy is first-order knowledge of exactly the same sort as science and history, but whether

---

[21] See, for example, Ludwig Wittgenstein, *Philosophical Investigations*, New York, 1953, also *The Blue and Brown Books*, New York, 1958; A. J. Ayer, *Language, Truth and Logic*, London, 1946, also *The Problem of Knowledge*, London, 1956; John Wisdom, *Philosophy and Psychoanalysis*, New York, 1953, esp. pp. 16–101, 229–282. In the collection edited by A. J. Ayer entitled *Logical Positivism*, Glencoe, 1959, see the essays by Moritz Schlick (pp. 53–59 and pp. 209–277), Rudolf Carnap (pp. 60–81), A. J. Ayer (pp. 228–243), F. P. Ramsey (pp. 321–326), Gilbert Ryle (pp. 327–344), and Friedrich Waismann (pp. 345–380). In another collection, edited by Edwards and Pap, entitled *A Modern Introduction to Philosophy*, Glencoe, 1957, see A. J. Ayer's "Demonstration of the Impossibility of Metaphysics" (pp. 555–564) and the debate about logical positivism between Ayer and F. C. Copleston (pp. 586–618).

philosophy is or can be first-order knowledge of a type that is as different from science and history as each of these in turn is different from the other.

As I have already said, I hope in subsequent chapters to make these differences clear. I hope also to be able to defend the position I am taking as against the one taken by the positivists, the analysts, and the linguistic philosophers, by showing that philosophy is able to answer first-order questions of its own and need not be restricted exclusively to inquiry on the plane of second-order questions. At this point I am simply positing, among the conditions of philosophy's respectability and especially of its educational value and its contribution to culture, that it should consist primarily of first-order knowledge.

(6)

All that I have done so far is to stipulate a number of conditions to be satisfied by philosophy in order for it to deserve the kind of respect now generally accorded science and history and in order for it to play the role in liberal education, in the organization of a university, and in the framework of our culture that is appropriate to it. I have not yet attempted to show that philosophy does satisfy these conditions; or if it does not, that it can do so or how it might do so. Nor have I answered questions about the conditions themselves, questions which the reader would be justified in asking. Are the five stipulations the right ones? Are all of them necessary, or can some be eliminated? Should others be added? Has the meaning or import of these conditions been correctly stated? Do these conditions raise difficulties or involve matters that need further clarification? The next two chapters should provide answers to some of these questions and background for answering the rest.

A conception of philosophy is obviously implicit in this set of five conditions. Other conceptions of philosophy, it might be expected, would reject some of the conditions posited. Considering alternative views of philosophy in relation to them should give us a better understanding of the conditions here laid down. That will be done in Chapter 3.

Any conception of philosophy, or any statement of the conditions it should satisfy, involves a number of presuppositions in the form of definite philosophical commitments. This holds true not only of the view of philosophy here being advanced; it holds true of alternative views as well. An explicit avowal of the philosophical presuppositions to which we are committed if we accept the conditions here laid down, but which can be avoided if we reject these conditions, cannot but help to throw light on their meaning or import. Chapter 4 will attempt to do this.

CHAPTER 3

Other Views of Philosophy

I HAVE ALREADY referred to the ancient, mediaeval, and even seventeenth-century view of philosophy, which conceives it as capable of achieving knowledge in the sense of *epistēmē*.[1] I mention it again only to point out that, though philosophy as thus conceived may satisfy the four other conditions, this conception of it, in attempting to satisfy the first condition, makes a demand upon philosophy which it cannot fulfill. By claiming too much for philosophy as an autonomous branch of knowledge, it had the effect of bringing philosophy into wide disrepute. Most of the views to which we now turn go the other way. In regard to the first condition, they tend to claim too little—denying that philosophy can achieve knowledge even in the

[1] See Chapter 2, pp. 27–28. The contrary view, which this book adopts, is well expressed by C. I. Lewis's statement that "proof, in philosophy, can be nothing more at bottom than persuasion." The philosopher can offer proof "only in the sense of so connecting his theses as to exhibit their mutual support, and only through appeal to other minds to reflect upon their experience and their own attitudes and perceive that he correctly portrays them. If there be those minds which find no alternatives save certainty . . . or skepticism, then to skepticism they are self-condemned" (*Mind and the World-Order*, New York, 1929, p. 23).

sense of *doxa*. In addition, none of them subscribes to all of the other four conditions.

I shall now briefly examine five or six alternative conceptions of philosophy, each of which is at variance on one or more points with the view of it taken in this book. This survey is hardly intended to be exhaustive; it serves only to indicate the consequences for philosophy which result from either ignoring or repudiating conditions which it should be able to satisfy, as science and history do.

(1)

Let me begin with the view of philosophy which has its roots in the famous statement that David Hume makes at the end of his *Enquiry Concerning Human Understanding*.

> If we take in our hand any volume of divinity or school metaphysics . . . let us ask, *Does it contain any abstract reasoning concerning quantity and number?* No. *Does it contain any experimental reasoning concerning matter of fact and existence?* No. Commit it then to the flames, for it can contain nothing but sophistry and illusion.

To translate this statement into more familiar terms: If we take in our hand any volume (which may be a book written by someone who regards himself as a philosopher), let us ask, *Is it a work of mathematics, as indicated by its subject matter and its method of analysis and reasoning?* No. *Is it a work of empirical science, or of historical scholarship?* No. Cast it aside, then, for it can contain nothing but worthless opinion, personal prejudice, superstition, or, worse, plain nonsense.

51

Twentieth-century positivism makes explicit the view of philosophy that is implicit in Hume's disjunction—his division of all the disciplines worthy of our consideration into (a) the formal disciplines of mathematics, to which the positivists would add the formal disciplines of logic and semantics, and (b) the empirical disciplines of the natural and social sciences, to which can be added historical research insofar as it employs observable data to determine what Hume calls "matters of fact and existence." Science and history exhaustively cover the modes of inquiry able to achieve first-order knowledge about that which is and happens in the world. Hence, philosophy must be relegated to the plane of second-order questions. While its subject matter is not the same as that of mathematics, it is, like mathematics, a formal, rather than an empirical, discipline; it is logical or semantic analysis devoted to structuring and clarifying science and mathematics.[2]

In his last book, *Some Problems of Philosophy*, William James, in an opening chapter which attempts to defend philosophy against its critics, makes certain statements about it which run counter to the conditions here stipulated. Far from defending philosophy, the view of it toward which these statements tend would, it seems to me, damage philosophy in the eyes of anyone who was concerned about its intellectual respectability. Though his view is not shared by many professional philosophers today, I call attention to it because it is widely held by specialists in other fields and by many otherwise well-informed laymen.

[2] This view clearly violates the fifth condition, which requires that philosophy should engage primarily in seeking first-order knowledge, pursuing its inquiries on the same plane as science and history.

James takes his departure from a generally accepted historical fact—that what are now the special sciences were once a part of philosophy and that they have developed to their present state by breaking off from the parent stem.[3] It is not this fact but the interpretation which James places on it that is so significant. "As fast as questions got accurately answered," he declares, "the answers were called 'scientific,' and what men call 'philosophy' today is but the residuum of questions still unanswered." [4] That may very well be what men, or most men, or those who are uninformed, do call "philosophy," as a matter of fact; but, unfortunately, James seems to agree with them instead of pointing out wherein and why this view of philosophy is wrong.

The special sciences have methods for answering questions accurately and for reaching a high measure of agreement about the right answers; but, according to James, "philosophy, taken as distinct from science or practical affairs, follows no method peculiar to itself." [5] Nor, it would seem, does philosophy have any problems of its own. The problems that it tackles and fails to solve are simply those which science has not yet got around to working on; they are "philosophical" problems only *pro tem* and they are that only as long as they remain unsolved.

"It is obvious enough," James says, "that if every step forward which philosophy makes, every question to which an accurate answer is found, gets accredited to science, the residuum of unanswered problems will alone remain to constitute the domain of philosophy, and will alone bear her

[3] "At this very moment," he writes, "we are seeing two sciences, psychology and general biology, drop off from the parent trunk and take independent root as specialties" (*Some Problems of Philosophy*, New York, 1911, p. 10).
[4] *Ibid.*   [5] *Ibid.*, p. 15.

name. In point of fact, this is just what is happening. Philosophy has become a collective name for questions that have not yet been answered to the satisfaction of all by whom they have been asked."

". . . because some of these questions have waited two thousand years for an answer," it does not follow, James adds, "that no answer will be forthcoming." [6] But by his own conception of philosophy in relation to science, it does follow that when definite and agreed-upon answers are found, they will belong to science, and we will realize that the long-unanswered questions were regarded as "philosophical" only because science had not yet succeeded in answering them. The only questions that will always be philosophical are strictly unanswerable questions—that is, questions which science will never be able to answer by its methods and which philosophy cannot answer either, because, apart from the sciences, it has no adequate method for solving problems or reaching agreed-upon solutions.

On the face of it, this view of philosophy hardly recommends itself to anyone who is concerned with philosophy's being worthy of the respect that is accorded science. It is difficult to see why a young man would choose to become a philosopher rather than a scientist. It is also difficult to see, in this view, why philosophy should be an essential part of liberal education or play a pivotal role in the organization of a university. For, in this view, philosophy is not a branch of first-order knowledge, nor does it even have autonomy as a mode of inquiry: it has no first-order problems that are genuinely and exclusively its own, at least none which it can solve as science does. It may have had an honorable historic career as the mother of all the sciences—

[6] *Ibid.*, pp. 22–23.

as that omnibus from which all the special sciences took their departure—but it now looks as if that career were almost, if not completely, finished; in which case, philosophy (as a first-order discipline) should be given a burial befitting the services it has performed. Its history may be worth studying, but—except as a second-order discipline —it no longer has any contributions to make, at least none which can be described as contributions to knowledge.[7]

Then there is the view that lurks behind many introductions to philosophy, surveys of the schools of philosophical thought, or courses in the history of philosophy. In various ways such books or courses present the succession and rivalry of conflicting "systems of philosophy" or "schools of thought," giving to each its due meed of praise and censure. Each system or school is pictured not only as conceiving the task of philosophy in its own special way, but also as setting itself problems that are fully intelligible only in terms of its own basic presuppositions. Since there are no common questions on which philosophers of diverse schools do or can agree, only thinkers of the same school can really disagree. As between diverse schools of thought, there are no genuine disputes (issues constituted by contrary answers to the same questions); and it is often not even clear whether disputes within a particular school are capable of being adjudicated. The conflict of the "isms" is persistent because it is intrinsically irremediable.

In this view, philosophy hardly deserves anyone's re-

[7] Philosophy thus conceived does not satisfy any of the conditions stipulated except, perhaps, the fifth; but while philosophy, in this view, does address itself to first-order questions primarily, these questions are really scientific questions if they are eventually answerable and only philosophical if they can never be answered.

spect as a branch of knowledge. It does not produce theories capable of being judged for their relative truth. It cannot possibly have the character of a public enterprise in which the participants engage in common tasks, deal with the same problems, cooperate, and make advances.[8]

A closely related view is that held by some historians of ideas. I have in mind here the type of historical relativism which tends to deny that two philosophers writing in different epochs and under different cultural circumstances can possibly be addressing themselves to the same problems. Like the immediately preceding view, this would make it impossible for philosophy to satisfy the third condition, requiring it to be conducted as a public enterprise in which the participants should be able to answer the same questions, able to agree or disagree, able to adjudicate their disagreements, and able to cooperate. In addition, philosophy seen through the eyes of historical relativism falls far short of what is required by the first and second conditions—that it be a branch of knowledge and that, among the theories or conclusions proposed by philosophers, some can be dismissed as false and some can be judged truer than others.

Historical relativism applies to scientific as well as to philosophical theories—and with the same effect. But, as I

[8] Philosophy thus conceived does not satisfy the first, second, and third conditions. The problems which the diverse "isms" try to solve may consist of first-order questions, as is required by the fifth condition; but the fourth condition, which requires that philosophy as a mode of inquiry have certain questions of its own, is satisfied only by lumping together the irreducibly different formulations that set different systems of philosophy or schools of thought apart from one another—almost in separate worlds or in logic-tight compartments.

shall subsequently try to show, there is a reason for holding that philosophy is better able than science to transcend the limitations imposed on human thinking by historical circumstances. Philosophers widely separated in time and space are contemporaries whom we can treat as dealing with the same problems and whom we can regard as talking to one another about them. This is not true, or much less true, of scientists working at different stages in the history of science.

We come next to a number of views which are somewhat akin in their conception of philosophy's relation to the special sciences and other disciplines. These views tend to deny that philosophy has first-order questions of its own, problems which it can deal with independently of the changing content of all the special sciences. While they do not restrict philosophy to second-order tasks of linguistic and conceptual clarification, they do focus its attention on problems arising from apparent conflicts, or at least lack of coordination, among the findings or conclusions of other disciplines, particularly the sciences.

According to John Herman Randall, Jr., for example, philosophy is "a clarification and criticism of the fundamental beliefs involved in all the great enterprises of human culture, science, art, religion, the moral life, social and political activity. It is especially the clarification and criticism of those beliefs that have come into conflict. . . ." This is philosophy's critical function; but it also has, Randall adds, an imaginative and poetic function—"the imaginative discernment and elaboration of new ideas, drawn from some special area; in modern times, usually from one of the sciences, but often from practical life or from religion as well." [9] If this were what philosophy is, then it would *not* be a relatively autonomous branch of knowledge, having first-order questions purely its own; all or certainly the primary problems of philosophy would consist of mixed questions involving the special sciences or other disciplines such as history, religion, art, law.

The effort to coordinate and see together what specialists in particular fields fail to relate C. D. Broad refers to as the synoptic function of philosophy; but he does not think that this is its exclusive function on the level of first-order problems.[10] W. F. Sellars seems to go further than Broad; he appears to make the synoptic task the sole function of philosophy. Philosophy, he writes, "has no subject-matter which stands to it as other subject-matters stand to other special disciplines. If philosophers did have such a special subject-matter, they could turn it over to a new group of specialists as they have turned other special subject-matters to non-philosophers over the past 2500 years, first with mathematics, more recently psychology and, currently, certain aspects of theoretical linguistics. What is characteristic of philosophy is not a special subject-matter, but the aim of knowing one's way around with respect to the

---

[9] *How Philosophy Uses Its Past*, New York, 1963, p. 100. Randall offers this statement of what philosophy *is* in the context of saying what philosophy *is not*: "not a narrow technical speciality, appealing only to a select few, with no relevance outside their limited circle . . . *not* the concern with a small group of inherited puzzles and dilemmas, insoluble because of the contradictory character of the assumptions that create them . . . *not* a collection of mistakes due to the confused misuse of language, to be cleared up by a proper analysis once and for all and then happily forgotten" (*ibid*).
[10] See "Two Lectures on the Nature of Philosophy," in *Clarity Is Not Enough*, edited by H. D. Lewis, London, 1963, pp. 60 ff.

subject-matters of all the special disciplines." [11]

The result of this conception of philosophy is the same as that which follows from Randall's view of it. If philosophy consisted entirely of such "know-how" in the performance of the synoptic function, and involved no "know-that" about a first-order subject matter of its own, it would not have the relative autonomy that is stipulated by the fourth condition. Nor would it be a branch of knowledge comparable to science and history. "The aim of the philosopher," as Sellars says, would not be "to discover new truths, but to 'analyze' what we already know." [12]

Philosophy would lack the autonomy it should have, in any view of it which emphasizes mixed questions, involving scientific or other special knowledge, to the exclusion of questions that are purely philosophical. There are passages in the writings of John Dewey and Alfred North Whitehead which appear to give adherence to this view. Each confesses that the shape which his philosophical thinking takes is determined by the current state of scientific knowledge—that, in short, his philosophical doctrines would have been different had he been writing in the seventeenth or in the fifteenth century, and that the positions he takes will have to be revised in the light of scientific knowledge a century or two hence. That could be the case only if all the problems with which they deal were to some extent dependent for their solution upon scientific knowledge; that

---

[11] *Science, Perception, and Reality*, New York, 1963, p. 2. Cf. Gilbert Ryle, *Dilemmas*, Cambridge, 1954.

[12] *Op. cit.*, p. 3. Judging from other essays in this volume (for example, "Being and Being Known"), Sellars does not restrict himself to the tasks of either analytic or synoptic philosophy.

is, only if they were all mixed questions.[13]

Actually, such is not the case, so far as Dewey and Whitehead are concerned. Their constructive philosophical writings deal with purely philosophical questions, which are in no way affected by the current state of scientific knowledge. If one were to name twentieth-century philosophers whose contributions to first-order philosophy not only were of the first magnitude, but also proceeded from a sound conception of what philosophers should be doing and how they should be doing it, the names of John Dewey, Alfred North Whitehead, and (I must add) George Santayana would lead the list.[14]

Their doctrinal or substantive differences do not obscure, nor should they cause us to overlook, their similarity of approach to the philosophical task and the extent to which their procedures converge. I am not saying that, from my point of view, they are procedurally sound in all respects,

[13] The view (if anyone were to take it) that all philosophical questions are mixed, involving the dependence of philosophy upon science, would not only run counter to the requirement that philosophy have a measure of autonomy derived from having certain questions of its own and a method of its own for answering them, but it would also raise a question about the other factor upon which the solution of the mixed question depends. Is it knowledge in the sense of *doxa* or mere opinion? If the latter, then philosophy is reduced to mere opinion and can have no intellectual respectability at all. If the former, then philosophy must be a branch of knowledge which has some autonomy, and then the very existence of mixed questions would entail the existence of purely philosophical questions which the philosopher must have a method of dealing with in a way that results in philosophical knowledge (*doxa*), not mere opinion.

[14] Unlike Whitehead and Dewey, Santayana nowhere acknowledges a debt to science for the direction of his philosophical thinking; on the contrary, he denies that it would have been different in any other age or culture. See *Skepticism and Animal Faith*, New York, 1923, pp. ix–x.

or that their philosophical work perfectly satisfies all the conditions which I think philosophy should meet.[15] But it moves in that direction, not away from it, as do the major movements in philosophical thought that now dominate the scene. I shall consider these in the pages to follow.

(2)

I have reserved for a somewhat more extended treatment the view of philosophy that is expressed, often quite explicitly, in the writings of the analytical and linguistic philosophers, especially since the end of the second world war. I refer specifically to the last fifteen or twenty years, because it is in this very recent past that the analytical and linguistic approach to philosophy has corrected the errors and excesses of Viennese positivism, logical atomism, and logical empiricism, with which it was associated in the period between the first and the second world wars.

In addition, it must be said of the analytical and linguistic writers in recent years that they continually ask themselves whether they have put philosophy onto the right track; whether they are at last doing what philosophers always should have been doing. They even ask themselves whether doing the things to which they have severely restricted themselves is enough—enough to deserve the high status that philosophy once claimed for itself in the family of disciplines.[16]

[15] For example, they are given to personal system building rather than to cooperative work in philosophy and to the piecemeal approach to philosophical problems. This is truer of Whitehead and Santayana than it is of Dewey.

[16] In this connection, I recommend two painstakingly honest reviews of the whole movement—one by J. O. Urmson, entitled *Philosophical Analysis*, Oxford, 1956; the other by G. J. Warnock,

Since the analytical and linguistic philosophers have the unusual merit of directly and publicly facing up to questions about the work they are doing—in a way that reveals their own doubts and misgivings—I think it important to comment, in a somewhat more detailed way, on their conception of philosophy in relation to the five conditions set forth in the preceding chapter.

It seems to me that the analytical and linguistic philosophers have taken a number of steps in the direction of making philosophical work intellectually respectable in precisely the same way that historical and scientific work is intellectually respectable.

They have excluded from the domain of proper philosophical work all efforts to construct vast speculative systems of thought which must be accepted or rejected as wholes. They have limited their efforts by strict observance of the heuristic principle that untestable statements are as out of place in philosophy as they are in science and history. They do not claim for their theories or conclusions any greater hold on truth than is claimed for scientific theories or conclusions; they eschew the certitude and finality of *epistēmē*. They carry on philosophical work in a way that manifests all the characteristics of a public enterprise: they address themselves to common problems; they make a piecemeal approach to these problems, question by question; they are able to agree and disagree, and when they disagree, their differences are adjudicable by reference

entitled *English Philosophy Since 1900*, Oxford, 1958. See also the title essay by H. H. Price in the collection, edited by H. D. Lewis, entitled *Clarity Is Not Enough*, *op. cit.*; and a collection of talks over the B.B.C., edited by D. F. Pears, entitled *The Nature of Metaphysics*, London, 1960.

to some common standard, such as the meaning of ordinary language; they have worked cooperatively on problems, as is shown by the many symposia in which they have engaged; and through cooperative work and sustained interchanges, they have made noticeable progress in a relatively short time, as is evidenced by errors corrected, insights sharpened, and points clarified.[17]

In addition to all this, they have demanded a certain proper autonomy for philosophy. They are not content, as were the early positivists, to have philosophy serve exclusively as the handmaiden of the empirical sciences—as their semantic clarifier or logical unifier. They have insisted that philosophy has a domain of its own, marked off from all others by a set of questions or problems that are purely philosophical.

So far, so good. What we have here is a program for philosophy, and philosophical work actually done, which satisfies the first four of the five conditions that I have proposed. *So far, so good, but still not good enough.* Analytical and linguistic philosophy fails to satisfy the fifth condition—the stipulation that the primary questions of philosophy, whether pure or mixed, must be first-order questions, seeking answers about that which is and happens in the world, answers that have the status of knowledge in the sense of *doxa*. The analysts and linguists restrict

---

[17] There are other examples in this century of cooperation in philosophy: the cooperative work of the members of the Vienna Circle (M. Schlick, R. Carnap, H. Reichenbach, and P. Frank); the joint undertaking of E. B. Holt, W. T. Marvin, W. P. Montague, R. B. Perry, W. B. Pitkin, and E. G. Spaulding in the production of *The New Realism* (New York, 1912); and a similar undertaking by D. Drake, A. O. Lovejoy, J. B. Pratt, A. K. Rogers, G. Santayana, R. W. Sellars, and C. A. Strong in the publication of *Essays in Critical Realism* (New York, 1920).

themselves to the plane of second-order questions—to the tasks of analyzing and clarifying the ways in which we think and speak and claim to know about that which is and happens in the world or what men should do and seek. Their rejection of the fifth condition is so crucial that it deserves further consideration.

It would appear that the analysts and linguists join hands at this point with the positivists, who also restrict philosophy to the plane of second-order questions. But they differ from the positivists in one very important respect. Their concern with everyday speech has led them to attempt to understand and clarify the concepts that are expressed in ordinary language, as well as the concepts of science. And this in turn has led at least some of them to deal with what they call "philosophical puzzles."

All or most of these puzzles seem to arise from the fact that certain lines of philosophical thought have reached conclusions which are incompatible with common-sense beliefs about such things as, for example, the existence of material objects, of other minds, or of the past. The analysts have been so concerned with these philosophical puzzles, bafflements, or embarrassments that they have at times appeared to regard the business of getting rid of them as the chief, if not the sole, function of philosophy, conceived then as a therapeutic effort to cure philosophy of its own self-induced headaches or blind spots.[18]

[18] Professor Price tells us how "the analytic conception of philosophy developed very naturally into a 'therapeutic' conception of it. The philosopher's job, it was said, is to cure us of muddles or headaches, generated by language; either by everyday language, or by the technical language of science. But it would appear that nobody could suffer from headaches of that particular sort unless he were already a philosopher. . . . And so we witness the curious spectacle of the professional philosopher deliberately and methodi-

Let us grant them complete success in the discharge of the therapeutic task (forgetting for the moment that all their troubles might disappear at once if they restated their problems about knowing material objects, other minds, and the past by expunging the properties of *epistēmē* from the meaning of the word "know"). Let us suppose that philosophy is at last rid of all the mistakes or unclarities in thought or speech that propagated the puzzles in the first place.

What then? With the philosophical theories or conclusions that conflicted with certain common-sense beliefs either eliminated or reinterpreted, we should be left with those beliefs—and many others—about the world in which we live, about ourselves and other men, and about how human life should be lived and human society organized and conducted. *What is philosophy's duty with respect to these beliefs?* Just to clarify them? To borrow a phrase from Professor Price, "clarity is not enough." Philosophy's duty is to examine them, to understand them, and above all to judge them—to say whether they are correct or incorrect and to offer adequate theories in support of such judgments.

I cannot guess whether the analytical and linguistic philosophers will ever break out of their present self-imposed restrictions and undertake this task.[19] Whether or

---

cally causing the headaches which he is subsequently going to cure. The student spends the first year of his philosophy course catching the disease, and then he spends the second year being cured of it. A strange sort of therapy! But unless things were done that way, the therapist would have no patients" (*loc. cit.*, p. 18). Cf. J. O. Urmson, *op. cit.*, pp. 173 ff.

[19] Some signs are now present of attempts to relax these restrictions or of efforts to transcend them. The analysts and linguists may be troubled by the question that Professor Price asks: "If philosophy

not they do, it seems to me that philosophers must attempt to answer first-order questions and must support their answers with reasonable theories, which can be submitted to appropriate tests, leading to a judgment of their relative truth. This is quite different from saying, as the analysts and linguists are wont to say, that the philosopher's only task is to understand what other men can possibly mean when they give this or that answer to such questions, without ever judging the relative soundness or truth of the answers given.[20]

(3)

The failure of the analytical and linguistic philosophers to satisfy the fifth condition, while satisfying the other four, underlines the importance of that last requirement. For philosophy to withdraw entirely from the field of first-order questions diminishes its educational and cultural importance to a point where it ceases to be anything more

---

is only clarification, does it deserve the place it traditionally had in liberal education? It acquired that place," he goes on to say, "on the strength of a claim to be something much more than this" (*loc. cit.*, p. 19). Cf. G. J. Warnock, *op. cit.*, pp. 157–159.

[20] These philosophers, as Iris Murdoch points out, "took it that the central question of ethics was the question 'What does "good" *mean?*'—but they refrained from answering the question 'What things are good?' and made it clear that this was a matter for the moralist, and not for the philosopher" (*The Nature of Metaphysics*, edited by D. F. Pears, p. 101). The analytic and linguistic philosophers, as G. J. Warnock remarks, "wish to say that philosophy has nothing to do with questions of *that* kind. Political philosophy involves the study of political concepts, but says nothing about the rights and wrongs of political issues. The moral philosopher examines 'the language of morals,' but does not as such express moral judgments" (*English Philosophy Since 1900*, p. 167).

than a professional occupation, of interest only to highly skilled specialists.[21] On the other hand, one aspect of the work done by the analysts and linguists suggests a sixth condition that philosophy should be able to satisfy. These philosophers, as we have seen, not only appeal to the ordinary usage of words; they also require philosophical theories or conclusions to illuminate and clarify common-sense beliefs. Some of them go further: they make compatibility with common-sense beliefs one of the tests of the soundness of a philosophical theory or position.

More than that needs to be said about the relation of philosophy to common-sense.[22] For the moment, I wish only to repeat what was said earlier—that, if technical or

[21] "No doubt one would not wish to deny," Warnock writes, "that there are very vital and interesting questions of this sort. But does it follow that philosophers ought to discuss them? Have they not perhaps, like physicists or philologists, their own special and specialized concerns in which in fact, for what the point is worth, they are evidently more interested. . . . Even if, as in fact is not perfectly clear, their present concerns are somewhat more confined than the concerns of philosophers historically have been, it is not clearly improper nor in the least degree unusual for such progressive specialization to occur" (ibid., pp. 168–169). A page or two later, Warnock adds: "There are after all a great many academic subjects in which, as they are at present pursued, the general public neither finds nor could well be expected to find any sort of interest. Yet no one is moved to complain of this state of affairs, or to urge the professors of those subjects to turn their hands to matters that would engage the concern of a wider audience. Why are philosophers not thus allowed to go their own way? No doubt there are many reasons. But one, I think, is this. There is a sense in which philosophy has only recently achieved professional status. . . . Second, it is only quite recently that the subject-matter, or rather the tasks, of philosophy have come to be clearly distinguished from those of other disciplines. . . . For these reasons I believe that philosophy has not yet been accepted as a subject which its practitioners should be left to practise" (ibid., pp. 171–172).

[22] See Chapter 8.

professional philosophy is to play the role it should play in liberal education and is to guide and improve the philosophizing done by the layman, it must avoid being esoteric. This, I think, should be added, as a sixth condition, to the other five. It can be considered as an addendum or corollary attached to the fifth condition: not only must philosophy be able to answer first-order questions, but it must also answer them in a way that makes contact with the world of common-sense; in a way that is continuous with common-sense rather than out of communication with it; in a way that makes sense, not nonsense, of common-sense.

In judging common-sense beliefs, philosophy may discriminate between those which are sound and those which are unsound and may correct the latter; but it is also the case that any philosophical theory which rejects all common-sense beliefs as unsound, or reduces the whole world of common-sense to the status of an illusion, has two strikes against it, or maybe three. It is with regard to this last point that some of the analytic philosophers seem to me to be moving in the right direction, even though they do not yet go the whole way. In order to do so, they would have to satisfy the fifth condition and do more than make a gesture in the direction of the sixth.

(4)

This brings me finally to a brief mention of the views of philosophy held by the phenomenologists and existentialists.

There can be no question that philosophy, according to the view of it held by those phenomenologists who are not also existentialists, is an autonomous branch of knowledge and that it has a method of answering first-order questions. They also think that the method of phenomenological analysis enables them to establish their principles and conclusions as necessary truths; in other words, they conceive their own philosophical doctrine as having, or more nearly having, the character of *epistēmē* rather than of *doxa*. In addition, the pursuit of their special methods tends to make their doctrine extremely esoteric. It soars transcendently above the world of common-sense and makes little, if any, contact with it.

The variety of the existentialists is such that it is almost impossible to say anything about them as a group, but two things seem to be clear. One is that they do deal with the most pressing problems of the ordinary man as well as with some of the traditional problems of philosophy—all of them important first-order questions: speculative questions about being and non-being; about the conditions of existence and its modes; about life and death; about being and becoming, about time and duration; about self and other; about matter and mind or consciousness; about freedom and indeterminacy; and practical questions about good and evil; about the conduct of life; about man's aspirations and life's goals; about man's relation to society and to his fellow men; and about the course of human history.

The other thing which is clear, unfortunately, is that in dealing with such questions—the kind of questions with which philosophers should be concerned—the existentialists proceed in a manner that reduces philosophy to a purely personal affair. The notion of conducting philosophy as a public enterprise would be an abomination to them. It would violate the privacy of the inner sanctum of the self, requiring them to relinquish the isolation of individual existence. The existentialists do not form an intellectual community, and they try even less to achieve communication with other thinkers. It is, therefore, difficult to say whether they agree or disagree with one another, and even more difficult to imagine them joining issue and arguing with philosophical outsiders.[23]

(5)

Three observations will bring to a close this examination of other views of philosophy.

(i) The analysts and the existentialists represent the two main currents in contemporary thought. There is a striking contrast between them, which should not be missed. On the one hand, the analysts are exemplary in the proper procedure of philosophy: they try to conduct philosophy as a public enterprise (and, in my judgment, succeed to a high degree); in contrast, the existentialists make no effort at all in that direction. On the other hand, the existentialists have a firm hold on the proper substance of philosophy; they address themselves to first-order questions that should be philosophy's primary concern. In contrast, the analysts have

[23] For a relevant portrayal of existentialism, see Abraham Kaplan, *The New World of Philosophy*, New York, 1963, pp. 97–128; cf. his account of analytic philosophy, *ibid.*, pp. 53–98. For one expression of the existentialists' position, see Karl Jaspers, *The Perennial Scope of Philosophy*, New York, 1949. For a brief statement of phenomenology, see the account of it by one of its founders and its most eminent exponent, Edmund Husserl, in the 14th edition of the *Encyclopaedia Britannica*, Vol. 17, pp. 699–702 (1929–1955). Husserl's essay is reproduced in a collection edited by Roderick Chisholm, entitled *Realism and the Background of Phenomenology*, Glencoe, 1960, pp. 118–128. For a comprehensive account, see Herbert Spiegelberg's two volumes, *The Phenomenological Movement*, The Hague, 1960.

turned their backs on problems of this sort.

(ii) I have so far done no more than compare other views of philosophy with the one being advanced in this book, by examining them in the light of the five or six conditions that I have proposed as requirements that philosophy should satisfy. I have shown in what respects these other views concur or diverge. While I have not concealed my judgment that these other views put philosophy in an unfavorable light, so far as its deserving the respect accorded science and history is concerned, I have not yet made an effort to persuade the reader that my view of philosophy is sounder or more tenable.

(iii) Underlying all these views of philosophy—the one being advanced in this book and the alternative views that have been examined in this chapter—there are a number of presuppositions, *themselves philosophical.* Any argument between conflicting views of philosophy, where they really disagree, would ultimately involve these basic presuppositions. Thus, for example, if the conflict we feel to exist between the analysts and the existentialists could be turned into real disagreements (logically tight issues), the dispute of the issues would involve arguments about the presuppositions underlying each of the opposing views. These presuppositions (in the case of analytic philosophy and existentialism) are more implicit than acknowledged; and so the conflict remains blind and is unlikely to become a reasonable and enlightened dispute. I will, therefore, try to state, as explicitly as possible, the presuppositions underlying the view of philosophy being advanced in this book, so that anyone who would take issue with it, or with the conditions that determine its character, can do so in a rational and enlightening manner.

CHAPTER 4

Presuppositions

IT WOULD BE NEATER, tidier, or at least less embarrassing if one could take a position *about* philosophy without having to commit oneself to certain positions *in* philosophy itself. One cannot, however; and this impossibility is, I think, peculiar to philosophy. We can hold this or that conception of science without committing ourselves to one scientific theory or doctrine as against another. The reason for this difference between philosophy and science should be evident.

A conception or theory of science, whether it is advanced by a scientist or a philosopher, is itself a philosophical and not a scientific theory. Such conceptions or theories belong to what we call the philosophy of science. A parallel use of words would suggest that the consideration of philosophy in which we are at present engaged should be called the philosophy of philosophy. The reflexivity is unavoidable. What is embarrassing about it is the feeling that we are caught in a circle.

On the one hand, to say that philosophy is or is not knowledge, that it is knowledge of one sort rather than another, that philosophical theories can or cannot be falsified by experience, or that philosophers should or should not be able to disagree in a way that is publicly adjudicable, commits one to certain philosophical theories about reality, knowledge, truth, reason, the human mind, and so on. On the other hand, any self-critical attempt to propound and defend such philosophical theories would seem to involve some conception of what one is doing when one propounds and defends philosophical theories.

Which comes first? The answer would seem to be dictated by the distinction between first-order and second-order questions. Questions about the nature of philosophy, like questions about the nature of science or of history, are second-order; questions about reality, truth, or the human mind are first-order, and, as I have pointed out, naturally take priority. But if one were to state and defend definite theories of these and other related matters before explicating the conception of philosophy that is involved in such theorizing, the postponement of the latter would be unduly protracted. I, for example, should be obligated to write several much longer books in order to lay the foundations for writing this one.

Instead I am going to try to do the next best thing, however inadequate that may be. In place of expounding and defending at length the philosophical theories which are presupposed by the conception of philosophy here being advanced, I shall simply state, as briefly as possible and without argument, the presuppositions to which I am committed. To present them in this way is merely to alert the reader to them. I should add that I regard them as fundamentally sound—much more tenable and truer than their contraries.

The view here taken of philosophy rests on two philosophical presuppositions—two assumptions that it requires us to make: one about the world and one about man. To the statement of them I will add a brief statement of their most obvious contraries, both to make their meaning clearer and also to enable the reader to see the positions that he would be rejecting if he were to adopt these assumptions as a basis for holding the view of philosophy being advanced in this book.

(1)

My first presupposition is a commitment to what is traditionally called realism. This involves: (1) the affirmation of a reality outside our minds—a world of real existences that are independent of our minds; (2) the affirmation that the world—the order of real existence—has a determinate structure of its own; that is, it is whatever it is regardless of how we think about it; (3) the affirmation that the world—the structure of reality—is intelligible; and (4) the affirmation that the world, having this knowable structure, provides us with a basis for determining whether our efforts to know it fail or succeed. This last point asserts that our theories can be falsified or confirmed by reference to something which is extrinsic to and independent of our minds.

To make this commitment to realism a little clearer, let me now briefly state two familiar alternative positions. One is Kantian idealism, which makes that which is knowable depend for its determinate structure upon the determinate structure of the human mind itself. The other is pragmatic conventionalism, which treats "reality" as if it were a plastic blob that can be given whatever shape or structure the

74

human mind finds it useful to impose upon it.

On either of these alternative presuppositions about reality, the world, or the knowable, the conception of philosophy here being advanced could not be sustained. But my commitment to realism does not preclude one aspect of pragmatic conventionalism: the admission that we have some freedom in choosing between conflicting theories by purely pragmatic criteria, but only *when all other tests fail*.[1] Nor does my commitment to realism preclude one aspect of Kantian idealism: the recognition that the human mind does have a determinate structure of its own which cannot help having some effect upon the shape our experience takes and upon our ways of thinking and knowing. This can be admitted without denying that the test of what we claim to know involves an independent reality.[2]

(2)

My second basic assumption concerns the constancy and character of man. It involves: the affirmation that man (or, more precisely the biological species *Homo sapiens*) has a determinate specific nature, which is itself a determinate part of the real world; the affirmation that among the

[1] The italicized qualification is of the utmost importance. We need not reject pragmatic criteria entirely in order to maintain that there are other tests of the relative truth of theories and that these other tests have priority over purely pragmatic criteria. To insist that pragmatic criteria are the only, or even the primary, criteria is to adopt the position of pragmatic conventionalism.

[2] C. I. Lewis's account of the mind's contribution to the structure of the experienced world, in terms of his theory of the "pragmatic *a priori*," also falls within the latitude of the realistic position as here stated. See *Mind and the World-Order*, New York, 1929, especially Chapters IV, VI, VIII–IX.

properties of man's determinate nature are cognitive powers adapted to knowing whatever is knowable about reality, including man himself as part of reality; and the affirmation that man's cognitive faculties are not exhausted by all his sensitive powers (his abilities to perceive, remember, and imagine), but also include the powers of understanding and reasoning, traditionally regarded as the powers of mind or intellect.

This presupposition can also be made clearer by setting it against two contrary views. The first is the assumption embraced by certain existentialists; namely, that man has no determinate nature and can make of himself anything that he chooses or wishes. Another version of the same assumption is the position taken by many sociologists and also by Marxists; namely, that man, lacking a determinate nature, is shaped or formed by the historic society or culture in which he happens to be born; hence, that what man is at any time and place is entirely relative to the historic social and cultural circumstances under which he lives. In a word, nurture is everything, nature nothing.

The second contrary assumption is to be found in a position taken by many psychologists, especially in the tradition of British thought; it is also, let me say in passing, the assumption that lies at the root of positivism, from Hume to the present day; namely, that man's cognitive powers are exclusively sensitive—powers of sense perception, memory, and imagination.

When I speak of my second presupposition as a commitment to the constancy of man, I am affirming not only that man has a determinate nature with determinate powers, including a mind or intellect that cannot be reduced to the functioning of the senses, but also that man's determinate

nature remains constant so long as man remains an identifiable and definable species of living organism. All the social
and cultural influences that mold the development of man
through the processes by which he is nurtured and conditioned operate on a determinate set of potentialities that
constitute the inherent properties of his specific nature.
These remain constant as long as the species *Homo sapiens*
endures.

(3)

I have already pointed out the respects in which the view
of philosophy that requires these assumptions differs from
the view of philosophy held by analytical and linguistic
philosophers and from the view of it held by existentialists. I
have done this by indicating which of the five or six
conditions they reject.[3] Their rejection of conditions which,
in my judgment, philosophical work should satisfy can now
be explained—or at least illuminated—by reference to their
rejection of one or both of the assumptions which underlie
the view of philosophy that has here been expressed in terms
of these conditions.

The existentialists reject both assumptions, most defi-
nitely the second. The analytic and linguistic philosophers
may, with some qualifications, adopt the realism of the
first assumption; but to the extent that they still accept the
positivists' relegation of philosophy to the plane of second-
order questions, they do so because they retain in some
measure the view of man's cognitive powers that lies at the
root of positivism—that is, a view opposed to at least that
part of the second assumption which affirms man's mind or

[3] See Chapter 3, pp. 63–70.

intellect as a cognitive power, distinct from and irreducible to all of his sensitive faculties.[4]

There is no need to add, as a third assumption, the statement that bodies of knowledge, such as science, history, or philosophy, have the character of *doxa*, not *epistēmē*. I asserted in Chapter 2 that they all have this character; but I did not argue for the reasonableness of that thesis there. Why, then, is it not here declared as one of my assumptions? My answer is that I hope, in the course of chapters to come, to be able to offer persuasive reasons for taking this view of organized bodies of human knowledge; as, in fact, I hope to be able to offer reasons for many other things that up to the present point I have merely asserted. Hence, it would be inappropriate to associate them with the two basic presuppositions stated in this chapter, for which no arguments whatsoever will be advanced in this book.

[4] That is the underlying reason why, in my judgment, they think that philosophy is unable to answer first-order questions or achieve first-order knowledge. I would also like to suggest that the very same reason why they think that philosophy cannot achieve first-order knowledge prevents them also from giving a satisfactory account of how science can and does.

CHAPTER 5

Logical Considerations

BEFORE UNDERTAKING the efforts at persuasion which constitute the main part of this book, I think some recapitulation is necessary to set the stage.

I have proposed a view of philosophy that differs from other views of this subject by virtue of the five or six quite specific conditions that philosophical inquiry is called upon to satisfy in order to be intellectually respectable—not only worthy of the same measure of respect that is accorded science and history, but also deserving of the respect that is appropriate to its own special character among the disciplines and in relation to liberal education and the organization of culture. I have stipulated:

(i) that philosophy should be an autonomous branch of knowledge, in the form of testable, falsifiable *doxa;*

(ii) that philosophical theories or conclusions should be capable of being judged by a standard of truth, to which appeal can be made in adjudicating disagreements;

(iii) that philosophical inquiry should be conducted as a public enterprise;

(iv) that it should have questions of its own (on which its autonomy is based);

(v) that, among these, some should be first-order questions (about that which is and happens or about
what men should do and seek); and

(vi) that none should be esoteric (out of touch with the
world and the beliefs of ordinary men).

These stipulations having been laid down, what must be
shown? As I see it, the reader needs to be persuaded,
principally, that philosophy can answer first-order questions of its own in a way that results in testable, falsifiable
doxa. This is bound up with philosophy's having a method
of its own for answering first-order questions—a method
which, if followed, produces answers having the desired
characteristics. This, too, needs to be argued. Persuaded by
these two things, the reader should be willing to acknowledge that philosophy can be a relatively autonomous branch
of knowledge, that its theories or conclusions can be tested
and judged for their relative truth, and that it can be
conducted as a public enterprise. But it would still have to
be shown that it can avoid being esoteric.

Let me clarify what is here at stake. There can be little
doubt that philosophy does have a method for answering
second-order questions of its own, and answering them in a
way that satisfies all the other conditions laid down.
Analytic and linguistic philosophy during the last forty
years has amply shown this. If we were to settle for this, as
many would like to, philosophy would have the requisite
autonomy as a branch of knowledge; it would have the
requisite character of a public enterprise, in which disputes
are adjudicated by reference to an objective standard of
correctness or soundness; and, to some extent at least, it
would not be esoteric. But it would still fall short of
satisfying the one condition that it must satisfy in order to

play its proper role in liberal education and in our culture. It would fail to provide answers to important first-order questions, examples of which were given in an earlier chapter.[1]

There can also be little doubt that some contemporary philosophers do try to answer such first-order questions; but they do so in a way that violates some of the conditions stipulated. The phenomenologists try to answer them, but in a manner that is quite esoteric. The existentialists try to answer them, but in a manner that does not permit the answers to be tested or disputes about them to be adjudicated.[2]

What remains to be shown, then, is that philosophy *can* satisfy all six conditions. The first, and the principal, step in that direction consists in showing, as I pointed out a moment ago, that philosophy has a method of its own for answering first-order questions of its own, and of doing so in a manner that subjects the answers to a variety of tests that measure the relative truth of opposed philosophical theories or conclusions. To bring this project into sharper focus, let us consider the relation between a discipline's having questions of its own and its having a method of its own, and the bearing of this relation upon the autonomy of a discipline as one of the branches of human knowledge.

[1] See Chapter 2, p. 43.
[2] If we turn from contemporary thought to the past, we must acknowledge that the great philosophical systems associated with the names of such thinkers as Descartes, Spinoza, and Leibniz, or Hegel, Fichte, and Schopenhauer, tried to answer first-order questions. But they, too, fail to satisfy the stipulated conditions, because system-building militates against the conduct of philosophy as a public enterprise, and because all these efforts aimed at giving philosophical knowledge the status of *epistēmē* rather than *doxa*. I shall have more to say on both these points in Chapter 14.

(1)

Let us start with the thesis that a discipline or mode of inquiry can have questions of its own if it, and it alone, has a method for answering that type of question. To avoid begging the question about philosophy, let us use the disciplines of science and history to illustrate the point, and let the particular science be taxonomic botany and the particular history be historical research concerning the development of the British constitution.

The botanist has a method of collecting and observing specimens which enables him to answer questions about the classification of the forms of plant life. The historian has a method of uncovering, dating, and interpreting documents and other traces or monuments of the past which enables him to answer questions about the succession of events relating to changes in the British constitution. The method of the botanist is totally inapplicable to the questions of the historian; so, too, is the method of the historian totally inapplicable to the questions of the botanist. The fact that each method is devised and designed to answer a certain type of question circumscribes the sphere of questions that the particular method is competent to answer. In addition, the fact that the method of the botanist or the method of the historian has a limited competence delimits each from criticizing the answers given by the other to the questions in his own proper sphere.

Let us now formalize this by substituting Discipline A and Discipline B respectively for taxonomic botany and British constitutional history. If Discipline A and Discipline B have clearly distinct methods, each designed to answer a certain type of question, then each has questions of its own which the other cannot answer; and, in addition, each is delimited by the limited competence of its method not only from answering the questions proper to the other discipline, but also from criticizing the answers given by that other discipline to questions that are properly its own, because they are within the limited competence of its special method to answer.

We can generalize this point still further. If the methods of all the particular sciences have enough in common to warrant calling all of them sciences, and if the methods of all the particular types of historical research have enough in common to warrant calling all of them historical research, then we can let Discipline A stand for science in general and Discipline B for historical research in general. This amounts to saying that science in general stands to historical research in general as taxonomic botany stands to historical research concerning the British constitution. Hence, we see that the relative autonomy of science and history as distinct branches of human knowledge rests on their being related to one another as Discipline A is related to Discipline B; and this in turn depends on each having a method of its own for answering questions of its own.

If we were now to designate philosophy in general as Discipline C, the claim that it is a relatively autonomous branch of human knowledge would be tantamount to asserting that Discipline C stands in relation to Discipline A and to Discipline B as they stand in relation to each other. To support this claim, we should have to show what few would dispute in the case of taxonomic botany and British constitutional history, or even in the case of science and history in general—namely, that philosophy has a method of its own for answering questions of its own, and that these questions cannot be answered by the methods of science and of history; with the further consequence that neither science nor history is competent to criticize the answers given by philosophy to questions within its own proper and limited sphere.

(2)

The way in which the thesis is stated above seems to make a discipline's autonomy depend upon its having a method of its own. Given a special method of inquiry, it would appear that there are certain questions which a discipline can, and certain questions which it cannot, answer.

The reverse would appear to be equally true. Given a certain type of question to be answered, the discipline must devise a method adapted to answering such questions. The relation would thus appear to be reciprocal. Having a certain type of question which it seeks to answer, a discipline may devise a method for answering questions of that type; just as having a particular method for answering questions, a discipline may formulate questions to be answered by that method.

The foregoing formulation needs to be qualified. If a discipline has a satisfactory method, not only will it be able to answer questions of an appropriate type, but it will also be able to arrive at answers that are testable and criticizable—answers that have the character of *doxa*, not of sheer, unfounded opinion. Hence, the reciprocal interdependence with which we are concerned obtains only between *questions that are answerable by knowledge* (*doxa*) and *a satisfactory method for answering questions* (where "satisfactory" means "able to result in knowledge").

Do type of method and type of question, taken together as reciprocal, suffice to differentiate one discipline from another, not only such main branches of knowledge as science in general and history in general, but also their particular subdivisions, such as taxonomic botany and organic chemistry (in the case of science), or British constitutional history and the history of musical instruments (in the case of historical research)?

I think not. There is at least one other critical element in the picture. Questions are questions about something. Let us use the phrase "object of inquiry" for that about which a question is asked. In some cases, the type of the objects of inquiry for a given discipline will be correlated with the type of question which that discipline seeks to answer and the type of method which it employs for answering such questions. The difference between science and history provides us with a clear example of this threefold correlation. As these two disciplines differ in type of method and type of question, so also do they differ in the type of objects about which they inquire.[3] But this is not always the case, as we can see if we consider certain subdivisions of science or of history. We may find two subdivisions that deal with different objects of inquiry; yet these materially different objects may nevertheless all be of the same formal type, as indicated by the fact that the questions asked about them and the method of answering are of the same type.

[3] It is equally correct to say that as these two disciplines differ in the type of objects about which they inquire and the type of questions they ask, so they also differ in the type of method by which they seek answers. The reciprocity in the relation of the three elements makes all permutations of statement equally correct.

Let M, N, and O stand for certain objects of inquiry; and let P, Q, and R stand for materially different objects of inquiry. Now, if all these objects of inquiry can be dealt with by Method A, then they are all objects of the same formal type—Type A. But a particular discipline may restrict itself to objects M, N, and O, while another may restrict itself to objects P, Q, and R. These two disciplines will then be subdivisions of Discipline A, differentiated from each other by the difference in the objects that fall within the scope of each.

Suppose for the moment that all historical research is of the same general type (that is, the same type of method, the same type of questions, the same type of objects). One subdivision of historical research deals with the development of the political institutions of the United States, another with the development of the political institutions of ancient Rome; or one is concerned with the development of economic systems and another with the development of musical instruments. These material differences in the objects of inquiry (all of the same formal type) would give us materially distinct disciplines that are subdivisions of a discipline having a certain formal type (historical research).

What has just been said applies to subdivisions of science, of mathematics, and of philosophy, as well as of history. For the most part, we shall not be concerned with these subdivisions; their existence, their number, and their differentiating characteristics do not affect our effort to show that philosophy as a whole is a branch of first-order knowledge distinct from the other three branches named above. Furthermore, our interest in distinguishing these four disciplines, as major types or main branches of human knowledge, is solely for the sake of showing that philosophy can have the requisite autonomy as a branch of knowledge. What must be shown is that philosophy can be a distinct type of knowledge and that philosophical inquiry can be a distinct type of inquiry, which it can be only if it has a formally distinct type of object, only if it asks a distinct type of question, and only if it employs a distinct method of inquiry that can result in testable and criticizable *doxa*.[4]

(3)

Two possibilities remain to be considered. One is that questions of the same type about objects of the same type are capable of being answered by methods radically distinct in type. The other is that the very same objects may be objects of different types of inquiry—that is, inquiry by disciplines distinct in the type of question they ask and distinct in the type of method they employ. Let us now consider these possibilities in the order mentioned.

Can questions of the same type about objects of the same type be answered by methods radically distinct in type? According to logical formalities which seem to me binding, I am compelled to say: either the statement of the possibility is mistaken, for there is only one type of method for answering questions of a certain type, and what is referred to as another type of method must turn out, upon examina-

---

[4] The foregoing discussion indicates to the reader the sense in which I am using the word "method." I hope it is clear that I am using it for what is distinctive or characteristic of the procedure of a discipline as a mode of inquiry (as, for example, the difference between the procedure of scientific investigation and the procedure of historical research), not for the detailed methodology by which that procedure is carried out.

tion, to be no method at all, but only a pseudo-method; or, if there really are two methods for answering questions of the same type about objects of the same type, then one of these methods must be the more effective method of answering them and the other the less effective method.[5]

Can the very same objects be the objects of different types of inquiry—inquiry by disciplines distinct in the type of questions they ask and distinct in the type of method employed in trying to answer them? Again, according to logical formalities which seem to me binding, I am compelled to say that the objects under consideration may be "the very same objects" *existentially* (that is, they may be the same real existences), but when the questions asked about them are different in type and the methods employed are different in type, then the objects which are the same existentially must be seen as objects formally distinct in type.

To illustrate what is involved here, I shall borrow an example from Gilbert Ryle.[6] The case he puts is as follows. "The very same objects" are the books in the library of an Oxford college. These are existentially the same for the college librarian and for the college bursar. But they are

[5] The possibility just analyzed is not fictitious. It is concretely represented by William James's conception of philosophy as struggling ineffectively with problems which are at some subsequent time effectively disposed of by science. (See Chapter 3, pp. 52–54.) That view of philosophy in relation to science would be accurate only if science had an effective, and philosophy an ineffective, method for answering the same type of question about the same type of object; or, conceivably, it might be an apt description of their relation if science had the only satisfactory method and philosophy had what turned out to be a pseudo-method for answering the same questions.

[6] See *Dilemmas*, Cambridge, 1954, pp. 75–81. The use I am going to make of this example departs radically from the use Ryle makes of it.

different types of objects for each: for the librarian, they are books to be classified according to their contents, and as such are distinctly different in type from the equipment in the college kitchen or the foodstuffs and wines in the college larder and cellar; for the bursar, they are consumable commodities purchased by the college, to be accounted for by reference to their purchase prices, their rate of depreciation, the cost of repairs, and so forth, in all of which respects they differ only quantitatively, not in type, from the kitchen equipment, the foods and liquors, the dormitory furniture, and the like.

The importance of the question with which we are here concerned lies in the possibility of its being exemplified by science and philosophy dealing with the very same objects, just as, in the foregoing example, the very same objects seem to fall under the purview of the college librarian and the college bursar. Ryle thinks there is no ground for imagining a conflict between these two officials because their approach to the same objects is so different and unrelated. I submit, on the contrary, that if scientific and philosophical inquiry both deal with what are existentially the same objects, there is at least the possibility of an apparent conflict between them, even though upon closer examination we may discover why and how that conflict is not real.[7]

(4)

The stage is now set for the efforts I shall try to make in Part Two, to show that philosophy can be what it should

[7] I shall have more to say on this subject later, when I deal with mixed questions involving both philosophical and scientific knowledge of the same objects. See Chapter 12.

be, according to the conditions laid down; and, first and foremost, to show that philosophy can have objects and questions typically its own because it has a method typically its own—a satisfactory and effective method for obtaining testable and criticizable *doxa*. As the reader examines these efforts at persuasion, he should bear the following alternatives in mind.

Either the conditions of philosophy as stated are correctly stipulated, or not. If not, then the burden falls on the reader of showing wherein and why they are incorrect. If they are correctly stipulated, then we can proceed in terms of them.

Proceeding in terms of them, either philosophy can satisfy all these conditions or not. It can do so *only* if it has a satisfactory method for answering first-order questions. If I succeed in showing that philosophy can have a method that is satisfactory for the purpose, then we can consider the consequences entailed by this view of philosophy. But if I fail, some alternative method that is satisfactory has to be found.

If the reader can discharge that burden, all is well; but if he cannot—or until he can—he is left with the following alternatives: either to be satisfied with analytical and linguistic philosophy, which confines itself to the plane of second-order questions, or to embrace esoteric doctrines, dogmatic systems, or a personal *Weltanschauung*—all of which put philosophy in a poor light as contrasted with science and history.

To avoid both of these alternatives, the reader must satisfactorily discharge one or the other of the two burdens that fall upon him if Part Two of this book fails to persuade him. If it fails to persuade him, and he fails to discharge one or the other of the tasks which then fall upon him, he must be prepared, as I should then be prepared, to admit that philosophy as an intellectual enterprise does not deserve the respect that is accorded history and science and that it cannot discharge the functions which no other discipline can perform in liberal education, in a university, and in our culture.

Part Two

Efforts at Persuasion

CHAPTER 6

A Method of Its Own

LET US IMAGINE once more a world in which philosophy as an academic discipline did not exist in any form or shape, but one in which all the other major branches of learning—science, history, mathematics—remained the same. We should have little difficulty in drawing the lines that separated these modes of inquiry or types of knowledge. Why would the introduction of philosophy complicate the picture? Why should we have to redraw the lines in order to fit philosophy in with a method and a place of its own?

The reason is that the picture into which we should be trying to fit philosophy is one the main lines of which were drawn by David Hume. His basic disjunction between two realms of learning and discourse dominates modern thinking about the order and relation of the disciplines. The whole field of reputable and reliable learning, it would appear, can be exhaustively divided into "abstract reasoning about quantity or number," which, since Hume's day, has come to be recognized as the sphere of *formal* or *analytic* statements; and "experimental reasoning about matters of fact or existence," which has come to be recognized as the sphere of *empirical* or *synthetic* statements. Since Hume's day, and especially since Kant's treatment of the distinction between analytic and synthetic judgments, this disjunction has been endlessly discussed, and the line between the two spheres has as often been made shadowy and unclear as it has been made sharper and clearer. I think I have a way of skirting the pros and cons of this discussion, by reinstating the Humean disjunction, freed of the Kantian overtones that were added to it. By "formal" or "analytic" statements, I shall always and only mean *statements that are neither verifiable nor falsifiable by appeal to experience;* and by "empirical" or "synthetic" statements, I shall always and only mean *statements that are verifiable (that is, incompletely verifiable) or at least falsifiable by appeal to experience.*

With the lines thus drawn, there would seem to be no question that mathematics represents one of the two principal archetypes of learning and discourse; mathematical statements are neither verifiable nor falsifiable by appeal to experience. There would also seem to be no question that science and history both fall under the other archetype; the conclusions of historical and of scientific research are to some extent, but not completely, verifiable by appeal to experience, and they can be empirically falsified. What about philosophy? How shall philosophy be distinguished in type from history and science without its becoming indistinguishable from mathematics? Or if philosophy—at least the part of it which claims to be first-order knowledge—cannot be associated with mathematics, how can it be placed on the other side of the line which separates the formal from the empirical, the analytic from the synthetic?

There are no satisfactory answers to these questions in the

terms in which they are asked. The terms are insufficient and the questions themselves are misleading, because they are based on the Humean disjunction. That disjunction is not the only way of exhaustively dividing human learning into its principal archetypes. There is another principle of division which makes it possible to accommodate philosophy without distortion. When that principle is introduced and added to the principle underlying the Humean disjunction, we shall, I think, be able to solve the problem of distinguishing philosophy from, and relating it to, science, history, and mathematics.

Why just these three? the reader may ask. What about the relation of philosophy to poetry? To common-sense beliefs or opinions? To religion? Let me remind the reader that we are concerned with organized bodies of knowledge (that is, knowledge having the status of testable and criticizable *doxa*). Even admitting the sense in which some writers speak of "poetic knowledge" or regard poetry as a form of knowledge, it would be difficult to claim that poetry constitutes an organized body of knowledge resulting from a specific mode of inquiry that involves submitting theories or conclusions to test and criticism. Common-sense beliefs or opinions can be excluded from consideration here on the same two counts, though it will become necessary, at a later stage of the argument, to consider common-sense beliefs or opinions not only in relation to philosophy but also in relation to science.[1]

But what about religion? Let us assume that the question does not cover religion in every aspect; for, in addition to being an organized body of knowledge, it is also a set of institutions, a set of practices (ceremonies, rituals, forms of

[1] See Chapter 8.

97

worship), and a way of life. Limiting ourselves to religion as an organized body of knowledge, we must admit that there are parts of it which appear to have the character of historical knowledge and parts which appear to resemble philosophy, at least in the character of some of the problems dealt with. Now it is sometimes claimed that religion as a body of knowledge rests on divine revelation (that is, the word of God as revealed to man). When it is thus construed, the ultimate warrant for religious doctrines or beliefs would lie in their having a supernatural origin; and religion would then be sharply distinguished from all other bodies of knowledge which have a purely natural origin—that is, which are acquired and possessed by man solely through his own efforts. Since the claim here being made is that philosophy is a branch of natural knowledge (and that this can be made clear by showing that it can have a method of its own for answering questions of its own), we need not for the moment be concerned with the relation of philosophy to religion conceived as supernatural knowledge, any more than we need be concerned with the relation of history or science to religion so conceived.[2]

Not everyone, however, accepts the view that religious doctrines or beliefs have a supernatural origin and should, therefore, be placed in a different category from all branches of natural knowledge. On the alternative view of religion as knowledge which man acquires solely by his own efforts, where does it stand in relation to science, history, mathematics, and philosophy? I fear that my answer to this

[2] This is not to dismiss as without interest or importance the whole problem of the relation of any of these branches of natural knowledge to religion conceived as supernatural knowledge. We shall return to the question, particularly as it affects philosophy, at a more appropriate place later in this book.

question may sound outrageous to certain ears, but there is no other answer I find tenable. When religious doctrines or beliefs are regarded as belonging to the category of natural knowledge, they are reducible or assimilable to historical knowledge in part and to philosophical knowledge in part, at least insofar as they have the character of testable and criticizable *doxa*. This is tantamount to saying that science, history, mathematics, and philosophy *exhaustively* represent all the distinguishable bodies of organized *natural* knowledge. Any set of doctrines or beliefs which falls under the category of natural knowledge must fall within the sphere of one or another of these four disciplines. To which one of these a particular doctrine or belief should be assimilated depends entirely on the type of question being asked and the type of method employed in arriving at the answer.

In what now follows I hope to show not only that philosophy can occupy a distinct place in the sphere of natural knowledge, but also that the principles by which the fourfold division is set up render it an exhaustive one. I shall proceed, first, by identifying the place of science in the picture; next, by differentiating history from science; then, by setting mathematics apart from both science and history; and finally, with all this done, by showing that there is still a distinct place that philosophy can occupy.

(1)

I shall use the word "science" to cover all the disciplines in the university catalogue which are usually called sciences, from astronomy to zoology. The enumeration of these particular subdivisions of science need not be exhaustive for the purpose of exemplifying what is here meant by science in general. In the sense intended, physics is a science, or a group of sciences; so, too, are chemistry and biology; so, too, are the social sciences.

While some of these particular sciences are experimental in the strict meaning of that term, not all are. All are empirical, but that is not their distinguishing mark. Historical research can also claim to be an empirical mode of inquiry, and it must be left an open question whether or not philosophy, too, is empirical—at least in the sense of testing its theories or conclusions by reference to experience. Nevertheless, it remains true that if we use this collection of disciplines to exemplify what we are referring to when we use the word "science," then whatever is a science is also an empirical mode of inquiry, though not every empirical mode of inquiry is a science.

This restriction on the use of the word debars us from calling mathematics a science or a group of sciences (including arithmetic, geometry, algebra). Clarity of analysis is served by this procedure. In deference to the prevalent convention of calling mathematics a science or a group of sciences, we might hereafter keep them distinct by referring to *empirical* science, on the one hand, and *formal* science, on the other. But I think that the nomenclature I have adopted will, in the long run, make things clearer. Since my aim is to show that science is only one of the four main departments of knowledge, and is not the only respectable branch of learning or mode of inquiry, no pejorative overtones attach to the statement that mathematics is not science.

With this restriction, we can ask, what characterizes science in general? What is common to science in all its forms? What unifying thread of method runs through all the subdivisions of science, tying them together as particular instances of one and the same mode of inquiry? The first part of the answer, but not the whole of it, is for me best expressed by using the words "investigation" and "investigative." I have chosen "investigation" in place of "research" because that word is used in too many ways and too loosely. Of course, any word is subject to the same difficulties; all I can do is to petition the reader—at least while he is reading this book—to use the words "investigation" and "investigative" with the restricted meaning that I am now going to assign to them. This is solely to facilitate communication. No questions will be begged or foreclosed by his acceding to this request.

By "investigation" I mean the process of deliberately making observations either for the express purpose of answering certain questions or solving certain problems or for the purpose of testing hypotheses, theories, conclusions, or conjectures. Accordingly, I shall call a discipline "investigative" in method if it proceeds to answer its questions, solve its problems, or test its answers and solutions by means of investigation as thus defined.[3]

I have already pointed out that, according to the Humean disjunction, science and history belong in what has come to be called the sphere of "empirical" or "synthetic" statements; and I have further defined this sphere by saying that nothing belongs there which is not testable by appeal to experience. By using the notion of investigation as just elucidated, it is possible to introduce a further distinction that is of the utmost importance for the fourfold division of

[3] In this connection, cf. an interesting discussion of observation, investigation, and experimentation in Claude Bernard's *Introduction to the Study of Experimental Medicine*, Part One, Chapter 1.

human learning being proposed. What I have in mind is a distinction between two kinds of experience, one of which I am going to call "special experience," the other "common experience."

Concerned as we are with types of knowledge and modes of inquiry, it is necessary to understand that experience as such is neither a kind of knowledge nor a kind of inquiry. We may know, or know about, the things we experience, but the experience of them is not knowledge of them. It is one thing to have the experience of breathing or not breathing, quite another to know about respiration and asphyxiation. Experience does not consist of assertions; it is neither true nor false; it is simply whatever it is. In contrast, knowledge (*doxa*) consists of assertions which may be either true or false. Unless we distinguish between experience and knowledge, we cannot say that our knowledge is based on experience or that what we claim to know can be tested by experience. Similarly, unless we distinguish between experience and inquiry, we cannot speak of empirical and non-empirical modes of inquiry.

With this understood, let me draw a line between special and common experience. By "special experience" I mean the experiences we have as the result of investigative efforts on our part, *and only as the result of such efforts*. By "common experience" I mean, in sharp contrast, all the experiences we have without any effort of investigation on our part. These are the experiences we have simply by virtue of being awake—with our senses alive and functioning, with an awareness of our inner feelings or states, but *without* asking any questions, *without* trying to test any conjectures, theories, or conclusions, *without* making a single deliberate effort to observe anything.[4]

I shall subsequently have more to say about the character of common experience. Here I shall confine myself to pointing out two things about it. One is that all men have common experience, but only some men—only those who investigate—have special experience. The other is that common experience is common not only in the sense that *all men have it,* but also in the sense that it is, at least in its rudimentary lineaments, *the same for all men.* Different groups of investigators with different interests and problems do not share the same special experiences, as all men, at least to a certain extent, share the same common experience.

To say that investigation is the *sine qua non* of science and, consequently, that science depends on special experience (on the so-called data obtained by investigation) is not to overlook the tremendous role that reasoning, imagination, theorizing, the formation of concepts and hypotheses play in the development and advancement of science. While observations made in the course of investigation are indispensable to science as a mode of inquiry, they are far from being the whole of it. Nevertheless, to say that they are indispensable is to say two very important things negatively.

First, all the theorizing in the world, and the very best

[4] What I have here called "special experiences" are usually called "the data of science" or "scientific data." But if the word "data" means that which is given to us without any effort on our part to get it, then it would be much more appropriate to use the word for our common experiences. These come very much nearer to being "data" or "givens." Stated another way, the *given* is the *immediate* in the purely negative sense of *not being mediated* by prior thought or action. In this sense of immediacy, common experience is immediate experience, and every type of special experience is mediated.

that the human mind can accomplish, could *not* by itself produce a single ounce of science without investigation and the data of special experience which it obtains. The scientific enterprise would never have got under way in the first place had men been content with the common experience of mankind.

Second, when we say that theories, hypotheses, reasoned conclusions, and conjectures are turned into scientific knowledge only by testing them empirically—that is, by looking for experiences which can falsify them—we always mean the special experiences which have been or can be obtained by investigation, *never* the common experience enjoyed and shared by men generally.

(2)

To sharpen the meaning of science, it is necessary to draw the line which separates it from history. I have already cautioned the reader about the word "history," which is usually employed in the titles of books that contain artfully constructed narratives. What distinguishes such narratives from works of fiction (which are sometimes also called "histories"—for example, *The History of Don Quixote de la Mancha, The History of Tom Jones, a Foundling*) is that they are supposed to be based on "historical facts" or "historical information." The information or facts about past events which historical narratives are based on or make allusion to, together with whatever can be inferred from such evidence, constitute items of historical knowledge and are the findings or conclusions of historical research. Since our concern here is with history as a type of knowledge and a mode of inquiry, I must ask the reader to keep remembering that I am always using the word "history" as short for "historical research" and "historical knowledge" and never using it to refer to historical narratives, which often contain much more than can be known by means of research.

When the word is used in this way, it should be clear at once that history is an investigative discipline and in this respect is like science. Now suppose that we were to divide all disciplines or modes of inquiry into the investigative and the non-investigative. This would give us a division of all disciplines into two archetypes:

I. Investigative disciplines
   These are dependent on the special experience or data obtained by investigation; negatively stated, they are unable to proceed on the basis of common experience alone

II. Non-investigative disciplines
   To whatever extent or in whatever way these are dependent on experience, they are dependent on common experience alone; negatively stated, they are able to proceed without any special experiences whatsoever

This dichotomous division of all disciplines is as exhaustive as the Humean division, which gives us the following two archetypes:

I. Empirical disciplines
   The sphere of synthetic statements; that is, statements that can be tested by appeal to experience

II. Formal disciplines
   The sphere of analytic statements; that is, statements that cannot be tested by appeal to experience

At first glance, it might be supposed that the two divisions simply coincide, but in fact they do not, for they are based on quite different principles. The principle of the Humean division lies in the distinction between what *is* and what *is not* capable of being tested by appeal to experience, whereas the principle of the division which I have introduced, for the purpose of expanding the picture, lies in the distinction between special and common experience—that is, between what *is* and what *is not* dependent upon investigation.

We can now see that history stands with science on the same side of each of the two divisions. Whichever way the archetypes of knowledge are set up, history and science fall under the same archetype. That being so, how is history to be differentiated from science as a distinct branch of learning or mode of inquiry? Everyone knows the answer. Science and history have different objects of inquiry—not just materially different objects, but objects different in type. Hence, the questions they ask and the methods they employ to find the answers are also different in type.

Scientific inquiry asks the kind of questions which call for *general* statements or formulae as answers; these are statements about classes of objects, not about particular instances. Historical research, on the other hand, asks the kind of questions which call for statements about *particulars;* these are statements about singular happenings or existences which have unique temporal and spatial determinations. In addition, it should be pointed out that these particulars are all *past* events or *past* existences; for, if they were present and capable of direct observation, they would not be objects of historical research.

There is more which might be said about history, but I do not think I have omitted anything which bears on the line that separates it from science. Men who are historians sometimes formulate theories or hypotheses about general patterns or causes of historical change; but when they do so, they go beyond the sphere of historical research and become philosophers—or, as Vico would say, scientists—of history. Men who are scientists (such as geologists, paleontologists, evolutionists) sometimes attempt to establish the spatial and temporal determinants of particular past events or to describe a particular sequence of such events; but when they do so, they cease to be engaged in scientific inquiry and become engaged in historical research.[5]

Let me repeat: though history, like science, is investigative and depends on the data of special experience, and though history like science makes statements that can be tested by reference to such experience, the method of history is distinct in type from the method of science, even as the questions it asks and the objects it asks about are distinct in type. Negatively, historical research performs no experiments, collects no statistical arrays, and so forth, as a basis for generalization. These are in the nature of the things that scientists do.

Positively, historical research looks for and probes particular remains from the past; examines documents, traces, and monuments; sifts testimony; and the like. These are the kinds of things that historians do. Hence, though both are

[5] Just as philosophy has pure and mixed questions, so do history and science. The solution of a problem that is a mixed question for science and history may involve a combination of scientific and historical knowledge and a combination of the methods of both disciplines. This would hold true for most of the problems in "natural history" which occur in such sciences as geology and paleontology. In contrast, the kind of questions that direct research in the fields of social and political history are likely to be purely historical—that is, answerable without the employment of scientific knowledge.

investigative, and though both submit their conjectures or conclusions to the test of experience (to the data obtained by investigation), history, by its method, can answer questions that science cannot answer; and science, by its method, can answer questions that history cannot answer.[6]

(3)

There is no need to identify the discipline or group of disciplines being referred to when we speak of mathematics; though, perhaps, it should be said that we are concerned exclusively with pure, not applied, mathematics—that is, mathematics divorced from all its physical or technical applications.

There is also no need to explain or argue the obvious distinction of mathematics from both science and history. In the framework of the dichotomy which divides all disciplines into the investigative and the non-investigative, mathematics is clearly on the latter side. It makes no use of special experience; if it has any dependence at all on experience, common experience suffices for all its purposes. This is just another way of saying that mathematics is "armchair thinking," which everyone recognizes to be the case.

In the framework of the Humean dichotomy, which divides all knowledge into the spheres of statements that are and statements that are not testable by experience, mathe-

---

[6] As an investigative discipline, history is coeval with science. The father of history, Herodotus, writing about the same time that the Ionian scientists were engaged in their physical inquiries, opens his book with the words, "These are the investigations of Herodotus of Halicarnassus. . . ." The Greek word from which our English word "history" is derived literally means "research" or "investigation."

matics is also clearly on the latter side. No one with any understanding of mathematics would ever try to refute a mathematical proposition by appealing to experience, common or special. This is simply another way of saying that mathematical statements are "formal" or "analytic," which almost everyone recognizes to be the case. The one outstanding exception is, of course, Kant; but even here the exception is more apparent than real, in view of the fact that Kant, though he treated mathematical statements as synthetic rather than analytic, also regarded them as *a priori* rather than as *a posteriori*, which means that for him they were *not* testable by appeal to experience. While these aspects would appear to be sufficiently clear, it may still be useful to stress the following three points.

(1) To say that mathematics is non-investigative does not entirely preclude dependence on experience. The mathematician has to get from somewhere his elementary notions or concepts—those which he subsequently uses to construct more elaborate and refined concepts. If these initial concepts are not innate or *a priori*, they must be experiential in origin. But the experience from which they originate is common experience, and the mathematician needs relatively little even of that. The existence of mathematical prodigies would suggest that mathematicians do not need more than the common experience enjoyed by the young.

(2) Though mathematics may depend on common experience for the origin of some of its primitive notions (certainly not for all its concepts), it does not resort to common experience in order to put any of its theories or conclusions to the test. Professor Popper's line of demarcation—between disciplines whose statements *can* and disciplines whose statements *cannot* be falsified by appeal to

experience—perfectly separates science and history, on the one hand, from mathematics, on the other.

(3) To say that experience, even common experience, plays a relatively insignificant role in mathematics does not preclude the importance of imagination, whereby the mathematician contemplates or manipulates one or another kind of symbolic representation of the abstract objects with which he is concerned. If the contemplation of mathematical symbols were to be regarded as observation on the mathematician's part, it would still be observation by the mind's eye, not the body's eye. Stated another way, the mathematician does not observe anything that he does not himself imaginatively construct for that purpose; and common experience is enough for all his imaginative constructions.[7]

I referred a moment ago to the abstract objects with which the mathematician is concerned. That the objects of mathematics are of this type—or, to use Hume's phraseology, that its objects are *not* matters of fact or real existence—will be understood by anyone who asks himself what kind of objects mathematicians can possibly ask questions about if their procedure is non-investigative and if the answers they give cannot be tested by appeal to experience.

We need not here be concerned with the problem—the important philosophical problem—of the mode of existence possessed by the objects of mathematical inquiry. For our present purposes, it does not matter whether the conceptualist or realist position offers the correct view of

[7] With regard to the three points mentioned above, and also with regard to the non-investigative character of mathematics, see John von Neumann, "The Mathematician," in *Works of the Mind*, ed. by Robert B. Heywood, Chicago, 1947, especially pp. 190–196.

the way in which numbers and geometrical figures exist. The only point that needs to be made here is the negative one that the objects of mathematics are *not* mutable, sensible, physical existents.

The negative statement just made does not preclude mathematics from being applicable to the world of mutable, sensible, physical existents. Physical measurements or other forms of special experience give us observed quantities, relations, orders, or sets, capable of fitting into mathematical formulae by serving as constants substitutable for the variables in terms of which mathematical formulae are constructed. Whether all of pure mathematics is thus applicable is not the question here. It may or may not be. The essential point is that the pure mathematician would not desist from his inquiries because he could not foresee the applications that might be made of the formulations he was trying to establish.

(4)

We finally come to the problem of putting philosophy into the picture. Where does it stand among the major types of inquiry? The answer depends, as I pointed out earlier, on our employment of two divisions instead of relying on the Humean dichotomy alone.

Let us take first the division of modes of inquiry into the investigative and the non-investigative, the principle of this division being rooted in the distinction between special and common experience. As we have seen, history and science stand on the investigative side of the line and mathematics on the non-investigative side. *Philosophy stands with mathematics.* Like mathematics, it has no need for the data of special experience to originate its basic notions or concepts. Like mathematics, it does not appeal to special experience to test its theories or to falsify positions taken or conclusions reached. To this extent, philosophy, like mathematics, is armchair thinking, for which the common experience of mankind suffices (though, as I shall point out subsequently, the philosopher needs the common experience of a mature human being, as the mathematician does not).[8]

Let us turn now to the Humean division of types of disciplines into the synthetic and the analytic, or the empirical and the formal—that is, into disciplines whose conclusions *can* and disciplines whose conclusions *cannot* be tested by appeal to experience. Here again history and science stand together on the synthetic or empirical side of the line, and mathematics lies on the other side; but now *philosophy stands with history and science.* We come then at last to an insight that is most critical for an understanding of how philosophy can be a distinct branch of knowledge with a method of its own. It consists in seeing that, while philosophy stands with mathematics on the non-investigative side of the first dichotomy, it stands with history and science on the empirical side of the second, or Humean, dichotomy.

The disposition of philosophy just made applies to it *only* on the plane of its first-order questions. So far as philosophy moves on the plane of second-order questions (semantical, syntactical, or logical), it belongs with mathematics on the

[8] What I have said so far about philosophy applies to it without regard to the distinction between first-order and second-order questions.

formal or analytic side of the picture.[9]

On the plane of its first-order questions (questions about that which is or happens in the world), the objects of philosophical inquiry are like the objects of science in two respects: they are, to use Hume's language once more, "matters of fact or real existence," not abstract entities, such as are the objects of mathematics; and they are, with one exception to be noted later, general objects, not particulars, such as are the objects of history.

On the plane of its first-order questions, the objects of philosophical inquiry are matters of fact or real existence. Asking questions about this type of object, philosophy, like science, strives for answers that can be tested by appeal to experience; but if, nevertheless, philosophy, like mathematics, is a non-investigative mode of inquiry, then to what sort of experience can philosophy appeal in order to test its theories or conclusions? It appeals to *the common experience of mankind*. The answer defines the method of philosophy, distinguishing it in type from history and science, on the one hand, and from mathematics, on the other: *from mathematics*, by virtue of testing its theories or conclusions by appeal to experience; *from history and science*, by virtue of the fact that the experience to which it appeals is the common experience of mankind, not the special experience obtained by investigation.

The reader will recall my reference to Professor Popper's line of demarcation between science and philosophy, with which I took issue.[10] Popper's line divides disciplines that

[9] This should not be construed to mean that mathematics itself is a second-order discipline, at least not in the sense in which we have defined the objects of second-order inquiries as the knowledge, conceptual stuff, and language to be found in first-order inquiries.

[10] See Chapter 2, pp. 33–36.

can falsify their theories or conclusions by appeal to experience from disciplines that cannot. But Popper does not distinguish between common and special experience; when he speaks of testing and falsifying conjectures by experience, he has in mind only the special experience obtained by investigation. Hence, he places science on one side of his line of demarcation and philosophy on the other. The picture is altered remarkably by introducing the distinction between common and special experience; for then, if we draw a line between disciplines that can and disciplines that cannot test their theories or conclusions by experience, philosophy stands with science on one side of the line, as against mathematics on the other; but if we draw a line between disciplines that employ and disciplines that do not employ the special experience obtained by investigation in order to test their theories, then philosophy stands with mathematics on one side of the line, as against science on the other. By combining these, we get a threefold division, separating science, whose conclusions can be tested by special experience; philosophy, whose conclusions can be tested by common experience; and mathematics, whose conclusions cannot be tested by experience, special or common.

(5)

Two diagrams present this picture graphically. Each diagram involves three principles of division. They are (i) investigative versus non-investigative—that is, dependence on special versus dependence on common experience; (ii) empirical and synthetic versus formal and analytic—that is, testable by appeal to experience versus non-testable; and

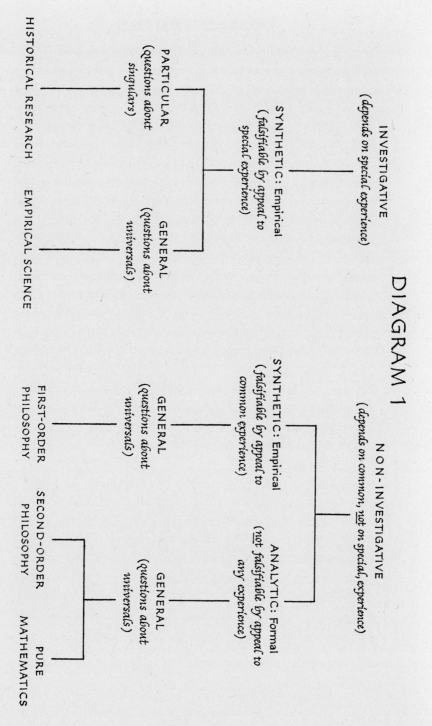

DIAGRAM 1

INVESTIGATIVE
(depends on special experience)

SYNTHETIC: Empirical
(falsifiable by appeal to special experience)

PARTICULAR
(questions about singulars)

GENERAL
(questions about universals)

HISTORICAL RESEARCH

EMPIRICAL SCIENCE

NON-INVESTIGATIVE
(depends on common, not on special, experience)

SYNTHETIC: Empirical
(falsifiable by appeal to common experience)

GENERAL
(questions about universals)

ANALYTIC: Formal
(not falsifiable by appeal to any experience)

GENERAL
(questions about universals)

FIRST-ORDER PHILOSOPHY

SECOND-ORDER PHILOSOPHY

PURE MATHEMATICS

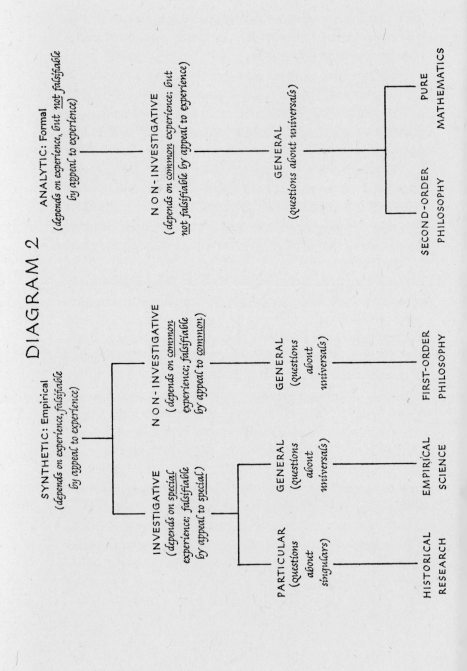

DIAGRAM 2

SYNTHETIC: Empirical
(depends on experience, falsifiable
by appeal to experience)

ANALYTIC: Formal
(depends on experience, but not falsifiable
by appeal to experience)

INVESTIGATIVE
(depends on special
experience; falsifiable
by appeal to special)

NON-INVESTIGATIVE
(depends on common
experience; falsifiable
by appeal to common)

NON-INVESTIGATIVE
(depends on common experience; but
not falsifiable by appeal to experience)

PARTICULAR
(questions
about
singulars)

GENERAL
(questions
about
universals)

GENERAL
(questions
about
universals)

GENERAL
(questions about universals)

HISTORICAL
RESEARCH

EMPIRICAL
SCIENCE

FIRST-ORDER
PHILOSOPHY

SECOND-ORDER
PHILOSOPHY

PURE
MATHEMATICS

(iii) particular versus general objects of inquiry—that is, objects singularly determined in space and time versus objects not thus determined.

Diagram 1, using investigative versus non-investigative as the primary principle of division, associates philosophy with mathematics. Diagram 2, using synthetic versus analytic as the primary principle of division, associates philosophy with science and history. In both diagrams, history stands alone by virtue of being the only discipline that seeks to know the singular, as opposed to the universal. If both diagrams are examined together, the dual character of philosophy will be seen clearly: associated with mathematics on the plane of second-order questions, it is allied with science on the plane of first-order questions.

Since the problem with which we have been mainly concerned centers on philosophy's ability to answer first-order questions, let us concentrate on the contrast between science and what I shall henceforth call first-order philosophy. Both have general, not particular, objects of inquiry. Both propound theories or conclusions that belong in the sphere of synthetic statements—statements that can be tested by experience. The crucial difference between them lies in the fact that science is investigative in method and philosophy is non-investigative. Whereas science must resort to the data of special experience in order to form its notions, generate its questions, and test its answers, philosophy needs only the common experience of mankind in order to shape its concepts, raise its questions, and test its answers.

In being non-investigative, like mathematics, philosophy is armchair thinking. In being able to test its formulations by experience, like science, philosophy is an empirical mode of inquiry. It is common experience that enables the philosopher to be empirical without having to get out of his armchair in order to solve his problems.[11]

(6)

I have shown that philosophy *can claim* to have a method of its own. If it were the case that no first-order discipline could form concepts, raise questions, or test answers except by means of special experience (that is, except by employing the data of investigation), then it would necessarily follow that a non-investigative first-order discipline, having the respectability of science and history, is impossible.[12] However, that is *not* the case; for common experience is available, and common experience can function in its own way, exactly as special experience does in its, to provide a basis for conceptual development, the materials relevant to which questions can be formulated, and the evidence by

[11] Those who accept Hume's disjunction are bound to say, as J. O. Urmson does, that philosophy has "to be logical rather than empirical—one cannot carry on empirical studies in an arm-chair" (*Philosophical Analysis*, Oxford, 1956, p. 127). He is right if "empirical" always and only means *investigation* and the appeal to *special* experience.

[12] To test this hypothesis, let us suppose that there is no such thing as common experience, distinct from the special experience that is obtained by deliberate and methodical investigation. Or let us suppose that, if there is, it cannot function as special experience does in the work of science. We know that philosophers do not undertake empirical investigations. We know that they do not observationally discover new facts. We know that they do not accumulate data. Hence, on either of the suppositions stated above, we would have to conclude that there is no place for philosophy among first-order disciplines. It would have to be bracketed with mathematics as a discipline that cannot give us knowledge of that which is and happens in the world.

which answers can be tested. This being so, philosophy can have a distinctive method which enables it to ask first-order questions typically its own and which enables it to test the answers it propounds.

Acceptance of this conclusion depends on two things principally: (i) on acceptance of the distinction between special and common experience, on there being such a thing as common experience, and on its being distinct from all the forms of special experience which result from the divers efforts at investigation in which men engage; and (ii) on acceptance of the proposition that common experience can function for first-order philosophy as special experience functions for science—on seeing that common experience can serve the philosopher in ways that are strictly comparable to the ways in which special experience serves the scientist.

CHAPTER 7

The Common Experience of Mankind

T HE DEFINITION of common experience just given involves two points, one negative, the other positive. The negative point is that it consists of all the experiences we have *without* asking a single question that calls for steps of observation especially contrived for the purpose. The positive point is that it includes experiences which are the same for all men everywhere at all times.

I did not say that everything which belongs to the common experience of a particular man is shared by all the rest of his fellow men. The ordinary day-to-day experiences of a twentieth-century Eskimo, a New Yorker, and a Hottentot are certainly not the same in all respects. The same must be said of an Athenian of the fourth century B.C., a Parisian of the thirteenth century, and a New Yorker of the twentieth.

I am contending, however, that the ordinary day-to-day experiences of these persons do not differ in *all* respects. There are a certain number of things about which they could immediately communicate with one another if they were to meet and engage in conversation: such things as some change in the seasons, the shift from day to night, living and dying, eating and sleeping, losing and finding, getting and giving, standing still and moving about in space, and so on. I am here assuming these communicators to be persons of no special learning—persons whose minds have been untouched by science and philosophy. Ordinary persons of such widely different location in time and space, and cultural background, could, I say, immediately communicate (with the aid of an interpreter) about the things common to their ordinary experience.

These universally shared elements of ordinary experience I shall refer to as "the core of common experience." It consists of those things about which communication is *universally possible* and with regard to which it is possible to translate certain of the statements made in any human language into equivalent statements in any other.[1]

(1)

I should like to quote and comment on two statements which I think throw some light on the role of common

[1] The following statement by A. J. Ayer is worth noting here: ". . . even if they are not strictly inter-translatable, languages of different structure may still be equipped to give substantially the same information; to every fact which can be stated in the one there will be a correlate which can be stated in the other. For example, a language without tenses, or other token-reflexive signs, cannot be an exact model of a language which possesses them. It will have no precise equivalent of a sentence like 'I met him yesterday.' Nevertheless, if the language affords the means of describing the persons to whom the pronouns refer, if it enables us to name the data which is indicated by 'yesterday,' and also perhaps, in order to get the full effect of the past tense, the date at which the sentence is formulated, then substantially the same result will be obtained. There will be a loss of economy, but no loss of information" ("Philosophy and Language," in *Clarity Is Not Enough*, London, 1963, p. 427). Cf. C. I. Lewis, *Mind and the World-Order*, New York, 1929, pp. 94-95.

experience in philosophy. The first is by Professor A. J. Ayer. It should be read in the light of the view, held by him and by other British writers, that philosophy does not discover new facts about the world, and does not test its conclusions by appealing to the data of special observation. Ayer writes:

> Philosophical theories are not tested by observation. They are neutral with respect to particular matters of fact. This is not to say that philosophers are not concerned with facts, but they are in the strange position that all the evidence which bears upon their problems is already available to them.[2]

Must we not ask Professor Ayer: What is the evidence that bears upon the problems of philosophy, evidence that is available to philosophers without investigation, without special observation, on their part? What is this evidence if it is not to be found in common experience? If there were no such thing as common experience, would philosophers be in the strange position of having all the evidence they need already available to them, where "already available" must mean "without special efforts of investigation on their part"? The only thing that is "strange" about the position of the philosopher is that, in this respect, he is unlike the scientist who does not have all the evidence he needs already available to him, but must investigate in order to obtain it. To call this "strange" reveals the prevalent modern propensity to regard the procedure of the scientist as standard and normal, and whatever differs from it as odd and somehow abnormal.

---

[2] *The Problem of Knowledge*, Baltimore, 1956, p. 7.

The second statement I want to quote is by George Santayana. It throws light on the elementary character of the things which constitute the core of common experience—the same for all men everywhere at all times because they are all sufficiently the same, and because all live in a world that is sufficiently the same. Santayana writes:

> For good or ill, I am an ignorant man, almost a poet, and I can only spread a feast of what everybody knows. Fortunately, exact science and the books of the learned are not necessary to establish my essential doctrine, nor can any of them claim a higher warrant than it has in itself: for it rests on public experience. It needs, to prove it, only the stars, the seasons, the swarm of animals, the spectacle of birth and death, of cities and wars. My philosophy is justified, and has been justified in all ages and countries, by the facts before every man's eyes. . . . In the past or in the future, my language and my borrowed knowledge would have been different, but under whatever sky I had been born, since it is the same sky, I should have had the same philosophy.[3]

Santayana refers to "public experience" as all that is needed to "prove" his philosophical views. I take it that what he means by "public experience" is what I have called "common experience," and that he is using the word "prove" in the sense in which it means "test." I would have added a few other things, but not many, to Santayana's enumeration of the things that belong to the core of common experience—such things as the multiplicity of

[3] *Skepticism and Animal Faith*, New York, 1923, pp. ix–x.

separate bodies that come to be and pass away, that move about in space and change in other respects; the multiplicity of other persons with whom we communicate by language or other means; pleasures and pains; doubts and misgivings; memories of the past and anticipations of the future; sensing and knowing; sleeping, waking, and dreaming; growing old.[4]

(2)

The reader may still have some unanswered questions about the meaning or reality of common experience. Guessing at what these might be, I shall try to state them in the form of objections, and append to each a reply.

Objection 1: Something as simple as the daily rising of the sun may not be the same experience for two men, one of whom sees it with Ptolemaic eyes, the other with Copernican eyes.

Reply to Objection 1: The interpretation of what they see is different, according to the theories they hold, but the experience they interpret differently is the same—the sun in different positions relative to the horizon at different times. Generally, the fact that men differ—for example, in the scientific, philosophical, or other theories that they hold —does not make it impossible for them to share certain

---

[4] What Santayana calls "public experience" Whitehead calls "immediate experience," Dewey calls "macroscopic experience," and C. I. Lewis calls "experience in general" or "common experience." Allowing for minor differences of expression and interpretation, the referent would appear to be the same. See Whitehead's *Process and Reality*, New York, 1929, pp. 6–7; Dewey's *Experience and Nature*, Chicago, 1925, pp. 2–3, 5–7, 9–10, 28; and Lewis's *Mind and the World-Order, op. cit.*, pp. 33, 36.

simple experiences not only with one another, but also with men whose minds are relatively devoid of theory.[5]

Objection 2: Men do not have to be scientists or historians in order to investigate, and acquire special experiences. Ordinary men ask questions in the course of daily life, questions which they try to answer by special efforts of observation on their part. The experience of ordinary men is not wholly or exclusively your so-called common experience—experience obtained without any investigation whatsoever.

Reply to Objection 2: Granting the objection does not affect the two points here being made: first, that not only ordinary men, but scientists and specialists of all sorts, have a certain body of experience that is common or ordinary in the negative sense that it is had without asking questions and without getting answers by special efforts of observation; and second, that though ordinary men do have special experiences in addition to common experience, it is only to the latter that the philosopher appeals when he wants evidence to test his theories or conclusions.

Objection 3: Common experience is not the same for all men everywhere, for the experience of the ordinary man necessarily varies with his time and place, with the circumstances of his environment, with the conditions of his life, and the elements of his education; more than that, the experience of the ordinary man grows or develops in the course of life; in other words, the experience of a mature man is different from that of a young man or a child.

[5] Cf. N. R. Hanson, *Patterns of Discovery*, Cambridge, 1958, Chapter I, "Observation."

Reply to Objection 3: This objection has been answered in the remarks made earlier about the Eskimo, Hottentot, and New Yorker, or about men in the fourth century B.C., the thirteenth century, and the twentieth century. What the objection maintains must be acknowledged. Common experience is not the same for all men in *all* respects; nor for a given individual is it the same in childhood, youth, and maturity. However, to admit this is not equivalent to saying that there are *no* respects in which common experience is the same for all men. The respects in which it is the same for all and does remain the same for the growing individual constitute what I have called "the core of common experience." All the evidence that the philosopher needs in order to test his theories and conclusions is to be found there.

(3)

Since the assertion that common experience exists cannot be tested empirically, by appealing to either common or special experience, and since it is a factual and existential rather than a formal and analytical statement, the only arguments for it have to be indirect.

One form the argument might take is that of a *reductio ad absurdum,* addressed to those who assert the existence of mixed questions involving science or history as one element in the mixture and philosophy as the other. In their understanding of the matter, does the solution of the mixed question call for the combination of knowledge drawn from science or history, with

(i) philosophical opinions conceived as having no foundation in experience whatsoever, or

   (ii) philosophical opinions conceived as having no need for any foundation in experience, or

  (iii) philosophical opinions conceived as needing and having an empirical foundation?

On the first alternative, philosophy is not knowledge even in the moderate sense of *doxa*. On the second, it would appear to be knowledge rather than opinion, transcendental knowledge, and knowledge in some sense that exceeds the claims made for *doxa*. Only on the third alternative is it empirical knowledge on the plane of *doxa*.

Now, on this third alternative, the empirical foundation which philosophy needs and has is either (a) experience obtained by investigation, as are the data of science, or (b) experience had without investigation. If there is no experience had without investigation—that is, no common experience—then philosophy, as empirical knowledge, must obtain the experience it needs by investigative processes (by specially devised means of observation, by experimentation, by data collecting, and the like). But everyone knows that philosophers do not collect data, make experiments, plan specially devised means of observation. Hence, either philosophy cannot be empirical knowledge or the experience on which it relies must be common experience.

Argument for the reality of common experience may take another form—that of questions addressed to the reader, without regard to any prior convictions about philosophy and science or about knowledge in its various senses. If the reader responds to one or more of these questions in the affirmative, he is affirming the existence of common experience. In other words, if I, as defender of the proposition that common experience exists, can elicit from the reader who may still be in doubt about it affirmative replies to the following questions, then, so far as I can see, he is sufficiently persuaded of the proposition.

Question 1: Do you have any experiences whatsoever that do not result from observations made by you purposively and deliberately in order to answer a question that you have explicitly asked? Only if you say, "No, not at all; without exception every single experience that I have ever had has been the result of an observation that I deliberately made in order to answer a question that was troubling me"—only if you say this do you deny having common experience. Otherwise, your response must be to affirm that you do have at least some experiences without any effort of investigation on your part; as, for example, when you wake up in the morning, when you dream, when you make love, when you fall downstairs, when you are eating a meal, taking a walk, and so on.[6]

Question 2: Do you think that you would be able to communicate about at least some things with any other human being who has ever lived on earth? If, considering this question carefully, you affirm the possibility of universal communication among the members of the human species about at least a limited number of things, your affirmation is tantamount to an affirmation on your part of common experience. Only if you say, "No, there are, and have been, some human beings so widely separated in time and space and so profoundly different in culture and language from me, that we could not communicate at all if we confronted one another"—only if you say this, do you

[6] This argument is intended to establish only the *negative* aspect of common experience—that is, its *not* resulting from planned or deliberate investigative efforts.

deny that common experience has a core which is the same for all men.[7]

Question 3: Do you hold certain opinions or beliefs—assertions about that which is and happens in the world or about what men should do and seek—which you hold as an ordinary man without the benefit of historical research, scientific investigation, or philosophical thought and which you find that many other human beings share? To answer "No" would be tantamount to saying that the only opinions or beliefs you hold are those that have been promulgated by men of special learning. Even if you did answer "No" (because you have made a valiant effort to adopt no opinion or belief that is not a product of special learning), would you not have to regard yourself as quite exceptional? In other words, would you not have to admit that there are many men—a vast multitude of them, in fact—who share with you opinions and beliefs about that which is and happens in the world or about what men should do and seek, opinions and beliefs that they have formed themselves or have imbibed from other men, all of whom have been untouched by special learning? If you answer the first question above, the one about yourself, affirmatively, or if you answer affirmatively the second question about other men, then you are admitting the existence of what I shall henceforth call "common-sense opinions or beliefs."

Let me now ask some further questions. *What is the basis of these common-sense opinions or beliefs, especially those*

[7] This argument is intended to establish only the *positive* aspect of common experience—that is, that it has a core of elements common to the experience of all men.

that are widely shared by men? Whence do they arise? On what grounds do we hold them? Unless you think (a) that they are wholly innate convictions of the human mind, (b) that they are of transcendental origin, or (c) that they are entirely arbitrary or unfounded prejudices on your part, you must attribute them to experience as somehow their source and must defend them, if they need defense, by appealing to experience as their warrant. The other alternatives being so unlikely, I am going to assume that you think these common-sense opinions or beliefs, in which you share, have some basis in experience.

What experience is their source and warrant? It cannot be the special experience acquired in the course of scientific investigation. There is nothing left for it to be, then, but the experience of ordinary men—the common experience of mankind. However, you may say: it was admitted earlier that even ordinary men may do some investigating and consequently have some special experiences. Granting this, one more question must be asked.

Is it not unlikely that the quite different special experiences of ordinary men would be the basis of the common-sense opinions or beliefs that they so widely share? To whatever extent certain common-sense opinions are shared by men, is it not likely that they are based on common experiences shared to the same extent? If you answer this last question affirmatively, you are once more affirming common experience; and, in addition, you are recognizing a core of common experience that is universal to the same extent that there are common-sense opinions shared by mankind.

CHAPTER 8

Common-Sense Knowledge

THE THIRD ARGUMENT, with which the preceding chapter ended, was an effort to persuade the reader that his or anyone else's acknowledgment of common-sense opinions or beliefs presupposes the existence of common experience, with its core of widely or even universally shared experiences. I regard the argument as persuasive, but two misinterpretations of it must be avoided.

The fact that common-sense opinions have their basis in common experience must not be construed to mean that they are all *ipso facto* true or beyond criticism. Like any other opinions, they are corrigible and subject to criticism.[1] One important exception must be mentioned here. If the axioms which Euclid calls "common notions" are self-

---

[1] In Chapter 2 (see pp. 28–30), where I suggested the use of the Greek word *doxa*, as opposed to *epistēmē*, as a qualifier attached to "knowledge" in order to indicate the use of that word in a moderate sense, I also said that I should use such phrases as "sheer opinion," "mere opinion," "unfounded opinion," to signify opinions that were held without any warrant and held in such a way that they were not subject to rational criticism or amendment. The reader will see at once that the phrase "common-sense opinion" is intended to signify something more reliable and having greater warrant than sheer or mere opinion.

evident propositions, such propositions express truths that everyone knows as a matter of common experience; but unlike all other common-sense opinions or beliefs, and unlike the conclusions of science and philosophy, these propositions do not constitute knowledge in the sense of *doxa*, but in the sense of *nous*.

The close relation between common experience and common-sense opinions must not obscure the clear distinction between them or lead us to merge one with the other. As I pointed out in the preceding chapter, experience is not knowledge. The experience of breathing is not knowledge of or about respiration. There are three elements here: my breathing itself, which I may or may not experience according as I am awake or asleep, attentive or inattentive to it; my experience of breathing when I am awake and attentive to that activity; and the opinions that I may form about my breathing—for example, the opinion that my breathing goes on when I am not experiencing it. Experience is a source of knowledge about the things experienced, and it provides a test for what claims to be knowledge of the things experienced. To function in these ways as a source and as a test, it must be distinct both from the things experienced and from the knowledge of those things.[2]

Knowledge in the form of *doxa* and common-sense opinions or beliefs (which have some of the attributes of *doxa*) are subject to criticism and correction. The only criticism that is applicable to experience as such takes the form of calling it "inadequate." Such criticism of experience usually stems from a criticism of the opinions which are based on the experience that is called "inadequate." This

[2] Cf. John Dewey, *Experience and Nature*, Chicago, 1925, pp. 18–21, 25–26.

type of criticism applies to special experience as well as to common experience. The data obtained by investigation can be inadequate. What is being said here is that other and better opinions would be formed if more and other experiences were had to replace or supplement the experience being criticized.

Though common-sense opinions or beliefs are subject to criticism and correction, common-sense[3] is not a self-critical faculty. It is not a methodical mode of inquiry. It does not produce an organized body of knowledge, but only an aggregate of separate opinions, with little or no compendency. It does not involve specific procedures for questioning opinions, refining or improving them, elaborating them, deriving some from others, relating and ordering them, and putting them to the test. Even in the exceptional case in which one common-sense opinion improves upon and replaces another, this does not occur as the result of a systematic and intentional effort. In all these respects, the aggregate of common-sense opinions differs from such organized branches of knowledge as science and philosophy.

Whence, then, come the criticism and correction of common-sense opinions or beliefs? Clearly, they must come from those branches of knowledge or modes of inquiry which are by their very nature self-critical—that is, which involve procedures for testing and refining the theories and conclusions that they themselves develop. Do they come from each and every one of the major branches of knowledge? From history and mathematics as well as from science

---

[3] I have been using and shall continue to use the hyphenated word "common-sense" to name our tendency to form opinions on the basis of common experience.

and philosophy? No, and for obvious reasons. Common-sense opinions have the character of generalizations; they are seldom if ever opinions about singular past events or existences. Hence, it is unlikely that common-sense opinions would provoke criticism from the historian, or undergo correction in the light of the special data of historical research. Furthermore, common-sense opinions concern matters of fact or real existence; they are opinions about that which is or happens in the world, not about abstract entities of the sort which are the typical objects of mathematical inquiry. Hence, it is unlikely that the mathematician, as such, would be a critic of common-sense opinions.

That leaves science and philosophy. Do both of these remaining disciplines engage in the criticism of common-sense opinions? And if they do, do they do so in the same way or in different ways? Let me state the answer in summary form and then try to explain it. It involves three separate points: (i) the criticism and correction of common-sense opinions come mainly from science, not from philosophy; (ii) philosophy by its very nature is directed to the examination and explication of common-sense opinions, and it undertakes to defend those opinions or beliefs which require and deserve defense; and (iii) in the rare instances in which philosophy criticizes and corrects common-sense opinions, it does so in a manner that is distinctly different from the manner in which science criticizes and corrects common-sense beliefs.

The reason for these differences between science and philosophy in relation to common-sense lies in the essential difference between science and philosophy as two modes of empirical inquiry and two types of empirical knowledge about that which is or happens in the world. When I refer to both science and philosophy as modes of empirical inquiry or as branches of empirical knowledge, I am speaking only of first-order philosophy and I am using the word "empirical" in the sense in which it is opposed to "formal," signifying knowledge that is testable by experience, whether that be common experience or the special experience obtained by investigation.

Science is empirical by virtue of the special experience on which it is based and to which it appeals in order to test its hypotheses and conclusions. Philosophy is empirical by virtue of the common experience on which it is based and to which it appeals to test its theories and conclusions. Both are empirical in the same broad sense; yet each is empirical in a typically different sense; and the specific way in which each is empirical is neither a superior nor an inferior way of being empirical—just different. One is neither more nor less empirical than the other. I shall amplify these remarks later, but now I wish to deal, first, with the correction of common-sense opinions by science; second, with the explication and defense of them by philosophy; and third, with the rare instances in which philosophy corrects common-sense.

(1)

Science, for the most part, simply goes beyond our common-sense knowledge of the world, by extending or adding to it.[4] It give us knowledge of matters totally beyond

[4] Since common-sense beliefs are not sheer or unfounded opinion, but have some of the characteristics of *doxa*, it is not inappropriate to speak of the aggregate of common-sense opinions or beliefs as constituting our common-sense knowledge of the world, even though that knowledge is not organized or attained in a methodical and self-critical way.

the reach of common-sense, for it is knowledge that can be arrived at only through investigation. Concerning most of the matters covered by scientific knowledge, common-sense forms no opinions at all because common experience provides no basis whatsoever for doing so. That is why, for the most part, the findings or conclusions of science, based upon special experience, do not correct or replace faulty common-sense opinions.

The exceptions to this general rule arise in those instances in which common experience does provide some basis for an opinion but in which common experience is also inadequate for the formation of a correct opinion and, therefore, needs to be supplemented by the special data obtained by investigation. In such cases, the investigative effort usually results in the correction or replacement of a faulty common-sense opinion by scientific knowledge. Consider the following common-sense opinions: that the earth is flat or that it is stationary, neither rotating nor moving through space; that living organisms spring spontaneously from decaying or putrefying flesh; that light is transmitted instantaneously—that it takes no time to travel from its source. It is not difficult to discern the common experience upon which each of these opinions is based. Were it not for the special data obtained by investigation in each case, the common-sense opinion, though false, would not have been falsified.

It is important to note that science falsifies the common-sense opinion, not the experience on which it is based. Even after the faulty common-sense opinion is corrected and replaced by scientific knowledge, our common experience with regard to each of the matters mentioned above remains exactly what it was before. But science has helped us to realize that that experience was inadequate to answer the question in response to which the faulty common-sense opinion was originally formed.

It should also be noted that the manner in which science corrects faulty common-sense opinions, by going beyond common experience through investigative efforts, is, in principle, the same as the manner in which later scientific work corrects earlier scientific errors when the earlier errors arose from insufficient data or from failures of observation which subsequent investigation remedies. Thus, for example, Harvey, by making observations which his predecessors failed to make, corrected the faulty scientific opinion, held by earlier anatomists, that the blood does not circulate.

What has just been said does not preclude purely theoretical advances or improvements in science. Harvey, for example, not only made observations that had not been made before, but he also corrected the reasoning of his predecessors about the observations they did make. He had a better theory of the function of the heart and blood vessels, one which gave a better account of all the data, both old and new. Science does not correct common-sense errors in this way, for common-sense is without theories or explanations of the opinions it holds.

(2)

Up to this point, I have skirted the issue about self-evident propositions, such as the axioms about whole and part and about the relation of equals and unequals, or such as the principle of being and non-being (namely, that one and the same thing cannot at the same time both exist and not exist, nor can it at the same time both be in a certain respect and not be in that same respect). The statement about being and non-being or the statement that a finite whole is always greater than any of its definite parts may look like the statement that the parent of a parent is a grandparent or the statement that plane figures are two-dimensional, but there is a subtle difference between them. In the one case, the statement merely makes explicit what is involved in our own linguistic conventions and therefore deserves to be treated as a tautology that gives us no information about the things of this world. In the other case, the statement expresses our understanding of things as they are and of their relationships, which would be the same no matter what words we used or how we set up our linguistic conventions.

Finite quantitative wholes exist and they have definite finite parts; for example, this page can be cut in half or in quarters. Now, as I understand a finite whole (that is, any finite whole) and as I understand any definite part of a finite whole, I understand the whole to be greater than the part, or the part to be less than the whole. So far is this from being a verbal matter that I cannot define the meaning of the words "whole" and "part"; these words express primitive or indefinable notions. Unable to define them, all I can do is to express my understanding of whole and part by a statement of how wholes and parts are related.

That statement is axiomatic or self-evident in the sense that its opposite is immediately seen to be false. I can use the word "part" for this page, and the word "whole" for a half of this page after I have cut it in two, but I cannot think that the page before it is cut is less than the half of it which I have in my hand after I have cut it. However I use language, my understanding of finite wholes and their definite parts is such that I am compelled to say that I know that the whole is greater than the part, and what I know is the relation between existent wholes and their parts, not something about the use of words or their meanings.

In contrast, when I say that plane figures are two-dimensional, I have merely spelled out the meaning that I attach to the phrase "plane figure." If I decide to use the word "plane" for figures that have only length and breadth, and "solid" for figures that have depth as well, then it becomes tautological to say that plane figures are two-dimensional, and solid figures three-dimensional.[5]

If there are axioms or self-evident propositions, as I think there are, they have the status of indemonstrable and incorrigible truths; that is, they are knowledge in the sense of *epistēmē*, not in the sense of *doxa*. Such truths are based on common experience alone and are part of our common-sense knowledge, for they belong to no organized body of knowledge; they do not belong to philosophy or mathematics any more than they belong to science or history. That is why Euclid called them "common notions." However, philosophy does stand in a special relation to them, as it stands in a special relation to common-sense knowledge because both, like philosophical knowledge, rest on common experience alone. If the truth of axioms or self-evident propositions is challenged, or if the effort is made to reduce them to tautologies or to statements of verbal usage, philosophy has the task of defending their status as first-order knowledge. Since they are indemonstrable, the defense must take the form of pointing to the common ex-

[5] To assert that the parent of a parent is a grandparent thinly conceals the verbal stipulation, "Let us call the parent of a parent a 'grandparent.' "

perience from which they are learned by intuitive induction.

The rest of common-sense knowledge consists of *doxai*—opinions that are intrinsically corrigible because they do not assert that which it is impossible to deny or that about which it is impossible to think the opposite. Not all intrinsically corrigible opinions, however, are subject to amendment or falsification by means of the data acquired by investigation. Some of the things we know by common-sense in the light of common experience concern matters about which investigation is simply impossible; in other cases, it may be possible but is quite unnecessary. If this were not so, then every first-order question would belong to science and, in addition, every common-sense opinion would ultimately be corrected or replaced by scientific knowledge of the same matter.

We are interested here only in those common-sense opinions which, while intrinsically corrigible, are not subject to amendment or falsification by science because they are knowledge of matters which are not subject to investigation. They cannot, therefore, be challenged by science. Hence, if they are challenged at all, they must be challenged by philosophy; and when they are thus challenged, their defense, if they can be defended at all, must also come from philosophy. At this point we are confronted by a split within philosophy itself—or, it would be better to say, a split among philosophers, between those who are opponents of common-sense and those who are its defenders.

To treat this matter illustratively yet briefly, I am going to characterize the philosophical opponents of common-sense as either skeptics or rationalists. The skeptics present arguments which try to show the untenability of certain common-sense opinions. Their arguments do not appeal to common experience; they ignore it. The rationalists offer theories which claim to be profounder or subtler than the shallow or gross common-sense opinions which they are intended to replace. Their theories do not appeal to common experience; they claim a higher warrant in the structure or revelations of reason itself. Both opponents of common-sense are alike in being non-empirical philosophers; that is, they share the same disregard for, or transcendence of, common experience. The proper contrasting appellation for the defenders of common-sense would, of course, be "empirical philosophers," since their defense rests on common experience.

For typical examples of what is here involved, I refer the reader to G. E. Moore's classic defense, against skeptics, of our common-sense knowledge about the existence of such things as my own body, bodies other than my own, the past, other minds; [6] and to Jacques Maritain's defense of our common-sense knowledge of the order and connection of individual, sensible, material things against rationalists who try to develop a system of the world from some preferential principle, such as Descartes' *cogito*, Spinoza's *substance*, Fichte's *pure ego*, Schopenhauer's *will*, Hegel's *absolute idea*. [7]

The reader will find the empirical philosopher appealing to common experience in order to repudiate erroneous philosophical doctrines or positions. He will see that com-

[6] "A Defence of Common Sense," in *Contemporary British Philosophy, First and Second Series*, London, 1924, pp. 193–208.

[7] *An Introduction to Philosophy*, London, 1930, Chapter VIII on Philosophy and Common Sense. Cf. *Degrees of Knowledge*, New York, 1938, Chapter II, esp. pp. 99 ff.

mon experience can serve the philosopher (that is, the
philosopher who adopts an empirical approach) in the same
way that the special data of investigation serves the empirical scientist, as a means of testing theories. He will also
discover that, just as Harvey's correction of the erroneous
view about the heart and blood involved the correction
of faulty reasoning by his predecessors, so the defense of
common-sense against skeptics and rationalists involves
logical criticism of their doctrines as well as the marshaling
of empirical evidence against them.

(3)

I said earlier that philosophy not only may defend but
also may correct common-sense opinions or beliefs. The
correction of common-sense opinions is usually the work of
science, for where they are faulty, the fault is most often
due to the inadequacy of common experience with respect
to matters about which investigation is possible. Philosophy,
being non-investigative, cannot supplement common experience where it is inadequate. Hence, it corrects common-
sense opinions only in those rare instances in which the
opinions represent an inadequate understanding of the
common experience from which they arise.

For example, from our common experience of the flow or
passage of time, the common-sense opinion is formed that
time is divided into three distinct parts or portions—past,
present, and future—each having a certain extent and each
separated by boundary lines, as three distinct parts of a
spatial area can be separated from one another. Philosophical analysis of our experience of time corrects this opinion
by showing (as Augustine and William James showed)

why it is incorrect to understand the parts of time as if they were separated from and related to one another as three parts of spatial area can be separated and related.[8]

This example illustrates how radically different are the ways in which science and philosophy correct common-sense. Science does it by going beyond common experience where it is inadequate, supplementing it by the special experiences turned up by investigation. Philosophy does it by staying with common experience but providing a better understanding or more accurate grasp of the things experienced.[9] The philosophical correction of common-sense opinions, where these represent a faulty or inadequate understanding of common experience, is, perhaps, one of the things which David Hume had in mind when he said that "philosophical decisions are nothing but the reflections of common life, methodized and corrected." [10]

(4)

To defend or correct common-sense is one thing; to rely on it, quite another. The proper method of philosophy calls for reliance upon common experience, but not for reliance on common-sense. The philosopher who adopted the empirical method would naturally respect the common-sense beliefs that have arisen from the same experiences to

[8] See St. Augustine, *Confessions*, Book XI, Chapters xiv–xxx; William James, *Principles of Psychology*, New York, 1890, Volume I, Chapter XV, especially pp. 608–610, 630–631.

[9] That science and philosophy differ in this way, with regard to faulty common-sense beliefs, follows from their essential difference in method—the one, investigative; the other, non-investigative; yet both empirical.

[10] *Enquiry Concerning Human Understanding*, Section XII, Part III, Number 129.

which he himself appeals; but he would not, in consequence, appeal to the authority of common-sense opinions in order to establish or defend his own theories or conclusions.[11]

When the empirical philosopher defends common-sense opinions, he relies on and appeals to the common experience from which those common-sense opinions arise; but since his own assertions are always supported by philosophical reasoning or amplified by philosophical analysis, they are always distinct from the unreasoned and unanalyzed common-sense judgments based on the same experience. When the empirical philosopher corrects common-sense beliefs, he acknowledges the common experience on which they are based, but he supplants those beliefs with a better understanding or more accurate grasp of the things experienced.

This brings us to an important question: can philosophy go beyond or add to the knowledge of the world that is

[11] It is significant that philosophers for whom the employment of common experience is a fundamental and distinguishing mark of philosophical method are also philosophers who understand the critical relation of philosophy to common-sense. Santayana, whose statement about common experience I quoted earlier (see Chapter 7, p. 123), also writes: "I think that common sense, in a rough dogged way, is technically sounder than the special schools of philosophy, each of which squints and overlooks half the facts and half the difficulties in its eagerness to find in some detail the key to the whole. I am animated by distrust of all high guesses, and by sympathy with the old prejudices and workaday opinions of mankind: they are ill expressed, but they are well grounded" (*Skepticism and Animal Faith*, New York, 1923, p. v). See Whitehead, *Process and Reality*, New York, 1929, pp. 25–26, and Lewis, *Mind and the World-Order*, New York, 1929, pp. 18–19. Cf. Maritain, *An Introduction to Philosophy*, op. cit., Ch. VIII; Etienne Gilson, "*Vade Mecum* of a Young Realist," in *Philosophy of Knowledge*, Philadelphia, 1960, p. 388; and D. J. B. Hawkins, *Crucial Problems of Modern Philosophy*, London, 1957, Ch. IX, especially pp. 124–125.

comprised in the aggregate of common-sense opinions about it? We have seen that science can and does do this. Whether it corrects and supplants faulty common-sense beliefs or simply goes beyond them where they are correct, science is continually amplifying our knowledge of the world, over and above everything that is known by common-sense. Can philosophy also amplify our knowledge of the world? Can it give us knowledge that we would not have if we were confined to the knowledge afforded by common-sense and by science?

A negative answer to this question would mean that philosophy provides us with nothing more than a better understanding of what we already know. Insofar as it gives us a reasoned analysis of common-sense opinions, philosophy does give us a better understanding of what we already know; but it can do more than that. Insofar as it corrects common-sense opinions, it not only gives us a better understanding of common experience, but it also gives us new knowledge of the world that is experienced.

It can go even further. In the process of developing theories to explain some of the things known by common-sense and by science, philosophy may posit theoretical entities, just as science does. The unobserved substances or causes posited by the philosopher are like the unobserved particles or forces posited by the scientist. In the case of philosophy, these theoretical entities serve to explain the observed phenomena in the field of common experience, just as in the case of science, they serve to explain the observed phenomena in the field of special experience. When, in either case, the posited theoretical entities are asserted to exist, the assertions, insofar as they can be supported or defended by appeal to experience, represent additions to our knowledge of that which exists. Philosophy can thus extend our knowledge of the world.

Finally, just as science goes beyond common-sense knowledge by asking questions that never even occur to common-sense, so can philosophy. When such questions are answered, as they are by scientific knowledge in the light of special experience and as they can be by philosophical knowledge in the light of common experience, our knowledge of the world is amplified by additions to the common-sense knowledge that we already possess.

CHAPTER 9

Tests of Truth in Philosophy

THE PRECEDING CHAPTERS have shown how philosophy can be a branch of first-order knowledge and can have a method of its own for answering questions of its own. What has been said about the reliance of philosophy upon common experience, and about the relation of it to common-sense, shows that philosophical knowledge can have the status of testable *doxa* and that philosophical thought can avoid being esoteric. So far, then, we have seen that philosophy can satisfy four of the six conditions.

What remains to be shown is how the relative truth of competing philosophical theories can be tested and judged and how disagreements among philosophers can be adjudicated by reference to objective standards of correctness or soundness in philosophical thought. If this can be shown, it will have a positive bearing on the possibility of conducting philosophy as a public enterprise in which philosophers cooperate and in which advances result from their cooperation.

Four distinct ways of testing a philosophical theory or judging its worth can be distinguished. These provide us

with criteria or standards for measuring the relative soundness of competing theories, for saying that one is truer—
sounder, better—than another. Let me name and describe
all four before undertaking a more extended discussion of
each.

THE EMPIRICAL TEST. This is the primary test, for it
eliminates from further consideration theories that common
experience falsifies. By itself, however, it is insufficient;
among theories that are *not* empirically falsified, one may be
better than another by other criteria.

THE LOGICAL TEST. One philosophical doctrine may be
free of the theoretical inconsistencies or embarrassments to
be found in another. One theory may be more comprehensive than another or may achieve comprehensiveness without committing the fallacy of reductionism to which
another theory must resort in order to deal with the same
problems.

THE "IS-OUGHT" TEST. On the plane of first-order
questions, philosophy is concerned not only with what *is*
the case (with questions about that which is and happens in
the world), but also with what *ought* to be (with questions
about what men should do and seek, questions about how
they should conduct their lives, organize their societies, and
the like). For want of better names, let us call the
is-questions "speculative," and the *ought*-questions "normative." Speculative and normative philosophy, as I shall
try to show later, are relatively independent subdivisions of philosophy, each with its own basis in common
experience. Thus, each can serve as a test for the other. If, in
the normative order, we have reason to think that a certain
philosophical doctrine is sound, it can be used to measure
the relative soundness of competing philosophical theories

in the speculative order. If, in the speculative order, we have reason to think that a certain philosophical doctrine is sound, it can be used to measure the relative soundness of competing philosophical theories in the normative order.

THE "MIXED QUESTION" TEST. There are certain mixed questions, it will be recalled, which cannot be answered by philosophy without taking into account relevant scientific knowledge. The relevant scientific conclusions sometimes appear to conflict with common-sense opinions which philosophy should uphold as being well founded in common experience. When this happens, philosophical thought should be able to resolve the conflict, or show that it is merely apparent, by applying to the mixed-question theories it has developed in its attempt to answer purely philosophical questions about that which is and happens in the world or about what men should do and seek. The measure of its success in doing this is a measure of the soundness of a philosophical theory.

Of these four tests, the last two—the "is-ought" test and the "mixed question" test—are applicable to philosophy, but not to science. They will be discussed at greater length in subsequent chapters.[1] In this chapter I shall deal with the other two tests, common to philosophy and science.

(1)

Before giving examples of the empirical test as it operates in philosophy, I should like to say a little more about the difference between science and philosophy in relation to experience. Let me begin by reminding the reader once

[1] The "is-ought" test in Chapter 11, and the "mixed question" test in Chapter 12.

more of the central and decisive difference between an investigative and a non-investigative mode of empirical inquiry. It is necessary to reiterate this because of the widespread error of supposing that a discipline cannot be empirical unless it investigates—that is, unless it acquires special data by means of deliberately devised steps of observation. That, as we have seen, is not the case. If a mode of inquiry is investigative, it will necessarily be empirical; that is, it will test its theories or conclusions by appeal to experience; but if a branch of knowledge is not investigative in method, it does not follow that it must be non-empirical—that is, makes no appeal to experience to test its theories. To suppose that it must is to suppose that any branch of knowledge that is not investigative must be like mathematics. While philosophy is like mathematics in needing only common experience as the ultimate source of its primitive concepts, it is unlike mathematics and like science in testing its theories or conclusions in the light of experience.

However, philosophy is like science with a difference—a difference that is rooted in the difference between common and special experience. We have seen this difference manifested in the relation of science and philosophy to common-sense opinions or beliefs. Science corrects common-sense opinions only where the latter are faulty because they rest on common experience that is inadequate and investigation is needed to supplement it. In contrast, philosophy corrects faulty common-sense opinions about matters in relation to which common experience is adequate and investigation is impossible.

The difference in method between science and philosophy—the difference between an investigative and a non-investigative empirical procedure—separates their fields of inquiry. Each is competent to answer certain questions about that which is and happens in the world and each is incompetent to answer the kind of first-order question that typically belongs to the other. This would not be so if, as it is sometimes supposed, there were no first-order questions which can be answered without investigation and no first-order answers which can be tested empirically without reference to the data of special experience.

On that supposition, all first-order questions of a general character would belong to science. To see that the supposition is incorrect, the reader need only re-examine the subjects of inquiry that were offered in an earlier chapter as examples of first-order questions in philosophy.[2] He may still have some doubt as to whether philosophers can answer such questions in a satisfactory manner; but whether or not he thinks that philosophers can answer them satisfactorily should not affect his being able to see that such questions cannot be answered at all by investigation. Some matters can be investigated; some cannot. We need the data obtained by investigation to test certain theories or conclusions; for others, common experience will suffice.

Let me offer one illustration which involves both matters which are and matters which are not subject to investigation. Galileo opens the Third Day of his *The Two New Sciences* as follows:

> My purpose is to set forth a very new science dealing with a very ancient subject. There is, in nature, perhaps nothing older than motion concerning which the books written by philosophers are neither few nor small;

[2] See Chapter 2, p. 43.

nevertheless, I have discovered by experiment some properties of it which are worth knowing and which have not hitherto been either observed or demonstrated. Some superficial observations have been made, as, for instance, that the free motion of a heavy falling body is continuously accelerated, but to just what extent this acceleration occurs has not yet been announced. . . . It has been observed that missiles and projectiles describe a curved path of some sort; however, no one has pointed out that this path is a parabola. . . . This discussion is divided into three parts: the first part deals with motion which is steady or uniform; the second treats of motion as we find it accelerated in nature; the third deals with the so-called violent motions and with projectiles.[3]

Galileo did not ask what motion is; but if he had, his answer to that question, like his definition of uniform motion or his distinction between natural and violent motion, would not depend upon prior investigation. Our common experience of moving bodies—bodies falling, bodies rolling down uneven slopes, and bodies being thrown—is all that we need to define motion, to state the properties of uniform motion, and to set violent motion apart from natural motion. No amount of investigation will contribute any light on these matters or test our statements about them. We may even know from common experience—or from "superficial observations," as Galileo points out—that "the free motion of a heavy falling body is continuously accelerated" (thus, we can see that a body falling from a great height drops faster and faster).

[3] *The Two New Sciences*, New York, 1914.

In contrast, the question which Galileo asked about the rate of uniform acceleration of a freely falling body is one that calls for investigation. Galileo confesses that it would be easy to "invent an arbitrary type of motion and discuss its properties"; but his aim is "to consider the phenomena of bodies falling with an acceleration such as actually occurs in nature and to make this definition of accelerated motions exhibit the essential features of observed accelerated motions." He tells us that, after repeated efforts, he succeeded in doing this and that his formula for acceleration was "confirmed by the consideration that experimental results are seen to agree with and exactly correspond with those properties which have been, one after another, demonstrated. . . ."[4]

To define the acceleration of a freely falling body, not just as a mathematician proposing this or that possible formula, but as a scientist trying to describe natural phenomena, Galileo had to perform the experiment of the inclined plane, making crude measurements of the distances traversed by notches along its side, and crude measurements of elapsed intervals of time by the pulses of a water clock.[5] These special data of investigation were indispensable to a decision between competing theories of uniform acceleration in free fall.[6]

[4] *Ibid.*, p. 160. Cf. Werner Heisenberg, *The Physicist's Conception of Nature*, New York, 1955, pp. 85–86.

[5] See Galileo, *ibid.*, pp. 178–179. The description of the experiment of the inclined plane is preceded in the text by the statement that "in those sciences where mathematical demonstrations are applied to natural phenomena . . . the principles once established by well-chosen experiments become the foundation of the entire superstructure."

[6] Cf. N. R. Hanson, *Patterns of Discovery*, Cambridge, 1958, pp. 37–49.

(2)

When philosophical theories or conclusions are put to the empirical test, they are either falsified or not. Only the negative result is decisive; the theories which escape falsification are not thereby established as true. Judgment concerning their relative truth must be based on other criteria or tests.

What is meant by saying that a philosophical theory is falsified by common experience, by the ordinary experience of our daily lives? Simply this: that we are faced with a choice between affirming the reality of our experience and dismissing the theory in question as false and accepting the theory in question as true and treating the world of our common experience as illusory. The conflict between the theory in question and common experience is such that both cannot be affirmed, the one as having truth and the other as having reality.[7]

There are philosophers, of course, who, confronted with this choice, do not hesitate to dismiss the world of common experience as illusory. They may even claim that one of the virtues of the theory which they espouse is that it punctures the illusions of common-sense about the world in which we lead our daily lives and go about our business. To be empirical in philosophy means making the opposite choice.

[7] A philosophical position can sometimes be expressed in a single proposition, but more often it is expressed in a set of related propositions, which is then called a theory. The falsification of a single proposition does not entail the truth of propositions that are inconsistent with it, but only of its formal contradictory. The falsification of a complex theory may turn on the falsification of one or more of its constituent propositions, the formal contradictories of which would then be seen to be true; but this would not establish the truth of other theories. See above, Chapter 2, p. 34, fn. 9.

It is not common experience, but the theory that conflicts with it, which must be rejected. The philosopher who proceeds in this way has put the theory to the empirical test and found it false.

In connection with the philosophical defense of common-sense beliefs, I mentioned the doctrines of Leibniz, Spinoza, and Hegel as examples of rationalistically constructed theories that ignore common experience and contravene common-sense. To say, as I would say, that the system of the world presented in Leibniz's *Monadology*, Spinoza's *Ethics*, and Hegel's *Phenomenology of Spirit* is falsified when tested by common experience amounts to saying that an acceptance of the doctrines set forth in these books would require us to reject what we think we know about the world in the light of our common experience of it. If that experience is not illusory, these philosophical theories must be false, at least in their central tenets.[8]

Two other theories which cannot survive the empirical test are the Heraclitean view that all things are always in flux and the opposite Eleatic view that whatever is, is both one and immutable. The relative permanence of things in common experience requires us either to say that that experience is illusory or that Heraclitus is wrong. The multiplicity and mutability of the things in our common experience require us to choose between treating that experience as illusory and rejecting the Eleatic view as false. The empirical test operates with the same result when applied to the view taken by materialists or atomists, ancient and modern (such as Democritus, Hobbes, Gassendi, Holbach), that the sensible things of our experience,

[8] Cf. C. I. Lewis, *Mind and the World-Order*, New York, 1929, pp. 8–10.

including our own bodies, are composed of material particles and void, *and nothing else*. Once again, unless we dismiss the world of our experience as illusion, we must reject as false the philosophical doctrine of atomism and materialism which requires us to treat it as such.

I have reserved for the last an example that has very special significance. It would appear to be paradoxical, to say the least, that a philosophical doctrine traditionally known as "empiricism" should not be able to meet the empirical test. Yet that is the case. I have in mind the view taken by the "British empiricists," from Locke, Berkeley, and Hume to many of their followers among contemporary positivists and analysts—the view that what we immediately perceive are our own sense impressions, usually called "sense-data," and that material objects, such as chairs and tables, cats and dogs, are only conceptual constructions from our sense-data. Unless our common experience is illusory, the very opposite obtains: for the most part, we immediately perceive chairs and tables, cats and dogs, not sense-data; only rarely do we perceive sense-data, and then only under very special circumstances which help us to understand why these exceptional experiences occur. Paradoxical as it may seem, the empirical test thus applied leads to the rejection of "empiricism" as a theory of experience. I will have more to say later about the fundamental error underlying the doctrine of sense-data;[9] for the present, my

[9] My critique of the doctrine of sense-data will be found in Chapter 16, pp. 266–270. Since the elimination of this doctrine, at the root and in all its consequences, is so essential to the restoration of sanity in philosophy, the reader may be interested in other critiques of it. I recommend the following: J. L. Austin, *Sense and Sensibilia*, Oxford, 1963; G. Ryle, *The Concept of Mind*, London, 1949, pp. 210–222, also *Dilemmas*, Cambridge, 1954, pp. 93–110; W. F. Sellars,

only point is that that doctrine, which has played such a central role in British thought, is falsified by common experience.[10]

(3)

In science as well as in philosophy, the empirical test is not the only way of assessing theories. In both, the logical test can also be applied. This test is of critical importance in judging competing theories or hypotheses which have not been falsified by experience.

The main criteria of theoretical excellence are (i) internal consistency; (ii) simplicity and elegance; and (iii) comprehensiveness or consilience, as illustrated by Newton's theory of gravitation which brought together, under one hypothesis, both celestial and terrestrial motions as well as such apparently disparate phenomena as the ebb and flow of the tides. Of these, the criteria of simplicity and elegance, as they are usually understood, apply particularly to scientific theories that are formulated in mathematical terms. Had the Ptolemaic hypothesis (the geocentric theory of the solar system) not been falsified by such special data of

---

"Empiricism and the Philosophy of Mind" (1956), republished in his *Science, Perception, and Reality*, New York, 1963, pp. 127–196; J. J. C. Smart, *Philosophy and Scientific Realism*, New York, 1963, pp. 18–27.

[10] With few exceptions, philosophers who regard themselves as empirical (in the sense that they conceive philosophical knowledge as knowledge that is derived from and tested by common experience) reject the central doctrine of British empiricism—that is, the doctrine of sense-data. See George Santayana, *Soliloquies in England*, New York, 1922, pp. 190–201; John Dewey, *Experience and Nature*, New York, 1925, pp. 1–2, 4–7; D. J. B. Hawkins, *Crucial Problems of Modern Philosophy*, London, 1957, pp. 126–137.

investigation as the phases of Venus and the rotary swing of the Foucault pendulum, it might still have been discarded in favor of the Copernican hypothesis (the heliocentric theory), because of the much greater simplicity and mathematical elegance of the latter. Even if the Ptolemaic theory had been able to account for all the observed phenomena—that is, had been able to save all the appearances—its cumbersome apparatus of epicycles and eccentrics would have still made it less elegant, as well as less useful, than its competitor in the treatment of the same phenomena.

It is difficult to compare philosophical theories with regard to their simplicity and elegance, in the precise sense in which these qualities are to be found in the formulations of mathematical physics. Nevertheless, of two philosophical doctrines attempting to deal with the same subject matter and problems, one may do so with a less complicated conceptual apparatus or may employ fewer theoretical constructions for explanatory purposes. A striking example of inelegance in a philosophical theory is the role which Descartes found it necessary to assign to "animal spirits" in his treatment of the body's relation to the mind.[11]

A sound philosophical theory should be free from internal inconsistencies or theoretical embarrassments. Their presence indicates serious flaws or defects—some mixing of error and truth. The "swerve of the atoms," invoked by Lucretius to explain free will, is a scandalous embarrassment to a theory which attempts to explain everything in mechanical terms. The necessity for psychophysical inter-

---

[11] See *The Passions of the Soul*, Articles 7–16. The fact that the problem with which Descartes is here dealing is not a purely philosophical matter, but a mixed question involving the science of physiology, does not alter the point.

action to explain sensation and voluntary movement is an equally scandalous embarrassment to the Cartesian theory of mind and body as separate substances. Bishop Berkeley's introduction of "notions" to account for our knowledge of spiritual beings is inconsistent with his basic principle that *all* the objects of human knowledge are "either ideas actually imprinted on the senses, or else such as are perceived by attending to the passions and operations of the mind, or lastly, ideas formed by the help of memory and imagination." The mind, soul, or spirit which knows or perceives is not itself an object of knowledge and cannot be, since we can have no idea of it. Nevertheless, Berkeley is compelled to assert that "we have some *notion* of soul, spirit . . . inasmuch as we know or understand the meaning of these words." [12]

Berkeley also affords us another example of internal inconsistency, one that is present in all nominalist attempts to account for "general ideas," or the meaning of common names, while at the same time denying the existence of abstract ideas. The Bishop finds himself forced to say that "an idea which, considered in itself, is particular becomes general by being made to represent or stand for all other particular ideas of the same sort." [13] The nominalist's embarrassment lies in the impossibility of his explaining how we can know that two or more particular ideas are "of the same sort" when we can have no idea whatsoever of any sorts or kinds.

The nominalist's inability to escape inconsistency appears in another way in Hume. The "absurdity of all scholastic notions with regard to abstraction and general ideas," he

---

[12] *Principles of Human Knowledge*, Sections 1, 2, and 27.
[13] *Ibid.*, Introduction, Section 12. Cf. 11, 12–19.

tells us, will be seen by anyone who tries "to conceive a triangle in general, which is neither *Isosceles* nor *Scalenum*, nor has any particular length or proportion of sides." [14] But when, in another place, he treats mathematics, he tells us that "though there never were a circle or triangle in nature, the truths demonstrated by Euclid would forever retain their certainty and evidence." [15] He offers as an example the proposition about the equality between the square of the hypotenuse and the sum of the squares of the other two sides; but he overlooks the fact, as he must, that this geometrical theorem applies to *all* right triangles, regardless of the length of the sides; and he must ignore the fact that other Euclidean theorems deal with the properties of triangles in general (prescinding from the special properties of triangles which are equilateral, scalene, or isosceles). How geometry can treat such objects when it is impossible for us to conceive of them is a matter that the nominalist must always find embarrassing to explain.

One more example of internal inconsistency is to be found in the thinking of the philosophical skeptic who seriously questions the truth of propositions about other minds and about the past and yet does not hesitate to argue against the contrary views advanced by other philosophers in the past. "Alluding to the existence of other philosophers," according to G. E. Moore, is only one of the ways in which philosophical skeptics "have betrayed this inconsistency. . . . Another way is by alluding to the existence of the human race, and in particular by using 'we' in the sense in which . . . any philosopher who asserts that 'we' do so

[14] *Enquiry Concerning Human Understanding*, Section XII, Part I, Number 122.
[15] *Ibid.*, Section IV, Part I, Number 20.

and so, e.g., 'we sometimes believe propositions that are not true,' is asserting not only that he himself has done the thing in question, but that *very many other human beings, who have had bodies and lived upon the earth,* have done the same." [16]

In addition to being free from internal inconsistencies and embarrassments, a sound philosophical theory should be comprehensive without being reductive. Of two competing theories, one is sounder than the other if it is able to deal with matters that the other cannot handle at all; or if, while both have the same scope of treatment, one can deal with the matters under consideration without recourse to the reductive analysis that the other must employ.

For example, the ethical theory of the ancient stoics, which holds that nothing external to our souls is able to harm us, cannot deal adequately with questions of justice and injustice. It must skirt this whole subject or skip over it lightly, since any adequate treatment of injustice presupposes that men can be injured by the actions of other men. The basic ethical principle of stoicism—that there is nothing good or evil in the world except a good or evil will—concentrates all attention on the fact that the unjust man injures himself, to the neglect of the fact that he could not be unjust if he did not also injure others. Such a theory, in addition to its obvious internal inconsistencies, is much less comprehensive than an ethical theory which can give reasons for the prohibition and punishment of injustice as

[16] "A Defence of Common Sense," in *Contemporary British Philosophy, First and Second Series,* London, 1924, p. 203. "The strange thing," Moore adds, "is that philosophers should have been able to hold sincerely, as part of their philosophical creed, propositions inconsistent with what they themselves *knew* to be true; and yet, so far as I can make out, this has really frequently happened."

well as explain how the unjust man who injures another suffers evil even if his unjust action goes unnoticed and unpunished.

Another example turns up in the theory of language which holds that all non-tautological or non-analytic sentences have to be empirical statements, i.e., descriptions of sense-experience. Such a theory either fails to account for many other types of sentences in our ordinary everyday speech, or accounts for them only by reducing them to statements of sense-experience, a distortion which a sounder, more comprehensive theory of language avoids without difficulty.[17]

Closely connected with the example just considered is the failure of logical atomism to handle the significant statements we make about states or nations (for example, "England declared war against Germany in August, 1914") without attempting to reduce all such statements to sentences describing the actions or properties of sensible particulars. The impossibility of carrying out such reductive analysis successfully means that the theory in question cannot be comprehensive without committing the fallacy of reductionism. It must, therefore, be judged less sound than a theory which can handle the significance of statements about corporate groups and statements about individuals without trying to reduce the one to the other.[18]

Finally, to take another example from the sphere of moral philosophy, the hedonist position, which claims that pleas-

[17] See L. Wittgenstein, *Philosophical Investigations*, New York, 1953, pp. 12 ff.; J. L. Austin, *How to Do Things with Words*, Cambridge (Mass.), 1962.

[18] See J. O. Urmson, *Philosophical Analysis*, Oxford, 1956, Chapter 10, on "the impossibility of reductive analysis." See also *ibid.*, pp. 180–187.

ure and pleasure *alone* is good and that one thing is *better* than another only insofar as it provides us with *more* pleasure, cannot comprehend the variety of pleasures without attempting—unsuccessfully—to reduce qualitative differences among pleasures to differences in the quantity of pleasure. This is recognized by J. S. Mill in his statement of the utilitarian theory. He finds it necessary to depart from the bare hedonist principle, and to admit that pleasures differ qualitatively as well as quantitatively, in order to comprehend the range of human satisfactions and preferences. He could not otherwise deal with the incommensurability of what he calls the "higher" and the "lower" pleasures.[19]

[19] See *Utilitarianism*, Chapter 2.

CHAPTER 10

Philosophy as a Public Enterprise: Agreement and Progress

W E HAVE DEALT with five of the six conditions and have seen that they do not pose insuperable obstacles for philosophy. One condition remains for consideration: can philosophy be conducted as a public enterprise? While the work of scientific investigation and of historical scholarship was not always thus conducted, it would be generally admitted that it now is, and has been for some time past. The participants in these intellectual enterprises address themselves to common questions, are able to disagree as well as to agree about the solutions of their problems, willingly submit to the policing of their work by standards commonly accepted, and make contributions which are both cumulative and corrective, so that their cooperation advances the state of the discipline.[1]

The same cannot be said for philosophy as it is now carried on. The analytical and linguistic philosophers have conducted their own program of work in a public manner, but they represent an exception to the prevailing pattern of

[1] See above, Chapter 2, pp. 36–38. Let me reiterate here that the possibility of progress is a consequence, not a requirement, of the public character of an intellectual enterprise.

philosophical work, both in the past and in contemporary thought.[2] Two charges repeatedly brought against philosophy bespeak the widespread opinion that philosophy differs from science and history in its character as an intellectual enterprise. Philosophers, it is claimed, never agree. Little or no progress is made in philosophical thought; it is not a cumulative discipline. Those who make such charges could go further and point out that philosophers, while appearing to differ, seldom really disagree, in the sense of joining issue (that is, giving mutually exclusive answers to questions of which they have a common understanding). They do not cooperate with one another in attacking common problems or in submitting their solutions to appraisal by standards commonly accepted by all participants in the enterprise.

To say that philosophy is inferior to science with respect to agreement (let us add, and disagreement) and with respect to progress (let us add, and cooperation) presupposes that they are comparable enterprises (that both are modes of inquiry attempting to solve problems and to advance knowledge); for if they are not comparable, then the charges are unjustly brought. One would not say that poetry or music is inferior to science because poets or musicians fail to agree, fail to cooperate, or make progress. No one expects poets or musicians to regard themselves as engaging in the kind of enterprise that has, or should have, these characteristics. If philosophy as a work of the mind is much more like poetry or music than it is like science, philosophers should be expected to behave like poets and musicians rather than like scientists; and when they behave in that way, they should not be criticized for it. Only if

[2] See above, Chapter 3, pp. 62–63.

philosophy and science are comparable intellectual enter-prises are we justified in comparing them and finding philosophy inferior in the respects mentioned—respects which are appropriate to that kind of enterprise.

Philosophy is frequently judged to be inferior to science in other respects. The prevalent opinion today (not only in learned circles but also among the general public) seems to be that philosophy is inferior to science not only with respect to agreement and progress, but also with respect to usefulness and understanding. Considering the degree to which each has practical value for or confers benefits on man and society, it is generally thought that philosophy has not been, and can never be, as useful to man as science has been, and is, through all its technological applications. Considering the degree to which each renders the world intelligible, it is generally thought that philosophy has never given, and can never give, an understanding of the world as penetrating as that which we obtain from science. Con-sidering the degree to which each is able to resolve disputes or settle differences among the participants in its enterprise, it is generally thought that philosophers have not achieved, and cannot achieve, agreement to the same extent as scientists do reach agreement by the resolution of their differences. Considering the degree to which each augments and accumulates the kind of knowledge it seeks, it is generally thought that philosophy has not made, and cannot make, progress to the same extent that science has and does.

I have enumerated four respects in which philosophy is often judged by many to be inferior to science. This opinion, shared by some of the leading figures in modern and contemporary philosophy, probably does not take into account the fact that philosophy may not yet have satisfied the conditions in terms of which it would be as respectable an intellectual enterprise as science. However, even if that were taken into account, it is my impression that the opinion would persist. It would still be thought that philosophy *at its best*—a state not yet achieved—could never equal the achievements of science in the four respects specified.

In this chapter, I shall examine the judgment that philosophy is inferior to science with respect to agreement and the judgment that it is inferior with respect to progress, because these two aspects, as we have seen, are intimately connected with philosophy's being—or with its capacity for being—conducted as a public enterprise.[3]

(1)

As forms of inquiry aimed at acquiring knowledge of that which is and happens in the world, scientific research and philosophical thought are comparable intellectual enterprises. We should, therefore, rightly expect that they can be conducted in a comparable manner. But is it right to expect that agreement can be achieved in philosophy in the same way or to the same extent that it is in science? Is it

---

[3] The consideration of the other two respects in which philosophy is judged to be inferior I shall postpone to later chapters. The question of philosophy's usefulness to men, as compared with the utility of science, can best be examined in the context of explaining what I have called the "is-ought" test for judging the relative truth of competing philosophical theories. (See Chapter 11.) To consider how philosophy compares with science in giving us an understanding of the world in which we live requires us to see these two types of knowledge in relation to the same objects of inquiry; and so this comparison can best be made in the context of explaining what I have called the "mixed question" test. (See Chapter 12.)

right to expect that progress can be made in philosophy in the same way or at the same rate as in science?

If philosophy and science were as much alike as two subdivisions of science are alike (for example, physics and chemistry or zoology and botany), the expectation of similar performance would be justified. That, however, is not the case. All the subdivisions of science involve essentially the same type of method: they are all investigative as well as empirical disciplines. Philosophy is an empirical discipline, but essentially distinct in type of method: it is non-investigative. Hence, the comparability of science and philosophy as modes of inquiry that seek knowledge in the form of *doxa* must be qualified by the essential difference between an investigative and a non-investigative procedure in acquiring knowledge and in testing theories or conclusions.

Three consequences follow from this essential difference. I call attention to them, not only because they help us to understand the divergent characteristics of science and philosophy as comparable disciplines, but also because they enable us to modify the prevailing judgments about philosophy's inferiority to science with respect to agreement and progress. The comparison—and evaluation—of science and philosophy in these respects must be made with an eye on the difference between them and with due account taken of the implications of that difference.

Because science is investigative and philosophy is not, specialization and division of labor are possible in science as they are not in philosophy—at least not to the same extent.

The multiplicity of the major subdivisions of science, and

the further subsectioning of the major subdivisions, is closely related to the multiplicity of specific techniques for carrying on the investigation of nature or society, each a technique for exploring a special field of phenomena. Men become specialists in science through mastering one or more of these techniques. No one can master all. The ideal of the generalist in science may, in the remote past, have had the appearance of attainability, but it does so no longer. To be a scientist now is to be a specialist in science. The total work of science is thus accomplished by the specialization of its workers and by an intensive division of labor, not only on the side of investigation, but also on the side of theoretical developments or constructions relevant to the data of investigation in a particular field.

Turning to philosophy, we find an opposite state of affairs. The core of common experience to which the empirical philosopher appeals is the same for all men; and common or ordinary experience involves no specialized techniques. Hence, there is and can be no basis for specialization or for division of labor in philosophy on the empirical side. These things which naturally pertain to the work of men when they investigate just as naturally play no part in the work of men when they do not.

On the theoretical side, there is some possibility of a division of labor in philosophy—as between logic and metaphysics, or between metaphysics and ethics. In fact, specialization has occurred both in the university teaching of philosophy and also in the concentration of this or that professor of philosophy upon this or that sector of philosophical inquiry. Nevertheless, it remains *possible* for one man to make contributions in all the major sectors of philosophical thought. The great philosophers of the past have certainly been generalists in philosophy; and in our own century the writings of Dewey, Russell, Whitehead, Bergson, Santayana, Maritain touch on all the major questions of philosophy. This sufficiently makes the point of contrast between science and philosophy; for, though in antiquity, before specialization took place, Aristotle could make contributions to the major fields of science, that is no longer possible. In fact, specialization and division of labor have now reached the point at which it is almost impossible for one man to do outstanding theoretical work in more than a single field of scientific research.

Because there is so much specialization and division of labor in science, and so little in philosophy, as a consequence of the fact that one is and the other is not investigative, it follows as a further consequence that the authority of experts must be relied on in science and cannot be relied on in philosophy.

The individual scientist accepts the findings of other scientists—both in his own field and also in other fields—without redoing the investigations on which those findings are based. He may, in rare instances, check the data by repeating the experiment, but for the most part, especially with regard to matters not immediately within his own special field of research, he proceeds by accepting the findings of reputable experts. He cannot do otherwise and get his own work done.

In many cases, though not in all, the individual scientist also accepts the theoretical conclusions reached by other scientists, if these have the authority of recognized experts, without checking all the steps by which those conclusions were originally reached or tested. In other words, a highly specialized scientist, working in some narrow corner of the whole scientific enterprise, accepts a large body of scientific opinions on the authority of other scientists. It would be impossible for him to do otherwise.

Since philosophers proceed entirely in terms of common experience to which all have equal access, and since it is by reference to common experience that philosophical theories or conclusions must be tested, philosophers need never accept a single philosophical opinion on the authority of other philosophers. On the contrary, whatever theories a philosopher holds and whatever conclusions he reaches he can and should arrive at by judgments he himself makes in the light of the very same evidence that is available to all other men, including all other philosophers. Where, in the case of scientific work, the individual cannot dispense with the authority of his fellow workers, he cannot, in the case of philosophical work, rely on it. One might go further and say that the man who accepts any philosophical opinions whatsoever simply on the authority of their spokesmen, no matter how eminent, is no philosopher.

Because science depends on special experience acquired by investigation, whereas philosophy relies on and appeals only to the common experience of mankind which, at its core, is the same for all men at all times and places, philosophers have a contemporaneity which scientists cannot have.

Philosophical questions which arise from and relate to common experience can make contemporaries of philosophers as far apart in time and place as Plato and Bradley,

Aristotle and Dewey, Augustine and William James. Another way of saying this is that there is no genuine unmixed
philosophical question which concerns us today to which it
would be impossible in principle to find an answer given by
a philosopher who lived at some prior time. Earlier philosophers may not have actually considered all the questions
with which we are concerned, but in many cases they did,
and in all cases they *could* have. Hence, in dealing with controversies about philosophical matters, the disputants may
be drawn from centuries far apart.

Not all philosophical questions have the timelessness
indicated above. This characteristic pertains only to those
purely philosophical problems which depend exclusively on
common experience for their solution and involve no
admixture of scientific knowledge. What I have called
mixed questions in philosophy, especially those which
depend, both for their formulation and for their solution, on
the state of scientific knowledge, vary from time to time.
Those which confront philosophers today are certainly not
the same as those faced by Aristotle or Descartes. The same
holds true of those mixed questions in philosophy which
depend on special historical knowledge, and of those which
lie athwart the border that separates philosophy from
revealed religion.

With these exceptions noted, let me repeat the point:
purely philosophical problems are of such a nature that the
philosophers who tackle them *can have the character of
contemporaries* despite their wide separation in time and
place. The accidents of their immersion in different cultural
milieus may affect their vocabularies and their notional
idioms, but this does not prevent them from being construed
as addressing themselves to the *same* problems and as

engaging in debate concerning the merits of competing solutions.

The very opposite is the case in science. A scientific dispute usually, if not always, involves men living at the same time. At any time, the current scientific problems to be solved are conditioned by the state of the data currently in hand or the state of the research currently being carried forward. Competing theories are sponsored by men who take account of the latest findings of research and of the directions taken by investigations going on. Archimedes, Galileo, Newton, and Einstein cannot function as contemporaries in the way in which Aristotle, Aquinas, Locke, and William James can.[4]

Let me state this point in still another way. The whole record of past philosophical thought can have critical relevance to current philosophical problems, whereas the whole record of past scientific work is not as relevant to current research and theorizing. A much larger portion of the scientific past has only antiquarian interest for scientists today. If there are philosophers today who would say that an equally large portion of the philosophical past can be similarly regarded, their view of this matter, I submit, stems from their relegation of philosophy to the plane of second-order questions, or to the supposition that all philosophical questions are "mixed questions," or to their not recognizing the role of common experience in the formulation and solution of first-order questions that are purely philosophical.

[4] Cf. the remark of Professor Cornelius Krusé, in his Foreword to Randall's *How Philosophy Uses Its Past*, New York, 1963, p. xii: "Not only the Greeks, but Spinoza and Kant, and, in fact, all the great leaders of philosophical thought of the past, are our intellectual contemporaries whom we ignore or neglect at our peril."

(2)

The differences between philosophy and science which we have just been considering have a critical bearing on the rate of progress that can be made by these two disciplines, and also on the diverse ways in which advances are made by these two modes of inquiry.

Two factors are mainly responsible for the progress that has been made in scientific knowledge. On the one hand, advances in observational techniques and their employment to explore new fields of phenomena result in the steady accumulation of more and more data of special experience. On the other, new theoretical insights are achieved by the development of better and more comprehensive theories. These two factors interact. The discovery of new data by investigation occasions or stimulates advances in theorizing; and new theoretical constructions often call forth experimental or investigative ingenuity in the search for supporting or refuting data. Furthermore, as we have seen, increasing specialization and ever more intensive division of labor occur in science; and this, in turn, is related to the ever growing number of scientists at work which, in purely quantitative terms, accounts for cumulative progress at an accelerating rate.

In philosophy, there is no accumulation of new data; there are no advances in observational techniques and no new observational discoveries; there is no specialization and no division of labor. Since common experience at its core always remains the same, it does not by itself occasion or stimulate advances in theorizing. Since these things are impossible in philosophy, precisely because it is non-investigative, it has made less progress and at a much slower rate.

If the same kind, amount, or rate of progress could be expected of philosophy, then it would be fair to say that science is vastly superior to philosophy in making progress. It is clearly wrong, however, to expect the same kind of progress—or the same rate of progress—from a non-investigative as from an investigative mode of inquiry, especially in view of the bearing of its investigative procedure on the main factors responsible for progress in science. To say that philosophy is inferior to science in regard to progress is like saying that a fish is inferior to a bird in locomotion. Both can move forward to an objective, each with a certain velocity, but the difference in the manner and the rate of their movement reflects the difference in the mediums through which they move.

What I have just said should not be interpreted as condoning philosophy's failure to make greater progress than it has so far made. Common experience being a constant factor, progress in philosophy must be made on the side of theorizing rather than on the empirical side—that is, in the development of new theoretical insights, improvements in analysis, the formulation of more precise questions, the construction of more comprehensive theories, and the removal of the theoretical inconsistencies, embarrassments, paradoxes, and puzzles that have long beset philosophical thought. Some progress of this sort has been made in the past, and some has occurred quite recently, but it must nevertheless be admitted that the total extent of it falls far short of what might be reasonably expected.

In my judgment, the central reason for this lies in the fact that, for the most part, philosophical work has been carried on by thinkers working in isolation, and not as a public enterprise in which thinkers make serious efforts to cooperate with one another. A little earlier, I pointed out that the ever growing number of scientists at work accounted, in part, for accelerating, cumulative progress. The creation of departments of philosophy in our institutions of higher learning, it could be said, has greatly increased the number of philosophers at work. If this has not produced the same kind of result that the same phenomenon has produced in science—and certainly it has not—the reason why, I submit, lies in the failure of the participants in the philosophical enterprise to cooperate, as scientists cooperate in their ventures.

That philosophy has not, for the most part, been conducted as a public enterprise does not entail that it cannot be. On the contrary, if philosophy can satisfy the other five conditions which I have laid down, it can satisfy this sixth condition as well; for if philosophy can have a method of its own for answering first-order questions of its own, if it can effectively apply tests of the relative truth of competing theories or conclusions, then it must follow that philosophers can tackle common problems, can join issue where they differ in their solutions, and can submit their differences to adjudication by standards commonly accepted. These things being possible, cooperation among philosophers is not a utopian dream; it has occurred to some extent; if it is ever fully realized, philosophy will be able to make advances at a rate and to a degree which conform to reasonable expectations.[5]

[5] Cf. Professor Krusé's observations on this point, *loc. cit.*, pp. x–xi.

What does this all come to? First, philosophy by its very nature cannot make the same kind and rate of progress that is made in science; to expect it to is to make a false demand; to denigrate philosophy for not doing so is unjustified. Second, because of the difference in the factors operative in the two disciplines, it is more difficult to make progress—and more difficult to make it steadily and at an ever accelerating pace—in philosophy than in science. Third, these difficulties can be overcome to a certain extent by the cooperation of philosophers in the conduct of their work as a public enterprise; and, when that occurs, philosophy will not be inferior to science, as it now is, with respect to progress. Philosophy is inferior to science now not because it fails to make the same kind or rate of progress, but because it fails to advance in a way and at a pace that is as appropriate to its non-investigative character as the manner and pace of scientific progress is appropriate to a discipline that is investigative in method. If philosophy were to do as well in its medium as science does in its, the correct statement of the case would not be that philosophy is inferior to science in progress, but only that it is distinctly different in this respect.[6]

(3)

One of the commonest complaints about philosophy is that philosophers always disagree. This complaint is given

[6] See my discussion of progress in science and philosophy in *The Idea of Freedom*, New York, 1958, Volume I, Book I, Chapter 9, pp. 74–78. Cf. Arthur O. Lovejoy, "On Some Conditions of Progress in Philosophical Inquiry," in *The Philosophical Review*, Vol. XXVI, No. 2 (March, 1917); James Ward, "The Progress of Philosophy," in *Mind*, Vol. XV, No. 58; and George Santayana, *Soliloquies in England*, New York, 1922, pp. 207–216.

added force by pointing out that, in contrast to philosophy, there is a large area of agreement among scientists. Furthermore, when they disagree, we expect them to work at and succeed in settling their differences. They have at their disposal and employ effective implements of decision whereby they can resolve their disagreements and obtain a concurrence of opinion among those qualified to judge the matters under dispute. Philosophical disagreements persist; or, to speak more accurately, since there is so little genuine disagreement or joining of issues in philosophy, differences of opinion remain unclarified, undebated, and unresolved. It is frequently far from clear that philosophers who appear to differ are even addressing themselves to the same subject or trying to answer the same question. This state of affairs gives rise to the widely prevalent judgment that, in this matter of agreement and disagreement, philosophy is plainly inferior to science. Nevertheless, as in the matter of progress, the comparison of science and philosophy with respect to agreement is falsely drawn and the judgment based on it is unfairly made.

One difference between science and philosophy, already pointed out, helps us to rectify the erroneous impression that agreement generally obtains in science while disagreement is rife in philosophy. Because philosophy relies solely on common experience in dealing with first-order questions, philosophers widely separated in time can be treated as contemporaries; whereas with the ever changing state of the data acquired by ongoing investigation, only scientists working at the same time can function as contemporaries. This basic difference between science and philosophy results in a different temporal pattern of agreement and disagreement in each, to whatever extent genuine agreements and disagreements do in fact exist.

The scientists of a given century or time tend to disagree with and reject the formulations of earlier scientists, largely because the latter are based on insufficient data. Disagreement in science occurs vertically across the centuries; and most of the agreements in science occur along the same horizontal time line, among scientists at work at the same period. In contrast, there is considerable and often unnoticed agreement across the centuries among philosophers living at different times; the striking disagreements—or differences of opinion—occur mainly among philosophers alive at the same time. In short, we find some measure of agreement and of disagreement in both science and philosophy, but we find the temporal pattern of it quite different in each case.

The judgment that philosophy is inferior to science with respect to agreement focuses entirely on the horizontal time line, where we find the maximum degree of agreement among scientists and the minimum degree of it among philosophers. If we shift our attention to the vertical time line, there is some ground for the opposite judgment; for, looking at the opinions of scientists in one century in relation to those of scientists in an earlier century, we come away with the impression of substantial and extensive disagreement, whereas we find a considerable measure of agreement among philosophers across the centuries.

To judge philosophy inferior by expecting or demanding that its pattern of agreement and disagreement should conform to the pattern exhibited by science is to judge it by reference to a model or standard that is as inapplicable as the model or standard of scientific progress is inapplicable to philosophy. To dismiss this judgment as wrongly made, however, is not to condone philosophy for its failure to achieve what might be reasonably expected of it in its own terms. The most crucial failure of philosophy so far is the failure of philosophers to face each other in clear and genuine disagreements, to join issue and engage in the debate of disputed questions. Only when this defect is overcome will they be able to settle their differences by rational means and achieve the measure of agreement that can be reasonably expected of them.

Here, as with respect to progress, the difficulties are greater for philosophy. The decision between competing scientific formulations by reference to crucial data obtained by investigation is easier than the resolution of philosophical issues by rational debate. Nevertheless, the difficulties which confront philosophy with respect to agreement and disagreement can be surmounted in the same way that the difficulties it faces with respect to progress can be overcome—namely, by the conduct of philosophy as a public, rather than as a private, enterprise. When philosophy is properly conducted as a public enterprise and philosophers work cooperatively, they will succeed to a much greater extent than they do now in addressing themselves to the same problems, in clearly joining issue where they differ in their answers, and in carrying on rational debate of the issues in a way that holds some promise of their eventual resolution.[7]

It is, therefore, fair to say that philosophy is at present inferior to science with respect to agreement and disagreement, but *only if one means* that philosophy has not yet

[7] See my discussion of these matters in *The Idea of Freedom, op. cit.*, Chapters 2–4, and Chapter 9, pp. 69–74. See also *ibid.*, Volume II, Book III, Part IV, Chapter 20.

achieved what can reasonably be expected of it—a measure and a pattern of agreement and disagreement appropriate to its character as a non-investigative discipline and hence distinctly different from the measure and pattern of these things in science. I reiterate that philosophy, like science, can be conducted as a public enterprise, wherein philosophers work cooperatively. In the very nature of the case that is possible, even though little has been done to move philosophy in that direction. Nevertheless, should philosophy ever fully realize what is inherently possible, its achievement with respect to agreement and disagreement will be as commendable as the achievement of science in the same respect, for each will then have done all it can do within the limitations of its method as a mode of inquiry and appropriate to its character as a type of knowledge.

CHAPTER 11

The Use of Philosophy:
The "Is-Ought" Test

KNOWLEDGE IS USEFUL. What is known may not always actually be put to use in the management or conduct of human affairs or in the control of man's environment, but it always can be. If it is not, its latent usefulness remains to be exploited in the future. Intrinsically useless knowledge is a contradiction in terms.

We often speak of knowledge in use as "applied knowledge." The Greek philosophers laid down a basic division in the use or application of knowledge, which is worth recalling. They distinguished between production and action—between the sphere of man's efforts to make things or to control the forces of nature in order to achieve certain results, and the sphere of human conduct, both individual and social. They also distinguished between knowledge itself, as capable of being used or applied, and a special type of knowledge which must be added in order to put knowledge to use.

The latter—the special knowledge that is operative when knowledge is put to use—the Greeks called *technē*. The English equivalent of that word is, of course, "technique," but I prefer the more colloquial rendering of it by "know-how." [1] In contradistinction to "know-how," let us call the knowledge that can be applied (for example, the knowledge to be found in what we call "pure science") "know-that." Pure science is turned into applied science through the addition of know-how to know-that.

Distinguishing between the spheres of application or use, we can speak of productive know-how and practical know-how—that is, the know-how which is involved in applying know-that to the business of making things or achieving desired effects or results and the know-how which is involved in applying know-that to the affairs of action, the problems of individual conduct and the conduct of society.[2]

Practical know-how, particularly that form of it which is involved in applying scientific knowledge, concerns the means for achieving whatever ends of individual or social action we set up for ourselves. It does not, and cannot, tell us what ends we ought to pursue, but it may tell us what ends are, or are not, practicable to pursue because adequate means are, or are not, available; it often gives us knowledge of the diverse means which are available for achieving a particular goal of action; and, with respect to alternative means, it often enables us to make a judgment about their relative efficiency or effectiveness.

[1] The English words "skill" and "art" are other names for technique or know-how. The distinction which we make between the artisan and the artist (between the practitioner of the useful arts and the practitioner of the fine arts) has removed the word "art" from its basic and general use as the name for each and every form of skill or technical competence, every type of know-how.

[2] Since the English word "practical" is derived from the Greek word for action ("praxis"), it seems the most appropriate word to use for this second type of know-how.

Productive know-how, again especially that form of it which is involved in applying scientific knowledge, concerns the steps to be taken in making useful tools, in improving their efficiency, and in shaping or controlling nature to our purposes. It does not, and cannot, tell us what our purposes ought to be; it merely helps us to realize whatever purposes we may have, so far as their realization depends upon instrumentalities that we can devise or controls that we can exercise over natural processes. Currently, such productive know-how, based on science, is called "technology."[3]

One other type of know-how must be mentioned. There is skill in inquiring or knowing as well as skill in making things and in controlling nature. In other words, there is skill in achieving knowledge itself; and for each of the major branches of knowledge that has a distinctive method or procedure of its own, there is a particular type of skill which is often called the "methodology" of that science, but which I would prefer to call the "heuristic know-how" of the discipline. Thus, the mathematician has a heuristic know-how for achieving the kind of know-that which constitutes mathematical knowledge; so, too, the scientist and the historian; so, too, the philosopher, if philosophy satisfies the conditions stipulated in this book.

I have introduced all these distinctions, and indicated the language I shall use in employing them, by way of preface to the discussion of the problems with which this chapter is concerned. I turn to those now.

---

[3] The word "technology," which, according to its Greek roots, should mean know-that about know-how, is thus currently used as if it had the same meaning as "technique" (that is, skill or know-how).

(1)

It would be reasonable to expect each different branch of knowledge to have, in addition to its own heuristic know-how, a kind of usefulness or application distinctively and characteristically its own. The heuristic know-how of mathematics differs from that of science; that is, the latter involves skills of investigation and experimentation which have no place in mathematical inquiry. Whereas science is directly useful through its technological applications in the sphere of production, mathematics is, for the most part, indirectly useful. Its application usually requires the mediation of science; applied mathematics usually involves one or another of the natural or social sciences.

What is the usefulness of philosophical knowledge? Science, as I have already pointed out, has two main types of usefulness or application—one in the sphere of production, the other in the sphere of action. Does philosophy, in addition to having its own heuristic know-how, also give rise to productive know-how and practical know-how?

With regard to productive know-how, it is generally recognized that philosophy is totally useless; it has no technological applications whatsoever. As William James said, it "bakes no bread"; it builds no bridges, makes no bombs, invents no instruments, concocts no poisons, harnesses no power, and so forth. Francis Bacon's famous remark that knowledge is power (that is, that knowledge gives man a mastery over nature and an ability to produce or control effects according to his wishes) is as false in the case of philosophical knowledge as it is true in the case of scientific knowledge.

With regard to practical know-how, philosophy is just as

deficient, though this is not as generally recognized as its deficiency with regard to productive know-how. Philosophical knowledge (insofar as it is know-that in the same sense in which scientific knowledge is know-that) does not instruct us concerning the means available for achieving whatever results we desire, or whatever goals or objectives we may set ourselves. By itself (without the addition of scientific knowledge), it does not tell us whether our practical purposes are or are not practicable, because there are or are not adequate means for achieving them. Nor does it enable us to judge the relative efficiency or effectiveness of competing means for achieving the same ends.

Is philosophy, then, totally useless? The answer must be in the affirmative if the usefulness of knowledge is exhaustively represented by the kinds of productive and of practical know-how that have their basis in scientific knowledge. But that is not the whole story.

As I pointed out earlier, science does not and cannot tell us what ends we *ought* to pursue; it does not and cannot tell us what our purposes *ought* to be. However useful it is productively, it does not tell us whether we *ought* or *ought not* to produce certain things (such as thermonuclear bombs or supersonic transport planes); it does not tell us whether we *ought* or *ought not* to exercise certain controls over natural processes (such as human procreation or changes in weather). However useful it is practically, it does not tell us whether we *ought* or *ought not* to employ certain means to achieve our ends, on any basis other than their relative efficiency; it does not tell us whether one goal *ought* or *ought not* to be preferred to another. It does not tell us, in short, what we *ought* or *ought not* to do and what we *ought* or *ought not* to seek.

For brevity, I shall refer to knowledge of all these *oughts* and *ought-nots* as "*ought*-knowledge." I have referred to such knowledge in earlier chapters (though not by that name) when I distinguished between two types of first-order questions with which the philosopher should deal: questions about that which is and happens in the world and questions about what men should do and seek. Tenable and defensible answers to the second type of question constitute what I am here calling "*ought*-knowledge." Answers to the first type of question might, in contradistinction, be called "*is*-knowledge."

Philosophy, properly constituted, consists of both types of knowledge. This is recognized by all who conceive of philosophy, on the plane of first-order inquiry, as divided into two main branches, which are traditionally called "speculative" and "practical" (the speculative branch consisting of *is*-knowledge; the practical branch consisting of *ought*-knowledge). The word "speculative" is appropriate for *is*-knowledge in view of its Latin root, which has the connotation of *seeing* or *beholding*.[4] But the word "practical," derived from the Greek *praxis*, which means action, has too narrow a connotation for *ought*-knowledge, since that is as applicable in the sphere of production as it is in the sphere of action. Hence, I will refer to the branch of philosophy which consists of *ought*-knowledge as normative rather than practical.

For reasons that will become clear presently, science is as deficient with respect to *ought*-knowledge as philosophy is deficient with respect to know-how. We will also see presently that the relation of applied science, technology,

[4] The same can be said for the word "theoretical," the Greek root of which has the same connotation.

and practical know-how to pure science (the know-that which is identical with scientific *is*-knowledge) is in a way comparable to the relation of normative philosophy (*ought*-knowledge) to speculative philosophy (the know-that which is identical with philosophical *is*-knowledge). In advance of these things' becoming clear, the essential point about the usefulness of philosophy can be made. In the spheres of action and of production, we need *ought*-knowledge as well as know-how. Philosophy, through its normative branch, supplies the one; science, through technology and other applications, supplies the other. Each, in short, is useful, though in quite different ways.

Diagram 3, on the opposite page, sets forth all these distinctions and relationships.

(2)

The difference in the usefulness of science and philosophy corresponds to the difference in their methods as modes of inquiry. No question properly belongs to science which cannot be answered by investigation or to the answering of which investigation can make no contribution. That is precisely why no *ought*-question is scientific and why, therefore, science includes no normative branch, no *ought*-knowledge.

Beginning in the seventeenth century, the natural sciences gradually separated themselves from speculative philosophy. More recently, the social sciences have declared their independence of philosophy in its normative branch. In order to establish themselves as subdivisions of science, such disciplines as economics, politics, and sociology had to eschew all normative considerations (that is, all *ought*-

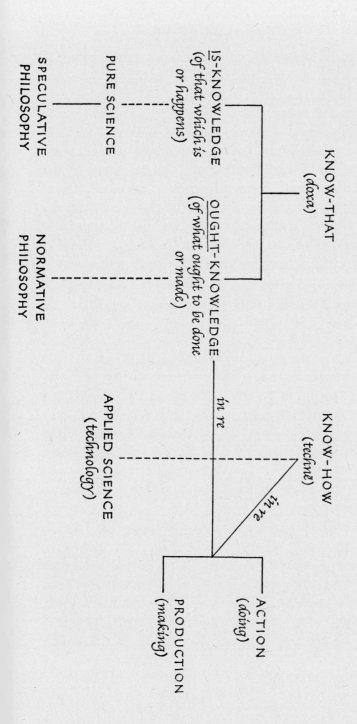

DIAGRAM 3

KNOWLEDGE

KNOW-THAT
(doxa)

IS-KNOWLEDGE
(of that which is
or happens)

OUGHT-KNOWLEDGE
(of what ought to be done
or made)

PURE SCIENCE

SPECULATIVE
PHILOSOPHY

NORMATIVE
PHILOSOPHY

in re

in re

KNOW-HOW
(technē)

APPLIED SCIENCE
(technology)

ACTION
(doing)

PRODUCTION
(making)

questions or, as they are sometimes called, "questions of value"). They had to become purely descriptive, becoming in this respect exactly like the natural sciences. They had to restrict themselves to questions of how men do in fact behave, individually and socially, and forgo all attempts to say how they ought in principle to behave.

It may be conceded by anyone who understands the distinction between *is* and *ought* that investigative science, natural or social, cannot deal with matters of *ought*. But it may still be thought that *ought*-knowledge can be derived from scientific know-that, just as productive and practical know-how are derived from it. To think so is to commit what has come to be recognized as the "naturalistic fallacy" in ethics.

The basic error which goes by this name consists in trying to derive an *ought*-conclusion from premises that are exclusively *is*-statements. It is fallacious to suppose that from knowledge of that which is and happens in the world, including knowledge of how men do or can behave, and *from such knowledge exclusively*, it is possible to know how men *ought* to behave, how society *ought* to be organized, and the like. If we avoid making this error, we will not make the mistake of supposing that scientific knowledge—all that we now have and all that we can ever acquire—will, taken by itself, establish a single normative judgment about what men *ought* to do or seek.[5]

[5] There are, of course, hypothetical normative judgments, of the form "If you want to achieve a certain end, you ought to do this"; and such judgments may be made in the light of scientific knowledge about available means and their relative efficiency. But such judgments beg a whole series of normative questions, such as: Ought you to desire the end in view? Ought you to employ this means, even if it is the most efficient means available? The question: Ought you to do this? cannot be properly answered without explicitly

What has just been said about the naturalistic fallacy applies to philosophical know-that exactly as it applies to scientific know-that. From premises which consist entirely of philosophical *is*-statements, no *ought*-conclusion can be validly drawn. The whole of speculative knowledge in philosophy—all that we now have together with all we may ever achieve—cannot by itself establish a single normative judgment about what men *ought* to do or seek.

We are thus faced with the following dilemma: either there is no philosophical *ought*-knowledge at all or, if there is, then normative philosophy must have principles of its own, in no way derived from speculative philosophy. If we were to take the first alternative, it would follow that speculative philosophy must be totally useless knowledge —which, I repeat, is a contradiction in terms. I take the second alternative, not only for that reason, but also because I think that philosophy can answer first-order normative questions and achieve *ought*-knowledge (in the form of testable *doxa*) under the same conditions that it can answer first-order speculative questions and achieve *is*-knowledge.

Before I explain my position with respect to normative philosophy, let me make clear how the existence of normative judgments in philosophy that are independent of its speculative knowledge relates to the usefulness of the latter knowledge.

---

answering these other questions. As we have seen, scientific knowledge can go no further than to tell us what means are available and which is most efficient; it cannot tell us whether we *ought* or *ought not* to seek the end in view; it cannot tell us whether we *ought* or *ought not* to employ a certain means on the basis of considerations other than efficiency. Hence, scientific knowledge as such cannot provide *all the answers we need* for the adequate solution of any normative question.

The statement of the naturalistic fallacy is largely negative in its import. It enjoins us from basing a normative judgment or *ought*-conclusion on premises or grounds that consist entirely of *is*-statements, whether these represent philosophical or scientific know-that. It leaves open the question whether normative judgments can be based directly on experience; and it allows, on the positive side, for the possibility that normative judgments can be based on mixed grounds—grounds which combine *is*-statements with *ought*-statements that are based on experience, not on other *is*-statements.

Hence, if normative philosophy includes some *ought*-knowledge that is derived directly from experience, it can reason to additional *ought*-knowledge (in the form of conclusions) by combining some *is*-knowledge with the original *ought*-knowledge (the normative principles derived directly from experience) to constitute adequate grounds for such conclusions. The *is*-knowledge which is thus combined with the normative principles may be either scientific or philosophical know-that. If the latter, speculative philosophy has been put to use through the mediation of normative philosophy, exactly as pure science is put to use through the mediation of technology or other forms of applied science.

When we consider the usefulness of philosophical knowledge, we must, therefore, distinguish between the direct usefulness of normative philosophy in the spheres of action and production and the indirect usefulness of speculative philosophy when the latter is put to use by normative philosophy—that is, when normative philosophy employs philosophical know-that as *part* of the grounds on which it bases *some* of its *ought*-judgments.

Scientific know-that may also be used by normative philosophy as *part* of the grounds for making *ought*-judgments. In other words, there are pure and mixed *ought*-questions, as there are pure and mixed *is*-questions. The purely philosophical *ought*-questions are those which can be answered by normative philosophy either by *ought*-knowledge derived directly from experience or by *ought*-judgments based on the combination of *ought*-principles with philosophical know-that. A mixed *ought*-question is one which cannot be answered except by combining *ought*-judgments with *is*-knowledge supplied by disciplines other than speculative philosophy. The answer involves scientific know-that or historical know-that, whether or not it also involves philosophical know-that.

(3)

Speculative philosophy can rely on common experience as the source of its basic notions and principles and also to provide one way of testing its theories or conclusions; so can normative philosophy. Each, however, relies on a different sector of common experience: speculative philosophy, on our common experience of that which is and happens in the world; practical philosophy, on our common experience of human desires, aspirations, preferences, regrets, and feelings of obligation and of relationship to others.

Speculative philosophy, as we have seen, may either defend or correct common-sense opinions or beliefs about that which is and happens in the world. Whichever it does, it does in the light of the very same common experience on the basis of which the defended or criticized common-sense opinions were originally formed. Normative philosophy may, similarly, either defend or correct common-sense opinions about how men ought to act individually or how they ought to conduct their social affairs. When it does so, it also reverts to the same common experience whence come the opinions it defends or criticizes.[6]

Speculative and normative philosophy are thus essentially alike as philosophical knowledge in that both stand in the same relation to common experience and to the common-sense opinions which are based on common experience. Yet they can be relatively independent branches of philosophical knowledge because the area or sector of common experience to which the one appeals is separate from the area or sector of common experience on which the other relies.

I said "relatively independent," not "absolutely independent." Normative philosophy is relatively independent of speculative philosophy in that it has some principles of its own, but it also makes use of speculative philosophy and so is not wholly independent of it. In this respect, normative philosophy stands in relation to speculative philosophy as technology stands in relation to pure science. But there the parallelism ends. Pure science often puts technology to use. It derives new techniques and new implements of investigation from the technological applications of earlier scientific knowledge. This reverse relationship does not obtain in the domain of philosophy; speculative philosophy never puts normative philosophy to use. In the process of reasoning by which the conclusions of speculative philosophy are

[6] See Henry Sidgwick's *The Method of Ethics*, 7th edition, London, 1962, Book III, especially Chapters XI and XIII. Cf. C. D. Broad's discussion of Sidgwick's treatment of "The Morality of Common Sense," in *Clarity Is Not Enough*, edited by H. D. Lewis, London, 1963, pp. 67–69, 73–74.

reached, none of the premises is ever drawn from normative knowledge about how men ought to conduct their lives or their social affairs. *Ought*-statements never function as grounds for *is*-statements as *is*-statements function to furnish part of the grounds for certain *ought*-statements.[7]

(4)

The reader will recall that one of the four tests of the relative truth of philosophical theories was called the "is-ought" test.[8] The analysis set forth in the preceding pages, of the difference and relation between speculative philosophy as *is*-knowledge and normative philosophy as *ought*-knowledge, makes it possible now to explain that test.

Looked at one way, the "is-ought" test appears to be merely a special form of the logical test—the test of internal consistency. Does a philosopher's view of the nature of things support or undermine his view of how men should conduct their lives? In the one case, he would be free from inconsistency; in the other, not. For example, a philosopher who denies the existence of individual beings which retain their identity over a span of time cannot consistently hold that men should be held morally re-

[7] Throughout the foregoing discussion and in what follows, everything said applies *only* to first-order inquiries, whether normative or speculative. First-order normative knowledge or common-sense opinions of a normative character can be put to use, in a sense, by speculative philosophy when that moves on the plane of second-order inquiry. The analytical and linguistic philosophers, moving on that plane, have devoted considerable attention to the language and meaning of normative statements.

[8] See Chapter 9, pp. 148–149.

sponsible for acts which they performed at an earlier time. If there are no such enduring entities, the agent who performed a certain act at an earlier time cannot be identical with the individual who is to be charged at a later time with moral responsibility for that act. Or, to take another example, a philosopher who precribes how men ought to act or who recommends any course of action that they should adopt cannot consistently hold the view that everything which happens is so completely determined that men are not free to choose between one course of action and another.

It would appear that the philosopher, confronted with these inconsistencies, could resolve them by taking either horn of the dilemma and relinquishing the other. If that were so, then the "is-ought" test would add nothing to the general requirement of logical consistency in a sound philosophy. The "is-ought" test is additive precisely because the reverse is the case. Our common experience of living and acting gives a certain primacy to normative over speculative philosophy. The denial of moral responsibility is immediately falsified by our common experience of human life, in which we feel responsible for our acts and hold others responsible for theirs. Hence, if we have to choose between denying moral responsibility, on the normative side of philosophy, and giving up, on the speculative side, the view that there are no enduring entities in the world, we must do the latter.

The primacy of the normative over the speculative gives special force to the "is-ought" test. It requires us to reject as unsound any philosophical theory about what *is* or *is not* which undermines our effort, on the normative side, to deal philosophically with how men *ought* to behave.

(5)

It was pointed out in the preceding chapter that philosophy is generally regarded as being less useful to
mankind than science.[9] If technological and practical
know-how were the only measure of the usefulness of
knowledge, we should be compelled to admit, not that
philosophy is less useful than science, but that it is totally
useless. As we have seen, however, *ought*-knowledge as
well as know-how is needed in the spheres of action and
production. Normative philosophy supplies us with the
ought-knowledge that we need for guidance or direction
in the conduct of our lives. We cannot go to any other of
the major branches of natural knowledge—to science, to
history, or to mathematics—for it. If we exclude from
consideration the claim of revealed religion to offer us
supernatural guidance (in the form of God-given laws)
and supernatural help (in the form of God-given grace),
philosophy alone, of all branches of knowledge, can tell us
what we ought to seek as well as both why and how we
ought to seek it. Philosophy alone gives us knowledge of
what is good and bad, right and wrong—the order of goods,
the moral law, ends and means, happiness, the human
virtues, and our duties.[10]

The power which science gives us through technology
can be used either for constructive or for destructive
purposes. The same scientific knowledge, put to produc-

[9] See Chapter 10, p. 166.

[10] The stories of human conduct that we find in narrative histories, like the stories told by writers of fiction, can be morally
instructive; but narrative history is not as such a branch of human
knowledge, and unless the stories are laced with normative judgments, either by the storyteller or by us, they teach no moral lessons.

tive use, can be used to emancipate man from labor or to enslave him, used to provide him with the comforts and conveniences of life or to kill and maim him, used to cure diseases or to inflict them. Precisely because it is ambivalent in this way, productive power is inherently dangerous and needs to be controlled by sound normative judgments about the pursuit of good and the avoidance of evil.

To overcome the dangers inherent in technological power, and to make its use beneficial rather than injurious to mankind, we must be able to direct and control technology. Science, which is the source of productive power, is entirely neutral with regard to the opposite ways in which that power can be used. Being non-normative, it makes no moral judgments—that is, no *ought*-judgments. It is by its very nature incompetent to guide or control the productive power which it has placed in man's hands and unleashed on the world. Therefore, it is to normative philosophy, not to science, that we must look for whatever help we can get in the direction and control of technology.

Far from accepting the prevalent opinion that philosophy has not been, and can never be, as useful to man as science has been, and is, through all its technological applications, I submit that the very opposite is the case. Of the two, philosophy has a superior usefulness, a higher claim on our respect for the benefits it confers upon us and the help it gives us. In one sense, the respective ways in which philosophical and scientific knowledge can be useful— through *ought*-judgments and through know-how—are incomparable, as incomparable as the ways in which philosophy and science make progress or achieve agreement. They are simply different. Yet things as different as normative philosophy and technology can be placed on a scale of values and judged, relative to one another, for their contribution to human well-being, to the happiness of men and the welfare of society.

Judged by such standards, the *ought*-knowledge which directs man in the achievement of the good life and the good society is superior to the know-how which puts at man's disposal productive power, power that may either facilitate or defeat man's achievement of the good life and the good society. In addition, one of the uses of philosophy is to give us rational control over the use of science; and it is in this very important respect, if in no other, that the superior usefulness of philosophy must be conceded by anyone who is persuaded that philosophy, both normative and speculative, can satisfy the conditions of intellectual respectability.

CHAPTER 12

Understanding the World:
The "Mixed Question" Test

WE HAVE CONSIDERED how philosophy should be compared with science in three respects—progress, agreement, and usefulness. A fourth respect remains: understanding. For our understanding of the world, should we go to science or to philosophy? Which renders the world more intelligible? Which penetrates more deeply into the nature of things?

These questions plainly presuppose some conflict, or at least competition, between the pictures that science and philosophy give us or between the stories that they tell; for if their views of the world concur, or if philosophy simply endorses the scientific account of things, there would be no reason to ask which gives us the better grasp of the world in which we live, and no sense in the generally prevalent opinion that philosophy has never given and can never give us an understanding of the world as penetrating as that which we obtain from science.

To examine the comparative merits of science and philosophy in this respect, I shall concentrate upon a single classic example of an apparent conflict between philosophy and science. I say "apparent" at this point only in order not to beg the question in advance, for if there were no appearance of conflict, we should have no problem. The crux of the problem lies in understanding why there appears to be a conflict. Once that is understood, I think the problem can be solved; and since, as I shall try to show, both the understanding of the problem and the solution of it are not scientific, but philosophical, achievements, I think it is arguable that philosophy is superior, not inferior, to science in rendering the world intelligible.

(1)

The example which serves our purpose can be stated as follows. It involves three points.

(1) A philosophy that is based on common experience would defend the common-sense opinion that the individual material objects of our experience really exist as they are experienced. Each has a *unity* of being, a *continuing identity* of being, and a *distinctness* of being; for example, this man and that man, this cat and that cat, this rose and that rose, or this chair and that chair. In addition, each is an individual sensible substance, having certain attributes and qualities. Among these attributes are its identity over a span of time and its material continuity or solidity.

This man, this cat, or this chair is not like a collection of marbles, so far as our common experience goes. We can divide the collection of marbles into two collections, or three, or four, simply by separating the discrete marbles into distinct piles; but we cannot divide this man or this cat into two or more men, or two or more cats; and though we may be able to take a chair apart and refashion its materials into two chairs, we have to destroy the original chair in order to do so. That process is ostensibly quite different from dividing a collection of marbles, precisely because the chair has material continuity, lacked by the collection of discrete marbles.

(2) Physical science, based on the very special data of experimental investigation, includes an elaborate and subtle theory of matter which involves certain so-called theoretical entities—not only discrete atoms of matter, but also the more minute particles which constitute atoms. Both the atoms and their constituent particles are intrinsically imperceptible to our senses. As N. R. Hanson points out, they are essentially unpicturable—"unpicturable-in-principle." But the elementary particles which constitute atoms are, if this is possible to say, even more radically unpicturable than atoms.

The atom of Democritus lacked all the sensible qualities which ordinary bodies have—such as color, texture, smell—but it still had basic quantitative properties, such as weight, shape or size, position, and motion. The qualities of perceptible bodies were called "secondary qualities"; the basic physical attributes of the atom, "primary qualities" or "primary properties." "Democritus' atomic theory avoids investing atoms," Hanson writes, "with those secondary properties requiring explanation. It provides a pattern of concepts whereby the properties the atom *does* possess—position, shape, motion—can, as a matter of course, account for the other 'secondary' properties of objects. The price paid for this intellectual gain is unpicturability." [1]

Until the end of the nineteenth century, and even for the

[1] *Patterns of Discovery*, Cambridge, 1958, pp. 121–122. Cf. Werner Heisenberg, *Philosophic Problems of Nuclear Physics*, New York, 1952, pp. 54–55.

first few decades of this century, modern atomic theory retained certain of the basic features of ancient atomism. So long as the atom remained the fundamental unit of matter, it had certain attributes in common with perceptible bodies, such as weight, position, motion; in addition, it had the special atomic properties of indivisibility, impenetrability, and homogeneity. But this "Democritean-Newtonian-Daltonian atom cannot explain what has been observed in this century. Its postulated properties . . . no longer pattern and integrate our data; to account for all the facts the atom must be a complex system of more fundamental entities," such as "electrons, protons, neutrons, positrons, mesons, anti-protons, anti-neutrons and gamma-ray photons. . . ." [2] Where earlier forms of atomic theory ruled out secondary qualities, the present theory of sub-atomic particles "denies its fundamental units any direct correspondence with the primary qualities, the traditional dimensions, positions, and dynamical properties. . . . The result," Hanson concludes, "is radical unpicturability." [3]

Heisenberg's statement of the matter confirms how radical, indeed, is the unpicturability of the present conceptions. "The indivisible elementary particle of modern physics," he writes, "possesses the quality of taking up space in no higher measure than other properties, say color and strength of material." They "are no longer bodies in the proper sense of the word." [4] They are units of matter only in the sense in which mass and energy are interchangeable; this fundamental stuff, according to Heisenberg, "is capable of existence in different forms," but "always appears in

[2] Hanson, *op. cit.*, pp. 122–123.
[3] *Ibid.*
[4] *Op. cit.*, pp. 55–56.

definite quanta." [5] These discrete quanta of mass/energy cannot even be described as particles, for they are as much waves or wave packets; Eddington coined the name "wavicles" for them to cover the fact that their behavior corresponds to both that of waves and that of particles.

(3) There would seem to be a conflict here between physical science and philosophy, if both are taken as giving us knowledge of the same real existences. It is easier to grasp this conflict in terms of the Democritean-Newtonian-Daltonian atom than in terms of the wavicle of contemporary sub-atomic physics, but *in principle* the conflict is the same. I shall state it in the easier form first.

Consider a particular real existence—a particular chair in a particular room, easily identified by all the persons in that room, who can all point to the same object, occupying the same space, and so forth. According to a philosophy based on common experience, the particular chair being pointed out is a solid material object, having certain sensible qualities and other experienceable properties. These are markedly different from the properties of a collection of marbles, no matter how the marbles are organized. According to the theory of atoms as the ultimate, indivisible units of matter, the chair is a congeries of minute and imperceptible bodies. The interaction of these bodies, with some resulting stable pattern of organization, does not abolish their discreteness or material discontinuity, made by the void or empty space which separates one from another.[6]

[5] *Ibid.*, p. 103.

[6] J. J. C. Smart, defending A. S. Eddington's contrast between the two tables (instead of chairs)—the table of common experience and the physicist's table—maintains that there is "a perfectly good sense in which it is true and illuminating to say that the table is *not* solid. The atoms which compose the table are like the solar system

Looked at the first way, the envelope of space (that is, the place) occupied by the particular chair appears to be completely and continuously filled with matter—in other words, by *one* body. Looked at the second way, the identical region of space is conceived of as being occupied by a vast multitude of discrete or discontinuous units of matter—by *many* bodies, in short. Can we hold these two views of one and the same place, or region of space, without a sense of conflict between them?

If we can see the apparent conflict between our common-sense view of the chair and the physicist's view of it, we should also be able to see it when we substitute the theory of sub-atomic particles or wave packets for that of atoms as the ultimate units of matter, for it is the same in principle. Let us go as far as Heisenberg would take us in the direction of divesting these quanta of matter (of mass/energy) of any of the properties assigned to sensible bodies, or even to atoms (such as position, shape, motion). The ancient contrast between atoms and the void, Heisenberg points out, can be translated into the most fundamental of all differences—that between being and non-being.[7] But if one recognizes that "to give an accurate description of the elementary particle—and here the emphasis is on the word 'accurate'—the only thing which can be written down as a description is a probability function . . . then one sees that not even the quality of being (if that can be called a 'quality') belongs to what is described." What, then, *is* the elementary particle or

---

in being mostly empty space. [This was Eddington's point.] So, though most common-sense propositions in ordinary life are true, I still wish to say that science gives us a 'truer picture' of the world" (*Philosophy and Scientific Realism*, New York, 1963, p. 47).

[7] *Physics and Philosophy*, New York, 1958, pp. 65–66.

205

wave packet? Heisenberg's answer is that "it is a possibility for being or a tendency for being." [8]

On this view, as on the view taken by old-fashioned atomism, the region of space occupied by the chair of our common experience is occupied by a vast multitude of material units. Where before that multitude consisted of units having some of the properties of bodies, including actual being or existence, now it consists of quanta of mass/energy having none of the properties of bodies, not even that of actual being. Where before the region of space occupied by the chair was not completely *filled* by atoms (since atoms, to be atoms, must be separated from one another by void), now the ultimate material units (whether in the form of particles or in the form of wave packets) are *discrete* quanta of mass or discrete quanta of energy. They may all be made of the same stuff, whatever that is, but there is a denumerable multitude of them.

We can now see why the conflict is in principle the same. It turns, not on the distinction between filled and empty space, nor even on that between being and non-being, but on the distinction between the one and the many. The chair of our common experience, the reality of which a philosophy based on common experience defends, is not only a solid body, but even more fundamentally a single being. The chair of physical theory (whether in terms of atoms or sub-atomic particles) consists of an irreducible multiplicity of discrete units, each having some kind of being, even that minimal grade of being for which Heisenberg used the words "possibility for being or tendency for being." Hence, whether we see the conflict in terms of one body in the region of space occupied by the chair versus many bod-

[8] *Ibid.*, p. 70.

ies (the atoms which together with the void make up the chair) or in terms of one being in that region of space versus many beings (the discrete sub-atomic units), the conflict is in principle the same, for it is a conflict between the one and the many.

If the unitary being which is the solid chair, with all its sensible qualities, is dismissed as a purely subjective fantasy on our part, then no conflict remains; for it can be said that what exists out there, where we have the illusion that there is a solid chair, is nothing but a multitude of material units, in a pattern of organization which occupies (whether or not it fills) a certain identifiable region of space. Or, if the physicist's atoms, particles, or wave packets are merely "theoretical entities," to which no real existence is attributed (that is, if they are *merely* mathematical forms, which have *no* physical reality), then their being posited for theoretical purposes does not challenge the view that what really exists out there is the solid chair of our experience.

If, however, real existence of the same kind is attributed to both the theoretical entities of physics and to the solid chair of common experience, then we cannot avoid what is at least an apparent conflict between science (in this case, physics) and philosophy.[9]

[9] For diverse considerations of this classic example of an apparent conflict between science, on the one hand, and philosophy together with common-sense, on the other, see William James, *Principles of Psychology*, New York, 1890, Vol. II, Chapter XXI, pp. 291–293, 299–301; Arthur S. Eddington, *The Nature of the Physical World*, New York, 1928, Introduction, pp. ix–xvii; L. S. Stebbing, *Philosophy and the Physicists*, London, 1937, Part II, pp. 45–140; Gilbert Ryle, *Dilemmas*, Cambridge, 1954, pp. 75–81; Jacques Barzun, *Science: The Glorious Entertainment*, New York, 1964, p. 63; and J. J. C. Smart, *op. cit.*, pp. 47–48.

Is this apparent conflict resolvable? If so, what is the resolution? Or is it only a pseudo-problem? If so, how is the misleading appearance of conflict to be removed? All of these questions bear on the relation of science and philosophy as first-order knowledge of the world, especially when each claims to give us knowledge of one and the same region of that world.

(2)

The first step to be taken in dealing with this problem is to consider two competing positions in the philosophy of science. One is the instrumentalist, the other the realist, view of science.[10]

THE INSTRUMENTALIST VIEW. Scientific theories are nothing but instruments of calculation and prediction, mediating between observed data and new data to be observed or effects to be controlled or produced by technology. They are not intended to be descriptions of reality. They are to be judged as operationally successful or unsuccessful, as effective or ineffective in yielding further experimental results or technological applications, but not as true or false in any sense of *true* or *false* that means agreement or non-agreement between theory and reality. According to the instrumentalist view, science, as James Conant points out, is not engaged in a process of map-making, progressively achieving better and better approximations in the charting of reality. "Science," he

[10] These two views of science are essentially philosophical in character, whether they are advanced or held by men who classify themselves professionally as philosophers or by men who classify themselves professionally as scientists.

writes, is "a series of interconnected concepts and conceptual schemes arising from experiment and observation and fruitful of further experiments and observations. The test of a scientific theory is its fruitfulness . . . its ability 'to suggest, stimulate, and direct experiment.' . . . A scientific theory is not even the first approximation to a map; it is not a creed; it is a policy—an economical and fruitful guide to action by scientific investigators." [11]

According to Karl Popper, "instrumentalism can be formulated as the thesis that scientific theories—the theories of the so-called 'pure' sciences—are nothing but computation rules (or inference rules); of the same character, fundamentally, as the computation rules of the so-called 'applied' sciences. (One might even formulate it as the thesis that 'pure' science is a misnomer, and that all science is 'applied')." [12] Still another way of making the same point would be to say that the instrumentalist treats scientific knowledge as essentially know-how instead of as know-that—heuristic know-how combined with productive know-how. Just as the line between pure science and applied science then disappears, so does the line between science and technology.

If we take a purely instrumentalist view of physics, such theoretical entities as atoms and the particles of nuclear physics become nothing but "convenient fictions," having operational significance only. They are not to be interpreted as referring to any existent reality. If one were to adopt an instrumentalist approach to the philosophical defense of common-sense opinions, the result would be

[11] *Modern Science and Modern Man*, New York, 1952, pp. 54–57.
[12] *Conjectures and Refutations*, New York, 1962, p. 111. For a fuller statement of the instrumentalist view, see pp. 107–114, *passim*.

similar. The experienced chair, conceived as an individual substance, would be regarded as a "theoretical construct," a convenient fiction posited to serve some theoretical interest or practical purpose.[13]

THE REALIST VIEW. There are several different versions of the realist view of science (or of philosophy), but all agree in regarding science (or philosophy) as knowledge of a knowable reality, as mapmaking in the sense in which maps can be more or less accurate, better or worse approximations to the actual shape of the terrain being explored, studied, or thought about. The realist view may involve different conceptions of knowledge—as *epistēmē* or as *doxa*—and, if knowledge is *doxa*, it may involve different accounts of how the relative truth of theories or conclusions is to be tested; but what is common to all versions of the realist view is the affirmation that theories can be true or false in the sense of agreement or non-agreement with an independent and determinate order of real existences. They can, at the very least, be falsified by experience, even if they can never be completely verified or rigorously demonstrated to be true. This minimum statement of the realist view presupposes that theories can be true as well as false, even though we may never be able to establish their truth in any final or certain manner.[14]

[13] Cf. W. V. O. Quine, "Two Dogmas of Empiricism," in *Clarity Is Not Enough*, edited by H. D. Lewis, London, 1963, pp. 129–132. Theoretical constructs, recognized as convenient fictions, may play a useful role in both scientific and philosophical thought. The character or limits of their usefulness is not in question here. The only point being made is that, in an instrumentalist view, the "theoretical entities" of atomic and nuclear physics are *nothing but convenient fictions*.

[14] Cf. Karl Popper, *op. cit.*, pp. 99–107, 114–119. It should be pointed out in passing that the realist view of scientific or philo-

Whatever version of the realist view is adopted, it stands opposed to the instrumentalist view of science on four counts, as indicated by the following statements, each of which directly negates an instrumentalist tenet. (1) Scientific theories are to be interpreted as descriptions of reality. (2) They are to be judged as true or false, where this means agreement or non-agreement with reality. (3) Progress in science does consist of better and better approximations to an accurate charting of nature. (4) Theoretical entities, such as atoms and sub-atomic particles, are not merely convenient fictions; if the physical theory which posits them is confirmed by empirical data, or at least is not falsified, then claiming truth for that theory amounts to asserting the real existence of these entities.[15]

(3)

The next step to be taken is to ask how the problem with which we are concerned is affected by these opposed views, not only of science, but also of philosophy; for, as we have

---

sophical knowledge can embrace a pragmatic or instrumentalist theory of truth, where that means no more than a statement of the ways of testing the truth and falsity of theories; but it firmly rejects the complete conventionalism (no determinate reality to be known, no agreement or non-agreement with reality, no truth or falsity to be tested, no standards of worth to be applied to theories except those of convenience or satisfaction of purpose) to which pragmatism sometimes leads and which is part and parcel of the instrumentalist view of science or philosophy. Cf. what was said on this point above, in Chapter 4, pp. 74–75.

[15] On this last point, see Grover Maxwell, "The Ontological Status of Theoretical Entities," in *Minnesota Studies in the Philosophy of Science*, Vol. III, Minneapolis, 1962, pp. 3–27. See also Ernest Nagel, *The Structure of Science*, New York, 1961, Chapter 6; and cf. J. J. C. Smart, *op. cit.*, pp. 16–18, 27–49.

seen, they are as applicable to philosophy as to science.[16] We are confronted with four possible combinations of these views: an instrumentalist view of science combined with an instrumentalist view of philosophy; an instrumentalist view of science combined with a realist view of philosophy; a realist view of science combined with an instrumentalist view of philosophy; and a realist view of both. What consequences does each have for the problem with which we are concerned?

AN INSTRUMENTALIST VIEW OF SCIENCE COMBINED WITH AN INSTRUMENTALIST VIEW OF PHILOSOPHY. For those who adopt this combination, the problem as here stated vanishes. As here stated, the problem arises from an apparent conflict between scientific and philosophical theories, when both are interpreted as know-that and as asserting that certain of their theoretical constructions give us knowledge of real existences. But even though the problem as stated becomes a pseudo-problem for the instrumentalist view of both science and philosophy, another question with which we are concerned remains of interest—the question of the relative superiority of science or philosophy. The question must be somewhat modified; for, instead of asking which gives us a better understanding of reality, we must ask, Which is more useful?

[16] As pointed out in Chapter 4, one of the two basic presuppositions of this book is that of realism; and this, as we saw, involves the rejection of pragmatic conventionalism, according to which the theoretical constructions of philosophy, as well as those of science, are nothing but convenient fictions which serve some practical purpose. In addition, we saw, in Chapter 3 (see pp. 58–59), that one view of philosophy, taken by Gilbert Ryle and W. F. Sellars, tends to reduce philosophical knowledge to know-how. To regard philosophy as nothing more than a kind of know-how or to regard its theoretical constructions as nothing but convenient fictions is to take an instrumentalist view of it.

As applied to the view of material objects taken by philosophy on the basis of common experience and the view of them taken by theoretical physics on the basis of experimental data, the question may not be answerable because each, serving a different purpose, may be useful in its own way. The scientific view has an obvious technological usefulness totally lacked by philosophy; and the philosophical view has an obvious usefulness in the ordinary transactions of life. We cannot say which is more useful.

This, however, does not completely dispose of the matter. If the judgment can ever be made that a particular scientific theory is more useful than a particular philosophical theory, both serving the same purpose, that judgment would not be a scientific, but a philosophical, judgment. Furthermore, it is not scientific know-how, but philosophical know-how which shows us that the apparent conflict between science and common-sense is only a pseudo-problem. It is also not scientific know-how, but philosophical know-how which helps us handle the apparent conflicts between different branches of science. In all these respects, philosophy can claim to be superior to science, even in an instrumentalist view of both. Its superiority is in the dimension of understanding; not, of course, in understanding reality or the nature of things, for there is no reality or nature to be understood in the form of know-that. Its superiority in understanding is a superiority of know-how in the realm of theorizing.

AN INSTRUMENTALIST VIEW OF SCIENCE COMBINED WITH A REALIST VIEW OF PHILOSOPHY. Again, our problem as stated vanishes, but now for a different reason. There can be no conflict, not even an apparent conflict, between the atomistic or nuclear theory and common-sense notions or philosophical theories about the sensible material objects of common experience. If it is improper to claim descriptive truth for scientific theories, then such theories, no matter what their content, cannot be involved in conflict with philosophical theories, for which the claim of truth is made. There can be no conflict between scientific know-how and philosophical know-that. If the theoretical entities of physics—the atoms and their elementary particles—*are nothing but convenient fictions*, their use in scientific calculations, predictions, or experimental processes cannot possibly challenge the reality of the familiar sensible objects of common experience.

There is, however, a second consequence here, and one that has a bearing on the comparative merits of science and philosophy. In the instrumentalist view, science gives us only know-how, no know-that—no knowledge of reality in that sense of "knowledge" which involves truth as agreement with reality. In a realist view of philosophy, philosophy does give us knowledge of reality. Hence to the question, *Which renders the world more intelligible?* we must answer, *Philosophy*. Science, in the instrumentalist view, offers us no understanding of reality at all.

Leaving aside history as knowledge of past particulars, philosophical theories and common-sense opinions would then constitute our only general first-order knowledge of that which is and happens in the world. In addition, there would be no mixed questions in philosophy, at least none involving both science and philosophy as knowledge (know-that) about the same objects or the same regions of reality.

A REALIST VIEW OF SCIENCE COMBINED WITH AN INSTRU-MENTALIST VIEW OF PHILOSOPHY. Here as before, the first consequence is the same (no problem, because no conflict);

but here the second consequence is exactly the reverse of what it was in the preceding case. It is science alone that gives us general first-order knowledge of reality; it is science alone that enables us to understand the world. Philosophical theories serve some other purpose, largely emotional in character; or they satisfy individual predilections and interests. Philosophy may even give us theoretical know-how that is useful in handling scientific theories, in themselves, in relation to one another, or in relation to common-sense; but philosophy does not give us any know-that about reality or the nature of things.

Professor Smart, who adopts "an unashamedly realistic view of the fundamental particles of physics," not only defends "the physicist's picture of the world as an ontologically respectable one," but also maintains that "the physicist's language gives us a *truer* picture of the world than does the language of ordinary common sense." [17] In an instrumentalist view of our common-sense opinions about the familiar objects of ordinary experience, or of the philosophical conceptions that are developed in defense of such opinions, the latter are not less true; they are simply not true at all. Atoms and their elementary particles are the ultimate realities; men, cats, roses, and chairs are now "philosophical constructions" or "theoretical entities," which may be useful as convenient fictions.

A REALIST VIEW OF BOTH SCIENCE AND PHILOSOPHY. The reader has already been reminded that a realist interpretation of philosophical thought is one of the two basic presuppositions of this book.[18] Hence, the state of affairs envisaged in the first and the third views above are not, for

[17] *Op. cit.*, pp. 18, 47.
[18] See Chapter 4, pp. 74–75.

me, tenable alternatives. The possibility described in the second above, however, is quite compatible with the position concerning philosophy taken in this book. Nevertheless, over and above the persuasive evidence and arguments that have been advanced for affirming the real existence of atoms and nuclear particles, the basic presupposition of realism, to which I am committed, inclines me to espouse a realist view of science as well as of philosophy. What consequences now follow from the adoption of this fourth alternative?

Insofar as science and philosophy have different objects of inquiry, no conflict occurs between them. As we have seen, certain questions cannot be answered by investigation; others cannot be answered without investigation. The answers that philosophy gives to questions of the first sort cannot conflict with the answers that science gives to questions of the second sort. There are, however, some mixed questions—questions which require us to relate what is asserted by scientific theory, on the one hand, and what is asserted by philosophical theory, on the other. These, as already pointed out, can arise only when both science and philosophy are regarded, realistically, as modes of inquiry aiming to achieve knowledge, or to arrive at relatively true descriptions of reality.

For example, there is the mixed question about the nature of man: any philosophical theory which defends the common-sense view of man as radically distinct from, and superior to, all other terrestrial organisms must be related to what is hypothecated in the biological theory of man's evolution, and to the conclusions about human and animal intelligence that have been reached by laboratory and clinical psychology on the basis of the special data obtained by investigation. Similarly, any philosophical theory of the human mind which sets the processes of reason or intellect apart from and above all the operations of the sensitive faculties, including memory and imagination, must be related to the conclusions about thinking and problem-solving that have developed out of cybernetic research and computer technology. Still another example of a mixed question is the problem with which we have been concerned in this chapter—the problem of relating the philosophical theory which defends the truth of the common-sense opinion about the sensible, material objects of everyday experience (or, in other words, affirms their reality as experienced) to the theory of matter developed by atomic and nuclear physics on the basis of much experimental evidence.

It would take an extended discussion to present a satisfactory solution of any one of these extremely difficult mixed questions. It cannot be done at the end of this chapter or even within the limits of this book.[19] What I propose to do, instead, is simply to state the criteria of a satisfactory solution of such questions; and I hope that, in doing this, I can throw some light on the one test of philosophical theories which has not yet been discussed (namely, the "mixed question" test) as well as assess the relative merits of science and philosophy for man's understanding of the world in which he lives.[20]

[19] I look forward to the possibility of a second series of Encyclopaedia Britannica Lectures at the University of Chicago in 1965, in which I shall deal with the mixed question about man and the related mixed question about the human mind.

[20] See Chapter 9, p. 149; and also Chapter 10, p. 166.

(4)

For the stated purpose, I am going to take the mixed question that we have been using as an example throughout this chapter—the one which presents us with an apparent conflict between philosophy and nuclear physics.

It is easy to say what cannot be done with regard to this problem. If we persist in holding a realist view of science, we cannot remove the conflict by treating the particles of nuclear physics as theoretical entities which serve as convenient fictions but have no reality. If we persist in regarding common experience as the basis of philosophical knowledge, we cannot remove the conflict by treating our common experience of material objects as illusory. If common experience is itself illusory, it can hardly be used to test philosophical theories; and if it is not illusory, then it provides some warrant for the truth of the common-sense opinions about the reality of the sensible, material objects of ordinary experience and also for any philosophical theory which employs certain conceptual constructions, such as that of individual physical substances, to defend and explain the truth of that common-sense opinion.

The validation of such conceptual constructions in philosophy is exactly like the validation of the theoretical entities of nuclear physics. Occam's Razor can be justly applied in both cases to excise these reifications if the data of experience—common or special—can be adequately accounted for without their employment; but if, in the case of nuclear physics, the experimental data cannot be satisfactorily accounted for unless certain theoretical entities are posited, and if, in the case of philosophy, the data of common experience cannot be satisfactorily accounted for unless certain conceptual constructions are posited, then the entities or constructs posited—elementary particles, in the one case, and individual physical substances, in the other—are validated in the only way that such things can be validated. Their validation by empirical evidence leads not only to the affirmation of the truth of the theory in each case, but also to the affirmation of the real existence of that which is signified by the theoretical concepts in each case.

So far we have rejected as unsatisfactory two ways of trying to solve the problem by removing the conflict. A third way is equally unsatisfactory. It is the effort made by some writers to show that the two theories are complementary, rather than conflicting, accounts of the same objects. Gilbert Ryle, for example, tries to treat the two theories by analogy with a librarian's and a bursar's account of the same books on the shelves of the college.[21] The analogy fails. The same books do have different properties (namely, their contents and their prices) which are of interest respectively to the librarian and to the bursar; but the real existence of this chair as an individual substance in a certain region of space and the real existence of an organized congeries of atoms or elementary particles in exactly the same region of space can hardly be treated as different properties of the same object, or even of the same region of space. There is no need to reconcile what the librarian records about the contents of the books when he classifies them with what the bursar records about the prices of the books when he enters them into his ledger; but I do not see how anyone can fail to question how the individual physical substance and the organized congeries of ele-

21 See *Dilemmas, op. cit.*, pp. 75–81.

mentary particles can *both really exist in identically the same region of space*. Stated thus, in realistic terms, the problem is genuine, not a pseudo-problem or a merely verbal one. Any satisfactory effort to arrive at a solution must begin by conceding that, in a mixed question of this sort, there is at least an apparent conflict between what science claims to know and what philosophy claims to know.[22]

To concede this is to concede that there is some truth in what each theory asserts—some truth in the assertion that atoms and sub-atomic particles really exist and some truth in the assertion that the solid material objects of our common experience really exist as solid material objects and, in addition, have the unity of individual physical substances. Can these apparently conflicting truths be reconciled?

The problem would be insoluble if the two assertions to be reconciled stood in relation to each other in the same way that the statement that Jones is sitting in a particular chair at a particular time stands to the statement that Smith, another man, is sitting in the same chair at the same time, and is not sitting on top of Jones or on the arm of the chair, but exactly where Jones is sitting. The statements about Jones and Smith are contradictory; both cannot be true; they cannot be reconciled. The assertion about atoms or nuclear particles as the imperceptible physical constituents of the chair and the assertion about the chair as an individual physical

[22] In view of the fact that Ryle tends to take the instrumentalist approach to both science and philosophy, it may be unfair to treat the librarian's and the bursar's account of the books in the college library as analogous to a scientific and a common-sense, or philosophical, account of the same material objects when these are regarded as know-that, not merely know-how. Ryle's analogy may work well enough for science and philosophy as know-how; it does not work when they are both interpreted as know-that.

substance having certain sensible properties are not contradictory and can be reconciled by a philosophical theory of matter and energy, of potential, virtual, and actual being, capacious and subtle enough to allow for a wide range of distinctions in the modes of existence among things *all of which really exist to some degree,* more or less.

Heisenberg hints at the solution to which we are coming. As we have seen, he refers to the elementary units of matter as "possibilities for being or tendencies for being." He also thinks that an "objective tendency or possibility" for being might be regarded as "a 'potentia' in the sense of Aristotelian philosophy. In fact," he writes, "I believe that the language actually used by physicists when they speak about atomic events produces in their minds similar notions as the concept 'potentia.' " [23] Later he adds the following concluding observation: "In the experiments about atomic events we have to do with things and facts, with phenomena that are just as real as any phenomena in daily life. But the atoms or the elementary particles are *not as real; they form a world of potentialities or possibilities rather than one of things or facts*." [24]

There are passages in Heisenberg (especially those dealing with the "Copenhagen interpretation of quantum theory") which make it difficult to determine whether he takes a realist or an instrumentalist view of nuclear physics.[25] There are still other passages in which he appears to adopt the extreme Pythagorean doctrine that the ultimate "building blocks" of the universe are mathematical forms, not material particles, quanta of energy, or physical entities of

---

[23] *Physics and Philosophy, op. cit.,* pp. 180–181.
[24] *Ibid.,* p. 186 (italics added).
[25] See *ibid.,* Chapters II and VIII, *passim.*

any sort.[26] In consequence, it is difficult to decide whether Heisenberg is of one mind on the question. But this does not affect the significance which I attach to his remarks about the potential being of elementary particles. This means, he says, that they are *not as real* as the things of daily life—the things of common experience. "Not as real" can hardly be read as equivalent to "not real at all." If the nuclear particles are real, *but less real* than the material objects of common experience, there must be diverse modes of real existence which differ in the grade or degree of reality which they respectively possess. Herein lies a clue to the solution of the problem. It involves two points.

(1) The reality of the elementary particles of nuclear physics cannot be reconciled with the reality of the chair as an individual sensible substance if both the particles and the chair are asserted to have the same mode of existence or grade of being. The same thing can also be said about the nuclear particles and the atoms of which they are component parts. The particles are less real than the atoms; that is, they have less actuality. This, I take it, is the meaning of Heisenberg's statement that the particles are in a state of *potentia*—"possibilities for being or tendencies for being."

(2) The mode of being of the material constituents of a physical body cannot be the same when those constituents exist in isolation and when they enter into the constitution of an actual body. Thus, when the chair exists actually as one body, the multitude of atoms and elementary particles which constitute it exist only virtually. Since their existence is only virtual, so is their multiplicity; and their virtual multiplicity is not incompatible with the actual unity of the

[26] *Philosophical Problems of Nuclear Physics, op. cit.,* pp. 56–59; 97 ff. Cf. *Physics and Philosophy, op. cit.,* pp. 71–75.

chair. Again, the same thing can also be said about a single atom and the nuclear particles which constitute it; or about a single molecule and the various atoms which constitute it. When an atom or a molecule actually exists as a unit of matter, its material constituents have only virtual existence and, consequently, their multiplicity is also only virtual.[27]

The virtual existence and multiplicity of the material constituents do not abrogate their potentiality for actual existence and actual multiplicity. If the unitary chair—or a single atom—were exploded into its ultimate material constituents, the elementary particles would assume the mode of actual existence which isolated particles have in a cyclotron; their virtual multiplicity would be transformed into an actual multitude.

The critical point here is that the mode of existence in which the particles are discrete units and have actual multiplicity cannot be the same as the mode of existence which they have when they are material constituents of the one chair in actual existence. If we assign the same mode of existence to the particles in a cyclotron and to the particles that enter into the constitution of an actual chair, the

---

[27] A basic insight of the theory of atoms or elementary particles, repeatedly stated by Heisenberg, Hanson, and others, is that, in order to explain the physical properties of composite bodies, it is necessary for their material constituents to be *without* the properties to be explained. This insight does not go far enough. It states only one of two prerequisites for the explanatory value of elementary particles or atoms. The other prerequisite, also negative, is the point mentioned in the text above; namely, that the material constituents *cannot* be actually present in the composite body in the same mode of existence which they have when they are not constituents of a composite body, but exist in isolation. In order to explain the physical properties of a composite body, the material constituents must be virtually, rather than actually, present in that body and lack the properties to be explained.

conflict between nuclear physics and the philosophical doctrine which affirms the reality of the material objects of common experience ceases to be merely an apparent conflict. It is a real conflict and an irresolvable one because the conflicting theories are irreconcilable. But if they are assigned different modes of existence, the apparent conflict disappears, for the theories that appear to be in conflict can be reconciled.[28]

Here, then, we have an example of the "mixed question" test in operation. One measure of the soundness of a philosophical theory or doctrine is its ability to solve problems of the sort with which we have been dealing; that is, its ability to reconcile what truth there is in a scientific theory with what truth there is in a common-sense opinion and in the philosophical elucidation of that opinion, when these several truths appear to come into conflict. No line of philosophical thought is sound which tries to avoid such mixed questions, or which tries to dismiss, as pseudo-problems, such apparent conflicts between science and common-

[28] Let no one suppose that the solution of this problem involves the acceptance of atomism or atomistic materialism as a sound philosophical doctrine. That doctrine, as expounded by the ancients or their modern followers, rests on the proposition that nothing exists except atoms and the void; that is, only the ultimate particles of matter have real existence, and all the material things composed of them are *nothing but* organized congeries of particles and involve no additional forms or principles of being. Materialism of this type, as I pointed out earlier, provides us with a good example of a philosophical doctrine that must be rejected on empirical grounds; if common experience is not illusory, this doctrine must be rejected as false; see Chapter 9, pp. 155–156. As Heisenberg remarks, "the ontology of materialism rested upon the illusion that the kind of existence, the direct 'actuality' of the world around us, can be extrapolated into the atomic range. This extrapolation is impossible, however" (*Physics and Philosophy, op. cit.*, p. 145). Cf. *Philosophical Problems of Nuclear Physics, op. cit.*, pp. 106–108.

sense or between science and philosophy. Among competing philosophical theories, one is sounder than another if it presents a more satisfactory resolution of such conflicts.

(5)

One matter remains: if we take the realist view of both science and philosophy, and treat both as offering us first-order knowledge of that which is and happens in the world, to which should we primarily turn for our understanding of the world? Which, if either, outranks the other in discharging the task of rendering the world intelligible to us? Philosophy, I submit, and for the following reasons.

In the first place, when there is an apparent conflict between science and philosophy, it is to philosophy that we must turn for the resolution. Science cannot provide it. When scientists such as Einstein, Bohr, and Heisenberg become involved with mixed questions, they must philosophize. They cannot discuss these questions merely as scientists; the principles for the statement and for the solution of such problems come from philosophy, not from science.[29]

In the second place, the two views of science that we have been considering are philosophical views of science, not scientific views of it. In other words, the understanding of

[29] The two books by Heisenberg from which I have quoted a number of times in this chapter impressively illustrate this point. In both, Heisenberg combines scientific knowledge with philosophical thought in order to state and try to solve the difficult mixed questions raised by nuclear physics. The excellence of both books, as compared with books by other scientists on these subjects, results from Heisenberg's philosophical competence and philosophical knowledge.

science itself is philosophical, not scientific. While psycho-analysts such as Freud and sociologists such as Mannheim may offer us what appear to be scientific accounts of philosophers and philosophizing, these are not comparable to the philosophical account of science that we find in such writers as Popper or Hanson. The relation is not reciprocal; for the psychological or sociological treatment of philosophy (*à la* Freud or Mannheim) is strictly *ad hominem*, whereas the philosophical treatment of science, history, or any other discipline is addressed to the nature of the discipline itself, not the nature, the activities, or the propensities of the human beings who do its work and produce its formulations.

In the third place, the first-order questions that philosophy tries to answer are more profound—both more elementary and more ultimate—than the questions that science tries to answer. It is philosophy, not science, that takes the over-all view.

Our initial concern with the conditions under which philosophy can be as intellectually respectable as science was accompanied by an additional concern with the special role which philosophy should play in liberal education, in the organization of a university, and in a culture. If science were superior to philosophy with respect to the understanding it gives us of reality and of the world of learning, science, not philosophy, should play that special role. It does not and it cannot; and philosophy can. Philosophy is indispensable to our understanding of science and, beyond that, to our understanding of the world that we know through science as well as through common-sense.

Hence, I conclude that when the philosophical enterprise satisfies, as it can, all the conditions laid down and when, in addition, philosophical thinking meets, as it can, all the appropriate tests of soundness or truth, philosophy will not only deserve the same kind of respect that is now generally accorded science; but, in addition, it will deserve a higher measure of respect, because of the two ways in which it is superior to science—in its practical usefulness and in its theoretic insights.

Part Three

Applications and Confirmations

CHAPTER 13

Retrospect and Prospect

I HAVE NOW DONE what I can to persuade the reader that philosophy, by being able to satisfy certain stipulated conditions, can be an intellectual enterprise that deserves the same kind of respect generally accorded science and history, and additional esteem for the pivotal role it can play in education and in the organization of the university and for the special place it occupies in the hierarchy of elements that constitute culture or civilization.

I think I have accomplished this principally by showing that philosophy can have a distinctive method of its own whereby it can be an empirical mode of inquiry resulting in a distinctive type of knowledge (*doxa*) about that which is and happens in the world or about what men ought to do and seek. The crux of the argument is, of course, the distinction between common and special experience. If that distinction is valid, as I think it is, philosophy can have its own limited sphere of inquiry, just as science has its own limited sphere of inquiry; it can have first-order questions of its own and various ways of testing the theories or conclusions it propounds, including an empirical test of what it claims to know, whereby some of its claims may be falsified. The other tests (the logical test, the "is-ought" test, and the "mixed question" test) serve to measure the relative truth of competing theories that have not been empirically falsified. These things being so, I have argued, philosophy can be conducted as a public enterprise, in which philosophers cooperate, adjudicate their disputes, and achieve some measure of agreement.

I have also tried to explain why philosophy is generally thought, especially in learned circles, to be inferior to science with respect to agreement, progress, usefulness, and the understanding it gives us of the world. That judgment, I have conceded, may be quite sound when it is made about philosophy in its present or past state, which falls far short of satisfying the conditions stipulated. However, the judgment is sometimes made in terms which suggest that philosophy can never achieve the kind or degree of agreement and progress that science so clearly manifests; and that philosophy by its very nature can never be as useful to mankind as science or as valuable a source of understanding. That deprecatory estimate of philosophy, I have argued, is mistaken and unfounded. The explanation of the mistake, I have tried to point out, lies in the fact that philosophy is here being judged by reference to standards that are appropriate to science and to science alone, instead of standards appropriate to its own distinctive type of inquiry, its distinctive method, its distinctive results. Philosophy, as a noninvestigative discipline, cannot be expected to make the same kind or rate of progress, achieve agreement in the same way or to the same extent, or have the same kind of usefulness, of which science, an investigative discipline, can rightly boast.

To recognize this is to see that in modern times—with the

ever increasing cultural pre-eminence of science from the seventeenth century on—philosophy has suffered from these mistaken comparisons with science (that is, from comparisons that involve judging philosophy by standards appropriate to science). However, it is not only in modern times that philosophy has suffered from its relation to other disciplines. As I see philosophy's historic development from its beginning to the present day, it has had a checkered career, full of misfortunes and disorders. In antiquity, it suffered confusion with science, on the one hand, and with religion, on the other; in the Middle Ages, it suffered from the cultural dominance of religion and theology; in modern times, it has suffered and is still suffering from the cultural pre-eminence of science. Throughout its history, it has been misled by false aspirations, arising from its misguided emulation of either the demonstrative and analytical procedures of mathematics or of the certitude of dogmatic theology or of the empirical procedures of investigative science; and at all times, it has suffered disorders within its own household resulting from the failure to understand itself—its separate sphere of inquiry, its own distinctive method, its characteristic procedure, and, above all, what it can and cannot hope to achieve.

In view of this, the kindest thing that can be said about philosophy in the twentieth century is that its present state reveals it to be, unwittingly, a victim of its past. The most generous comment to add is that there are no intrinsic obstacles to its having a future much brighter than its past. Such optimism should not be expressed as a prediction, but as a hope that what it is possible for philosophy to become, it will become in the future. In the third and concluding portion of this book, I therefore propose to deal with philosophy's past and with its future. Here I wish to make a few points prefatory to what is to be undertaken in the chapters to follow.

(1)

Let me begin by recalling something said in the opening chapter. It was pointed out there that concern with philosophy's intellectual respectability—both in itself and in its relation to other disciplines, especially in relation to science—is a peculiarly modern phenomenon. Ancient and mediaeval philosophers never asked themselves whether philosophy was respectable. Rightly or wrongly, they not only assumed the intellectual worth of the philosophical enterprise, but they also took for granted its value in liberal education and in the organization of human culture; and they expected general public recognition of philosophy's worth and value. It is only in modern times that the most eminent philosophical writers have manifested a persistent worry about the condition of philosophy—about its achievements, its progress, its utility, especially relative to the achievements, progress, and utility of science. It is only in modern times—it might be more accurate to say that it is only in recent times, only in our own century—that the general public and the learned world in particular have come to question or even to reject philosophy's traditional status.

How should we interpret these facts? Should we say that the ancient and mediaeval view of philosophy was right and the modern view of it wrong; or should we say the reverse? The reader might suppose that I would defend or espouse the ancient and mediaeval view of philosophy. Have I not been arguing for philosophy's intellectual respectability and, beyond that, for its superiority to science in practical usefulness and theoretic insight?

While the answer to the last question is certainly affirmative, the reader has misunderstood the whole tenor of my argument if he supposes that it leads me to espouse the ancient and mediaeval view of philosophy and to reject the modern worry or concern about philosophy's state. I have not argued that philosophy, either in the past or at present, *ever has satisfied* the conditions which it must satisfy in order to warrant the ancient and mediaeval view of it or to dismiss as unjustified the modern worries or doubts about it. The whole tenor of my argument has been, on the contrary, to show that philosophy *can satisfy* these conditions, not that it has ever done so or is now doing so.

Hence, my position with respect to the ancient and mediaeval view of philosophy is that it is correct if it is interpreted as presenting us with an ideal to be realized—a sense of the public esteem it should deserve, a vision of the position it should occupy in the family of disciplines, and of the status it should have in our culture; but that it is wrong if it is interpreted as claiming that the philosophical enterprise, as conducted in ancient and mediaeval times, lived up to this ideal. Concurrently, my position with respect to the modern view of philosophy, and especially the view taken of it in the twentieth century, is that it is wrong if it is interpreted as claiming that, for reasons intrinsic to the very nature of the philosophical enterprise, it cannot ever realize or approximate the ideal which is to be found in the ancient or mediaeval view of philosophy; but that it is quite correct if it is interpreted as saying simply that, from its beginnings to the present, philosophy has not yet succeeded in satisfying all the conditions it must satisfy in order to deserve the respect accorded science or to occupy the cultural role assigned to it in ancient and mediaeval thought.

(2)

If I thought, *as I do not*, that it is only in modern times that philosophy has fallen into a parlous condition, then I should undertake in the following chapters to depict the high estate achieved by philosophy in ancient and mediaeval times, to explain how and why it is only in modern times that philosophy has fallen from that high estate, and to recommend the ways and means by which philosophy, in the future, can once more regain it by returning to its ancient past.

However, thinking, *as I do*, that philosophy has at no time ever satisfied all the conditions of respectability and worth as an intellectual enterprise—conditions which I think that it *can* and *should* satisfy—I am going to try to show the various cultural circumstances and other influences that have so far prevented the philosophical enterprise from being conducted as it should be, circumstances and influences which, it will be seen, differ in each of the major epochs of Western civilization; the mistakes that have been made, especially in modern times, by the various efforts to reform philosophy and to restore it to the status it was once thought to have; and the tendencies in the present century which, if developed in a certain way, might substantiate the hope that philosophy can have a future brighter than its past.

One recurrent theme runs throughout the story I am about to tell. It is that almost all the misfortunes and disorders which philosophy has suffered come, directly or indirectly, from the state of its relation to other disciplines, especially its relation to mathematics; its relation to religion in general and, in particular, its relation to the dogmatic theology of a religion that regards itself as revealed; and its relation to science, especially as that has developed in the modern world. These relationships, it will be seen, are not the same in all epochs because these other disciplines are in different stages of development in different epochs.

The difficulties that have beset philosophy, *vis-à-vis* its relation to other disciplines or their influences upon it, are of two sorts. On the one hand, philosophy has suffered from a lack of distinction between itself and other disciplines; that is, at certain times in the past, the line which should sharply separate philosophy from science or religion has either been non-existent or shadowy and indistinct. On the other hand, philosophy has suffered from the tendency to emulate and imitate other disciplines, without regard to the differences between itself and them which make such imitation inappropriate. In this connection, another misfortune which has befallen philosophy should also be pointed out—namely, that when, at certain times in the past, philosophy has failed in its effort to imitate other disciplines that it has erroneously set up as models to emulate, it then has suffered from a falsely induced sense of inferiority and failure.

(3)

Before I embark on the venture of retelling the story of philosophy in three short chapters, I must enter one disclaimer. I know that it is impossible to encompass the history of philosophy within such limited space if the story were to be told, as it usually is, in substantive terms—that is, in terms of theories held, doctrines propounded, systems developed, and arguments advanced by individual thinkers for or against particular positions. I propose to do something else, something which can be done with the brevity required.

I propose to deal with the history of philosophy almost exclusively in procedural terms—that is, in terms of philosophy's understanding of itself in different epochs and also its various misunderstandings of its own nature, tasks, methods, limitations. With one or two exceptions, which will be duly noted in the proper place, I propose to tell the story of philosophy's checkered career in terms of the soundness of its procedures at various times and in terms of the adequacy and correctness of philosophy's understanding of itself, without regard to the truth or falsity in substance of its doctrines or theories.

One final remark: I am not substituting a procedural for a substantive history of philosophy merely for the sake of brevity. Only a procedural history of philosophy is directly relevant to the argument of this book, since an examination of philosophy's career from the procedural point of view will reveal the steps by which philosophy, past and present, has moved toward satisfying the conditions herein set forth, or turned its back on them and moved in the opposite direction. The procedural history of philosophy set forth in the following chapters will necessarily take the form of applying the conditions stipulated to the historic materials and judging the course of history in the light of them. If it conveys to the reader the general impression that I hope it does, then the historical applications of the argument should also serve to confirm its validity.

CHAPTER 14

The Misfortunes of Philosophy in Antiquity

WITH THE SPECULATIONS of the pre-Socratic philosophers, with the dialogues of Plato, and with
the treatises of Aristotle, philosophy got off to a
good start in three respects.

(1) The Greek philosophers managed to pose, and to
pose quite clearly, many of the fundamental questions of
philosophy. The fecundity of the Platonic dialogues lies in
this: they raise so many of the basic questions—questions
about the nature of things, about being and becoming,
about the one and the many, about matter and spirit, about
the divine, about knowledge and truth, about language,
about the senses and the intellect, about ideas, about
virtue and the virtues, about justice and happiness, about the
state and the individual. These questions, at the very beginning of philosophy's career, indicated its scope and character as a first-order discipline, both speculative and practical.

Neither the refinement of these questions in later periods
of thought nor the later addition of questions that open up
new lines of philosophical inquiry should be allowed to
diminish the magnificence of the Platonic achievement,

which richly deserves the tribute paid by Alfred North Whitehead when he said that the whole of European thought can be read as a series of footnotes to the dialogues of Plato.

(2) The Greek philosophers—here Plato to a lesser extent, and to a much greater extent Aristotle—also managed to lay down the lines of correct procedure in many of the respects that are essential to the proper conduct of the philosophical enterprise. The way in which Aristotle carefully considers the questions raised by his predecessors or contemporaries, and takes their opinions into account, is an amazingly clear first approximation to what is meant by the conduct of philosophy as a public, rather than a private, enterprise.

Consider these two statements by Aristotle, which eloquently express his sense of philosophy as a cooperative enterprise. The first is from the *Metaphysics*, Book II, Chapter 1:

> The investigation of the truth is in one way hard, in another easy. An indication of this is found in the fact that no one is able to attain the truth adequately, while, on the other hand, we do not collectively fail, but everyone says something true about the nature of things, and while individually we contribute little or nothing to the truth, by the union of all a considerable amount is amassed.

The second is from *On the Soul*, Book I, Chapter 2:

> It is necessary to call into council the views of our predecessors, in order that we may profit by whatever is sound in their thought and avoid their errors.

Pondering these statements, it is difficult not to attribute to Aristotle a conception of philosophical knowledge as testable *doxa*. If he regarded philosophical knowledge as *epistēmē,* he would hardly recommend, as he does in the above statements, a type of procedure that befits sifting opinions and testing them for their relative truth. If philosophical truths consisted of self-evident principles and rigorously demonstrated conclusions, one would not proceed in this way.[1]

In addition, Aristotle is an empirical philosopher in the proper sense of that term; namely, a philosopher who submits theories and conclusions—his own and those of others—to the empirical test, by appeal to the common experience of mankind. Moreover, he employs the empirical test as primary; and only secondarily resorts to the logical test and the "is-ought" test in judging the relative soundness of competing philosophical views that have not been falsified by common experience.

(3) The Greek philosophers—here both Plato and Aristotle, though in quite different ways—managed to detect and expose a large number of typical fallacies, paradoxes, and puzzles that result from linguistic or logical inadequacies, imprecisions, or confusions in the discourse that is generated by philosophical problems. What I am saying here is that Plato and Aristotle initiated philosophy, not only on the plane of first-order questions, both speculative and normative, but also on the plane of second-order questions about human thought and speech, especially when these are concerned with difficult first-order questions in philosophy. To the major contributions previously mentioned, they added a third—an amazingly rich beginning of what is now

[1] However, see what is said on this point below, pp. 247–249.

241

called "analytic and linguistic philosophy"—a contribution which, by the way, the more learned of contemporary analysts properly acknowledge.

These three contributions can be recognized and given their due meed of praise without any regard to the substantive truth or error in the philosophical positions taken by Plato and Aristotle on particular problems. When we take all three into account, it is hard to see how philosophy could have had a more auspicious beginning. Nevertheless, the circumstances under which philosophy was born and went through its first state of development were not wholly auspicious. I have three misfortunes in mind.

(1)

First and most important of all, there was in antiquity no clear line between philosophy, on the one hand, and either science or religion, on the other. The ancients did not clearly and explicitly separate questions that cannot be answered *without* investigation from questions that cannot possibly be answered *by* investigation. As a consequence of this, Aristotle treated, as if they were properly philosophical questions, questions that can be properly answered only by investigative science—questions about the nature and motions of the heavenly bodies, questions about the nature, number, and operation of the human senses, questions about the elementary forms of matter, questions about the species of living things, their order, relation, and origin.

Many of the treatises of Aristotle exhibit him as dealing with what we now know to be philosophical questions, on the one hand, and what we now recognize to be scientific questions, on the other; but he deals with them as if they were all philosophical questions. A great many of the errors with which Aristotle is charged are errors that he made in his effort to answer scientific questions without being aware that they require a different method from the one he employed in answering questions that are genuinely philosophical. This is not to say that he failed to resort to investigation in certain fields, especially in biology. *We* know that he was an investigative scientist as well as a reflective philosopher; but *he* did not know it. He did not separate—and, in his day, probably could not have separated—these two modes of inquiry in which he engaged, as we, looking back at him, can retrospectively separate his efforts at scientific inquiry from his lines of philosophical thought.

This, then, is one of the misfortunes of philosophy in antiquity: by virtue of the inchoate togetherness of science and philosophy, philosophy took upon itself a burden that it could not discharge—the burden of answering questions that did not properly belong in its domain. We can see the particular sciences—such as physics, astronomy, chemistry, physiology, zoology—in the womb of ancient philosophy. Philosophy is, historically, their mother; but they have not yet broken away from her and established themselves as branches of a separate and autonomous discipline, the discipline of investigative science. Until this happens—and it does not begin to happen until the seventeenth century— they constitute a burden and a distraction to philosophy; worse than that, the errors which philosophers make in unwittingly trying to deal with matters that properly belong to science insidiously affect their treatment of matters which are properly their own concern.

What I have just said about science and philosophy in

243

antiquity can also be said about science and religion; they were also inchoately confused. The ancients did not realize that certain questions were of a sort that exceeded the powers of all human inquiry to answer—questions that could not be answered either by investigation or by reflection on the common experience of mankind. Both Plato and Aristotle tried, as philosophers, to handle such questions—Plato in the *Timaeus*, in the *Phaedo*, and in the *Laws*, Aristotle in the eighth book of the *Physics*, the twelfth book of the *Metaphysics*, and the tenth book of the *Ethics*. Certain of the matters therein treated are matters beyond the reach of testable *doxa*. If men are ever to possess knowledge of such matters, it must come to them by way of divine revelation and supernatural faith. They cannot acquire it by the exercise of their natural faculties and by recourse to the evidences of experience and the light of unaided reason.[2]

The confusion of philosophy with religion in antiquity has still another unfortunate consequence. Religion, as we have seen, is more than a type of knowledge; it is a group of institutions, a set of ceremonial or ritualistic practices, and a code of observances and performances having a sacerdotal or sacramental character.[3] When these things are taken

[2] As we shall see in Chapter 15, the line separating the domain of philosophy from the domain of dogmatic theology and revealed religion was clearly drawn only toward the end of the Christian Middle Ages. Some of the speculations of Plato and Aristotle about theological matters lie athwart the line which separates natural theology (which is a part of philosophy) from dogmatic theology (which belongs to revealed religion).

[3] See above, Chapter 6. pp. 97–99. It was pointed out there that if religious beliefs are not derived from divine revelation and are not held by supernatural faith, they do not have the character of a special type of knowledge.

together, they constitute what we understand by "a way of life." When we speak of religion as a way of life, we think of it as enrolling the individual in a community of men who share certain beliefs, engage in certain ceremonials or rituals, and practice certain obligatory observances. A religious way of life can, of course, be lived anchoritically as well as communally, but it still involves more than beliefs; it involves observances and actions of a sacerdotal or sacramental character, observances and actions that have as their goal a spiritual transformation of some sort. Whatever the nature of that goal, one thing is clear: the goal of the religious way of life is not simply more knowledge of the type which the religious person already has.

This last point confirms what should be otherwise clear —namely, that such disciplines as scientific investigation and historical research, as we understand them today, are not, strictly speaking, ways of life in the sense in which religion is. Scientists and historians may belong to learned societies; they may have codes of professional behavior; they may engage in certain practices; but all these, taken together, have only one end in view, and that is the advancement of knowledge, knowledge of exactly the same type which they already possess to some extent.

What has just been said about science and history must be said with equal force about philosophy when we understand it as a comparable branch of knowledge and a comparable mode of inquiry. Whatever rules there are for the conduct of philosophy as an intellectual enterprise, and whatever code of professional behavior philosophers should subscribe to, these, as in the case of science and history, have only one aim—the advancement of knowledge, the same type of knowledge that philosophers already possess in some degree.

Philosophy is, therefore, no more a way of life than science or history.[4] The fact that normative philosophy consists of *ought*-statements, rules or prescriptions for the conduct of life and the management of society, does not alter the case one bit. These are not rules or prescriptions for philosophers or aspirants to follow in order to lead a philosophical way of life; they are rules or prescriptions for all men to follow in order to lead a good human life. Even if it is true, as Socrates, Plato, and Aristotle seemed to think, that the good life for man involves a certain amount of philosophizing, it does not follow that philosophy is a way of life.

I have tried to make this clear in order to call attention to the fact that, in the ancient world, philosophy was sometimes mistaken as a way of life. The most obvious example of this is the Pythagorean cult which combined ceremonies, rituals, and observances with a certain line of philosophical speculation about the primary reality of numbers or mathematical forms. Another example is to be found in the dialogues of Plato, wherein Socrates, with Plato's approval, preaches an almost Christian asceticism, not only as prerequisite to philosophizing itself, but also as a philosophical way of life aiming at not just knowledge, but at the elevation or transformation of the soul.[5] My point is, in short, that in a culture which enrolled the less sophisticated in the beliefs and practices of the popular Olympian religion

[4] A simple test can be applied. A truly religious man deplores his own moral failings and tries to rectify them in order to bring his character and conduct more into accord with the precepts and practices of his religion. But a scientist, a historical scholar, and a philosopher may each recognize that he has certain moral deficiencies without any sense of need to overcome them for the sake of serving better the objectives of scientific research, historical scholarship, or philosophical thought. This is one way of seeing that religion is a way of life and that science, history, and philosophy are not.

[5] See, for example, the *Phaedo*, 64–70.

or in those of less populous cults, such as the Orphic or Eleusinian mysteries, philosophy tended to set itself up in competition with religion as a way of life better suited to men of learning and sophistication.

(2)

Both Plato and Aristotle were bewitched by the conception of philosophy as *epistēmē*—as something much more certain and incorrigible than opinion because it is grounded in incontestable, self-evident axioms or first principles and proceeds therefrom to demonstrate its conclusions. They both drew a sharp line between knowledge and opinion (*nous* and *epistēmē*, on the one hand, and *doxa*, on the other), and they both placed mathematics and philosophy on the knowledge side of the line.[6] This misfortune, at the very beginning of philosophy's history, plagues it throughout its history, not only in antiquity, but also in the Middle Ages and in modern times.

It may be said in Plato's defense that there are passages in which he seems to say that only God has knowledge or wisdom (in the sense of *epistēmē*), and that man seldom, if ever, rises above the plane of opinion. We know that Plato regarded all physical or cosmological speculations as, at best, "likely stories"; and a careful reader of the dialogues is compelled to admit that they never present a single doctrine in the form it should have if its truths had the character of knowledge (*nous* and *epistēmē*) rather than that of debatable opinion (*doxa*).

It may also be said in defense of Aristotle that, though his

[6] See Plato, *Meno*, 97–99; *Republic*, Book VI, 509b–513d; and Aristotle, *Posterior Analytics*, Book I, Chapters 2–11, 19–22, 32–33, Book II, Chapter 19; also *Ethics*, Book VI, Chapters 3, 6, and 7.

exposition in the *Posterior Analytics* of the structure of knowledge (*nous* and *epistēmē*) as distinct from arguable opinion (*doxa*) as that is treated in the *Topics* suggests that mathematics and philosophy or science are knowledge rather than opinion, his own philosophical treatises at their very best do not exhibit this structure at all. The conclusions which Aristotle presents in his *Physics* and his *Metaphysics*, his *Ethics* and his *Politics*, are offered as defensible, reasonable, and tested opinions (*doxa*), not as conclusions rigorously demonstrated from self-evident principles. Nowhere in the treatises of Aristotle can we find a body of knowledge that conforms to the requirements set forth in the *Posterior Analytics*.[7]

Nevertheless, the subsequent history of philosophical thought was grievously influenced by the exaltation and idealization of knowledge (*nous* and *epistēmē*) as over against the best that can be achieved in the realm of opinion (*doxa*). Later philosophers, whether they agreed or disagreed with the substance of Platonic or Aristotelian teaching, adopted the ideal of *nous* and *epistēmē* as one to be aimed at in philosophical work. Some of them went much further and did what Plato and Aristotle refrained from doing; they expounded their own philosophical thought in a form and with a structure that made it look as if it conformed to the ideal.

If subsequent ages had paid more attention to the actual sifting of philosophical opinions that goes on in the dia-

[7] I am concerned here only with Aristotle's work as a first-order philosopher. His *Prior Analytics* (which is second-order work) contains an informal axiomatization of syllogistic. See William C. and Martha Kneale, *The Development of Logic*, Oxford, 1962, pp. 78–79; and I. M. Bochenski, *History of Formal Logic*, South Bend, 1959, p. 72 ff.

logues of Plato, and had recognized that the *Posterior Analytics* does not describe the structure or movement of philosophical thought as it occurs in all the major treatises of Aristotle, philosophy might have been saved many centuries of misdirection in the fruitless effort to conform itself to an inappropriate model.

(3)

The third misfortune that befell philosophy in antiquity is closely connected with the second. It is the baleful influence of mathematics, mainly in the form of geometry.

Geometry provided the ancients with what they took to be the model of a deductive system. When Plato and Aristotle want to exemplify what they mean by *epistēmē*, they usually offer the demonstration of geometrical theorems. Again it must be said in defense of Plato and Aristotle that they never made the mistake of Spinoza and other moderns, who actually try to expound a philosophical theory *in ordine geometrico*. Yet we cannot overlook the frequency with which they point to geometry as an actually developed body of knowledge which approximates their ideal better than any other and which, therefore, serves as a model to be imitated.

The bewitchment of philosophy by mathematics—not only by geometrical demonstration, but also by the analytical character of mathematical thought—is a much more serious illness of philosophy in modern times than it was in antiquity. Nevertheless, the first signs of that illness can be found in antiquity, not only in connection with the illusions about *epistēmē*, but also in the extensive use that Plato makes of geometrical figures and of numbers as exemplary forms.

CHAPTER 15

The Disorders of Philosophy in the Middle Ages

AFTER THE FIRST flowering of philosophy in Greece in the fifth and fourth centuries B.C., there is a long period of sterility and stagnation. This is not to say that the fifteen hundred years from the end of the fourth century B.C. to the eleventh century of the Christian era are totally devoid of substantive contributions to philosophical thought. The stoics, the epicureans, and the neo-platonists of the Hellenistic period add to the stock of philosophical theories and arguments, and so do some of the early Fathers of the Church, especially St. Augustine. However, looking at what happened in procedural terms, we find no development of the philosophical enterprise as such, no refinement of method, no clarification of purpose, no sharpening of boundary lines, no clearer definition of philosophical objectives.

From the perspective of this survey of philosophy's history—looking for self-understanding on the part of philosophy—the long period that follows Plato and Aristotle adds little or nothing. If anything, there is a loss of energy and clarity. Philosophy is done in a lower key and without the conscious effort at self-examination—the effort to philosophize about philosophy itself—that distinguishes the work of Plato and Aristotle.

Beginning in the middle or at the end of the eleventh century, and running to the end of the thirteenth or the middle of the fourteenth century, there is another brief period in which philosophy takes new steps forward, especially in the direction of ordering itself in relation to religion and theology. Unhappily, these gains also involve new disorders. Let us look first at the positive side of the picture.

(I)

We need not judge the validity of Christianity's claim to possess, in the Old and the New Testament, the revealed word of God in order to see how the theological effort to understand revealed truth—the dogmas of the Christian faith—not only stimulated philosophical thought, but also relieved it of a burden.

I shall refer to philosophical thought that is stimulated by the exigencies and intellectual demands of Christian faith as Christian philosophizing. The faithful refer, instead, to Christian philosophy and mean, by that term, philosophical thought carried on in the light of faith and elevated or rectified thereby. In order not to beg the question about the validity of this conception of a Christianized philosophy, inwardly transformed by the admixture of faith with reason, I shall use the phrase "Christian philosophizing" to call attention to the fact that something happened to philosophy when it became involved in the effort to construct a rational system of dogmatic theology in order to explain, so far as that is possible, the articles of Christian faith.

What happened was an extension of the scope of philosophical inquiry by the introduction of new questions— questions that did not occur to Plato and Aristotle, and probably could not have been formulated by them in the terms or with the precision to be found in Christian philosophizing. The most obvious example of this is the whole discussion of the freedom of the will, occasioned by the need to assess man's responsibility for sin, both original and acquired, and complicated by the doctrines of divine grace, foreknowledge, and predestination. Though St. Augustine and later mediaeval thinkers find much to draw upon in the writings of Plato and Aristotle with regard to other philosophical problems, they develop their elaborate doctrine of free will almost from scratch. Plato and Aristotle appear to take man's freedom of choice as an obvious fact of experience; they offer no analysis or defense of free will; it was not for them a problem, full of thorny issues, as it was for Christian philosophizing.[1]

Another example involves the contrast between the treatment of time and eternity and the approach to the problem of the world's having or not having a beginning, as these things are discussed in Plato's *Timaeus* or Aristotle's *Physics*, Book VIII, and as they are expounded in the theological doctrine of the world's creation by God. While the latter is strictly theological, ultimately based on the opening words of Genesis, it influences the philosophizing that is done within the framework or in the context of dogmatic theology. It leads Christian philosophizing to raise questions about the real distinction between essence and

[1] See my discussion of this subject in *The Idea of Freedom*, Volume I, New York, 1958, pp. 469–473, 499–505; Volume II, New York, 1961, Chapter 11, *passim*.

existence, about the difference between time and eternity, and about the causation of being or existence as compared with the causation of becoming, change, or motion. These questions do not appear in the corpus of Greek thought.

Still another example involves the refinement in later Christian philosophizing of the Aristotelian conceptions of substance and accident, essence and nature, matter and form, occasioned by the difficulties encountered in the theological employment of these conceptions to deal with the three great mysteries of the Christian faith—the mystery of the Trinity, the mystery of the Incarnation, and the mystery of the Eucharist.

As the examples given above indicate, dogmatic theology raised new questions for philosophy, and these new questions led to conceptual advances—the addition of new terms to the vocabulary of philosophical thought as well as the refinement of concepts that mediaeval thinkers inherited from the Greeks. These advances were accompanied by another benefit, of a more distinctly procedural character. In citing the misfortunes of philosophy in antiquity, I pointed out that, in the absence of any religious belief which claimed a divine origin for itself in the express revelation of God's word, Greek philosophers could not draw a sharp line between the domains of philosophy and religion. They could not separate questions that were answerable in the light of reason and experience from questions that were answerable only in the light of faith. In consequence, philosophy unwittingly assumed tasks it was not competent to discharge.

That burden persisted in the first phase of Christian philosophizing, during which men engaged in the fruitless effort to demonstrate the dogmas of the Christian faith as if they were philosophical conclusions. Instead of saying that the burden persisted, I should perhaps have said that it grew heavier and that the resulting distraction of philosophy from its own proper tasks became aggravated. In addition, the excesses of rationalism on the part of philosophers who tried to bite off religious matters that they could not chew generated a reaction on the part of theologians in the opposite direction. This resulted in the excess known as "fideism," which, instead of telling philosophers to mind their own business, told them that they really had no business of their own to mind—that philosophy had no autonomy as a mode of inquiry, that all important questions were answered by faith, and that all others represented idle curiosity and the vanity of worldly learning.

These opposite excesses, together with their cause—the inappropriate burden that philosophy was still carrying on its back—provoked the effort, in the second phase of Christian philosophizing, to define the spheres of faith and reason and to straighten out the tangled involvement of philosophy with religion. The work of Aquinas culminates this effort. Being both a philosopher and a dogmatic theologian, he carefully drew the line which both related philosophy to theology and also separated their domains.

On the one hand, Aquinas preserved the relative autonomy of philosophy *vis-à-vis* dogmatic theology. On the other hand, he restricted philosophy to its proper domain by limiting it to questions that are answerable by experience and reason and delimiting it from matters beyond the competence of experience and reason to treat. The achievement of Aquinas, in thus relieving philosophy of the burden—the undue tasks and the distractions—of involvement in religious matters, deserves to rank with the contributions made by Plato and Aristotle to the formation and constitution of the philosophical enterprise.[2]

Before I turn to the negative side of the picture, I must mention one other procedural gain that is made in the later Middle Ages. The universities of the thirteenth century, especially the faculties of Paris and of Oxford, instituted public disputations of both philosophical and theological questions. In the *Disputed Questions* and the *Quodlibetal Questions* of Aquinas, we have a one-sided record of debates in which he was himself involved, but that record nevertheless reveals a procedure in which philosophers confronted one another, joined issues, and entered into debate. Problems are taken up in piecemeal fashion; questions are attacked one by one; objections are raised and answered. We have here, then, in these mediaeval disputations, a good procedural model for the conduct of philosophy as a public enterprise. The spirit of this procedure persists in somewhat altered form as late as the seventeenth century, in the philosophical correspondence in which both Leibniz and Spinoza engaged with critics or adversaries, and in the seven sets of objections and replies which Descartes appended to his *Meditations on First Philosophy*.

(2)

Some of the things which plagued philosophy in antiquity continued to plague it in the Middle Ages. Though not

[2] In connection with the condition of philosophy in the Middle Ages, especially as concerns its relation to religion, it must be pointed out that no mediaeval philosopher ever made the mistake of turning philosophy into a way of life. Philosophers who were also religious Christians, Jews, or Muslims could not possibly make that mistake.

caused by philosophy's relation to theology, they were aggravated by it. I have two manifestations of this in mind.

One is the persistence of the illusion about *epistēmē*. This was aggravated by philosophy's involvement with dogmatic theology. The latter, rightly or wrongly, made claims to certitude and finality which had the effect of intensifying philosophy's quest for a kind of perfection in knowledge that it could never attain. If dogmas and dogmatism are proper anywhere, it is in theological doctrines that claim to have their foundation in the revealed word of God. While philosophy, strictly speaking, could not claim to have any dogmas or dogmatic foundations, it tried to rival theology with a certitude and finality of its own by giving its principles and conclusions the high status of knowledge in the form of *nous* and *epistēmē*.

The other is the persistence of philosophical efforts to solve, *without investigation*, problems that belong to investigative science. This, too, was aggravated by philosophy's involvement with dogmatic theology, the latter imbuing philosophy with an undue confidence in its powers. It should be noted here that the well-deserved respect accorded Aristotle by the later Middle Ages often turned into undue reverence and misplaced piety, in consequence of which many of the scientific errors committed by Aristotle acquired the status of unquestionable philosophical truths. When they were questioned by scientific investigators at the end of the Middle Ages, they were defended by specious philosophical reasoning, which brought philosophy itself into disrepute.

In addition to the two persistent disorders just mentioned, philosophy is plagued by a new trouble—one which had its origin in the Middle Ages, but which mainly worked its mischief at the beginning of modern thought, in the age of Descartes, Spinoza, and Leibniz. In the Middle Ages, theology was placed on the throne as queen of all disciplines, and philosophy stood at its side, its serving-maid or handmaiden. Though Aquinas tried to convert theology from an absolute monarch into a constitutional ruler and to transform philosophy from a menial into a free and loyal subject, he nevertheless left the two in a hierarchical relation of superior and inferior. And though Aquinas also tried to relieve philosophy of the questions that are answerable only by faith, he left to philosophy a number of theological questions, about God and the human soul, the answers to which he called "preambles to faith."

These questions were assigned to a branch of philosophy which came to be called "natural theology" to distinguish it from "dogmatic theology." Since Aristotle, in a book that he probably would have called "First Philosophy," but which his editors entitled "Metaphysics" (meaning the books which came after the books on physics), also treated such questions, particularly questions about an immaterial, immutable, and eternal being; and since Aristotle himself used the words "theology" and "first philosophy" interchangeably for the discipline that concerned itself with these questions, natural theology gradually became established as a part of metaphysics. This helps us to understand how it came about that, at the end of the Middle Ages, when such secular philosophers as Descartes, Leibniz, and Spinoza emancipated themselves from dogmatic theology, they still retained, in their role as metaphysicians, an absorbing predilection for theological problems, as witness Descartes' *Meditations*, Leibniz's *Theodicy* and *Discourse on Meta-*

physics, and Spinoza's *Ethics*.[3]

In the later Middle Ages, influenced by the conception of philosophy as a body of knowledge having the character of *epistēmē*, which philosophy's association with dogmatic theology intensified, philosophers, in dealing with the questions relegated to natural theology, tried to give their reasoning a demonstrative and rigorous appearance that it could not actually possess. Thinking that they succeeded, they often went further and took over into natural theology matters with which reason, apart from faith, was even less competent to deal. They undid the good work of Aquinas by extending the bounds of natural theology to include much more than the few simple preambles to faith that he had placed on the philosophical side of the line which he drew to divide its domain from that of dogmatic theology.

This overexpanded natural theology not only set much of subsequent scholastic philosophy off on a wild-goose chase; it also helped to get modern philosophy off to a bad start. I have in mind the work of the three great philosophers of the seventeenth century, to whom I have already referred: Descartes, Leibniz, and Spinoza. They were brought up and educated in a tradition of metaphysics and natural theology that was a heritage from the later Middle Ages and the decadent scholasticism of the fifteenth and sixteenth centuries. Though two of them were Christians, none was a Christian philosopher in the sense of accepting the guidance of faith through the subordination of philosophy to dogmatic theology. On the contrary, they represent the revolt

---

[3] When one examines the content, the language, and the style of argument of these works, there is good reason to say that they represent the end of the Middle Ages as well as the beginning of modern times.

of philosophy from theology which, in spite of Aquinas's efforts to prevent it, had provoked the rebellion of secular thinkers by the abuse of its authority and by tyrannical misrule. The misfortune was not that philosophy emancipated itself from dogmatic theology, but that, having declared its independence, it did not leave dogmatic matters to the theologians. Instead of doing that, it did almost the very opposite. It shook off the authority and the restraints of theology while taking on itself not only problems that lay on the borderline between philosophy and theology, but also problems that were central in the latter domain. To make matters worse, the illusion of *epistēmē* was now doubly aggravated—on the one hand, by rivalry with the dogmatic certitude claimed by theology; on the other hand, by emulation of the demonstrative rigor attributed to mathematics. Misled by it, Descartes, Leibniz, and Spinoza initiated modern thought with dogmatic systems of philosophy, constructed in a pretentiously rigorous manner, and dealing with scientific, theological, and genuinely philosophical matters as if they were all susceptible to the same kind of treatment.[4]

The reader must carefully examine Descartes' *Principles of Philosophy*, Spinoza's *Ethics*, and Leibniz's *Monadology* and *Discourse on Metaphysics* to see for himself the style and manner of philosophizing which I call "system build-

---

[4] "Philosophy," writes A. N. Whitehead, "has been haunted by the unfortunate notion that its method is dogmatically to indicate premises which are severally clear, distinct, and certain; and to erect upon these premises a deductive system of thought" (*Process and Reality*, New York, 1929, pp. 11-12). Whitehead goes on to say: "The combined influences of mathematics and religion, which have so greatly contributed to the rise of philosophy, have also had the unfortunate effect of yoking it with static dogmatism" (*ibid.*, p. 14).

ing." He will then, I hope, readily understand why I use that term in a wholly derogatory sense, especially if he bears in mind my central contention that philosophy, as a mode of inquiry, aims at knowledge in the form of testable *doxa*, not unquestionable *epistēmē*. He will realize that system building defeats or violates the procedures proper to philosophy, especially its being conducted as a public enterprise in which common questions are faced, issues are joined, and disputes can be adjudicated.

The philosophical system which is so private and special that it comes to be called Cartesian, or Spinozist, or Leibnizian assumes the character of a great painting or poem, an individual artistic achievement calling for rejection or acceptance as an inviolable whole. There are, of course, Platonic and Aristotelian, Augustinian and Thomistic, doctrines in philosophy, but there is no system of Platonic, Aristotelian, or Augustinian philosophy in any comparable sense of that term. There is some accuracy in speaking of a Thomistic system, but this should always be understood as referring to the system of theology which Aquinas presented in his *Summa Theologica*, not to a system of philosophical thought, for none can be found in or extracted from his writings.

We have here one clue to what is wrong with system building in philosophy, as well as an explanation of how it arose. Since dogmatic theology rests on the dogmas of religious faith, a system of dogmatic theology can be properly constructed by an orderly exposition and defense of these dogmas. It is the order and relation of the dogmas, with which sacred theology begins, that gives the dogmatic exposition of theology its systematic character. Clearly, I mean more here by "systematic" than thinking in an orderly and coherent way. I mean a monolithic structure, rising from a firm foundation in unchallengeable premises, such as dogmas are.

Even though they reacted against the *Summa Theologica* of Aquinas and other theological systems, the thinkers of the seventeenth century were greatly influenced by the model of system structure it offered. They were also influenced by another model of system structure—that of Euclid's *Elements*—which was as inappropriate as the theological model for philosophers to try to imitate. Yet this is precisely what Descartes, Spinoza, and Leibniz tried to do, each in his own way. Each laid down a few "unchallengeable" premises from which he thought he could erect, by the deductive elaboration of their consequences, the whole vast structure of his thought. Each proceeded in an ostensibly deductive manner to "demonstrate" conclusions which, for him, had the certitude and finality of *epistēmē*. Thus there came into being, for the first time in the history of philosophy, individual systems of thought, an event that caused drastic reactions and consequences in the centuries to follow.

CHAPTER 16

The Vicissitudes of Philosophy
in Modern Times

I N EACH of the two historical epochs that we have so far
surveyed—antiquity and the Middle Ages—we have
found both positive and negative features. I have
called the latter the "misfortunes" or "disorders" which
philosophy has suffered; and the former, the good starts or
gains which it has made in understanding its tasks and
acquiring sound procedures for accomplishing them.

In the ancient world, philosophy made two good starts:
an admirable, though not exhaustive, exploration of the
questions with which philosophy should be concerned; and
a first approximation to the method which philosophy
should employ, together with an approach to the way in
which the philosophical enterprise should be conducted. It
also experienced two misfortunes: unclarity with regard to
philosophy's limited domain, resulting in the combination of
competence in the handling of genuine philosophical problems with unwitting incompetence in the handling of
scientific and religious questions; and bewitchment by the
illusion of *epistēmē* as the model to which philosophical
knowledge should conform.

In the mediaeval world, there were also two procedural

262

advances: clarity with regard to the distinction between the domain of religion and dogmatic theology and the domain of natural knowledge, which at least made it *possible* for philosophy to rid itself of the burden of theological questions beyond its competence; and the public disputation of philosophical questions, in which philosophers attempted to face common problems, join issue, and engage in rational debate, thus providing a procedural model for the conduct of philosophy as a public enterprise. These gains were attended by two misfortunes that persisted from antiquity: the continuing bewitchment of philosophers by the illusion of *epistēmē*, now reinforced by the association of philosophy with dogmatic theology; and continuing unclarity with regard to the distinction between philosophy and science in the domain of natural knowledge, with the result that philosophers still carried a burden of alien problems beyond their competence to solve.

In addition, there was the disorder which arose from an undue expansion of the domain of natural theology. This had adverse effects on the thought of the seventeenth century. As we have seen, all the misfortunes and disorders of both the ancient and the mediaeval periods are compacted and intensified at the dawn of modern times with the introduction, for the first time, of the worst procedural misfortune—the construction of philosophical systems by Descartes, Leibniz, and Spinoza. This is the root cause of all the other miscarriages that have occurred in modern times —that series of vicissitudes which was initiated by the critical reaction to the great dogmatic systems of the seventeenth century.

Nevertheless, the modern period, like the ancient and the mediaeval, has its positive as well as its negative features—its turns for the better as well as its misfortunes and disorders. In telling the story of philosophy in modern times, I am going to reverse the order and postpone a consideration of philosophy's gains until I have described what I regard as the four major misfortunes or disorders which it has suffered since the seventeenth century.

(1)

The first of these misfortunes occurred in the context of an otherwise sound critical reaction to the dogmatism and pretentiousness of the philosophical systems of the seventeenth century. The critical movement in philosophy, from Locke to Kant, looked askance at these systems and challenged their unwarranted claims to be able to demonstrate and to know with certitude. It questioned as well their competence to deal with matters (both theological and scientific) beyond the proper scope of philosophical inquiry. In both of the respects just indicated, this critical reaction was sound, and it might have been wholly on the side of gain if it had insisted, positively, on the substitution of *doxa* for *epistēmē* as the standard or grade of knowledge at which philosophy should aim. That by itself would have dealt a death blow to system-building and provided an effective antitoxin against any future recurrence of the disease.

Unfortunately, the critical reaction to the systems of the seventeenth century took another course, and resulted in two serious disorders. To explain the first of these, it is necessary to recall that, in the ancient and mediaeval worlds, metaphysics was called *philosophia prima* or "first philosophy." Let me now extend the meaning of "first philosophy" to include all first-order inquiries, not only speculative questions about that which is and happens in the world but also normative questions about what ought to be done and sought. All such questions, as I pointed out earlier, take precedence over second-order questions of the sort concerned with how we can know the answers to first-order questions. A sound approach to the examination of knowledge should acknowledge the existence of some knowledge to be examined. *Knowing what can be known* is prior to *asking how we know what we know*.

Using the word "epistemology" for the theory of knowledge and especially for inquiries concerning the "origin, certainty, and extent" of our knowledge, I have two things to say about this part of the philosophical enterprise. First, it should be reflexive; that is, it should examine the knowledge that we *do* have; it should be a knowing about our knowing. Second, being reflexive, epistemology should be posterior to metaphysics, the philosophy of nature, ethics, political theory—these and all other branches of first-order philosophical knowledge; in other words, our knowing what can be known should take precedence over our knowing about our knowing.

Both of these procedural points were violated in the critical movement that began with Locke and ran to Kant. Epistemology became "first philosophy," taking precedence over all other branches of philosophical inquiry; and, with Kant, it became the basis for "prolegomena to any future metaphysic." Epistemology more and more tended to swallow up the whole philosophical enterprise. It is this retreat from the known world and our knowledge of it to the world of the knower and his efforts to know which prepared the way for the later total retreat of philosophy (in our own century) to the plane of second-order questions, relinquishing entirely any claim to have a respectable method for carrying on first-order inquiries.

The critical force of all this epistemologizing spent itself in showing that philosophy was not, and could not be, a respectable body of knowledge, which is true enough if the word knowledge is used in the sense of *epistēmē*, but far from being true if it is used in the sense of *doxa*. As a result, epistemology itself became misdirected. Instead of asking how we know what we *do* and *can* know (in the form of *doxa*), it asked how we *can* know what we *do not* and *cannot* know (in the form of *epistēmē*).

I think it is apt, and not too harsh, to call this first unfortunate result of the critical reaction to dogmatic systems "suicidal epistemologizing." Epistemology, fashioned by philosophers as a scalpel to cut away the cancer of dogmatism, was turned into a dagger and plunged into philosophy's vitals.

The second unfortunate result can, with equally good reason, be called "suicidal psychologizing." Like the first, it is also a retreat from reality. Where the first is a retreat from the reality of such knowledge as we actually do have, the second is a retreat from the reality of the world to be known. What I mean by "suicidal psychologizing" is sometimes less picturesquely described as "the way of ideas," fathered by Descartes, but given its most unfortunate effects by the so-called British empiricists—Locke, Berkeley, and Hume—who made the psychologizing of common experience the whole of philosophy and substituted that for the use of common experience as one of the principal tests of the soundness of philosophical theories or

conclusions about the experienced world. The psychologizing of common experience deserves to be called suicidal;
for, in effect, it cuts away the very ground on which the
philosopher stands.

To explain this briefly, I must depart from my purely
procedural approach and allow myself a brief digression on
a point of substance in the theory of ideas. This point is
indispensable to our understanding of the basic procedural
error in the psychologizing that is so rampant in modern
philosophy, especially in the British tradition.

In the ancient and mediaeval worlds, there was a clear
distinction between the first and second intentions of the
mind. This distinction applied to the contents of the
mind—its sensations, memories, and images as well as its
abstract ideas. I shall hereinafter call all such contents of the
mind "ideas," as modern philosophers are wont to do.

A first intention of the mind is an idea functioning as an
instrument of knowing. It is *that by which* we know
whatever the particular idea is an idea of. It is *that by which*
we have before us whatever object we are thinking of, and
trying to know or understand. It is *not* itself the object of
which we are thinking; it is *not* the object we are trying to
know or understand.

The mind—or, to be more precise here, the intellect or
power of understanding—is reflexive. It is able to consider
its own contents—its ideas, whether these are of sensitive or
of intellectual origin. As a consequence, an idea, in addition
to being *that by which* we have before us whatever objects
we are thinking about, may also be *that which* we can
reflexively think about. It then becomes the object of the
mind's second intentions, which are the ideas we employ to

think about our own ideas—that is, the first intentions of the mind.[1]

The distinction between first and second intentions has a parallel in the sphere of language. It is the grammatical distinction between our first and second impositions in the use of words. When we use a word as a name for some non-verbal object, we employ it as a first imposition. We thus impose "cat" as a name to signify members of the feline species. But we can also consider the word "cat" itself, and we can say of it that it is a noun. The word "noun" as applied to the word "cat" is a second imposition.

It should be noted here that when the word "cat" is said to be a noun, the word "cat" must still be functioning as a first imposition. Otherwise it would be a meaningless mark or sound, not a name which means something—namely, the class of non-verbal objects which, as a first imposition, it is used to name. The same holds true in the sphere of thought. When we, employing second intentions, think about our own ideas, we can do so only while they are still functioning as first intentions. In other words, they must still be *that by which* we know some object which is not itself an idea in order for them also to be *that which* we know reflexively as the object of our second intentions.

What Locke did was to make the simple but disastrous error of obliterating all first intentions by treating all ideas as if they were either primarily *objects* of the mind or *second intentions* employed by the mind to consider its own

[1] Only the intellect is reflexive; the senses are not. Hence, if man's cognitive powers were entirely sensitive and did not include intellect or understanding, there would be no distinction between first and second intentions of the mind; and it would be impossible for ideas of a purely sensitive origin to be objects of attention or consideration.

ideas. He laid down the basic principle of "the way of ideas"—which led to the suicidal psychologizing of experience—when he announced that ideas are the objects of our mind when we are having any conscious, wakeful, thoughtful experience.[2] Ideas ceased to be *that by which* we know the world about us, and became *that which* we know—almost all that we know.

I need not dwell here on the far-reaching consequences of this fundamental substantive error—the subjectivism and the solipsism that resulted from proceeding in this way, together with all the skeptical excesses that it led to, and the epistemological puzzles and paradoxes that confronted those who tried to hold on to the most obvious features of our experience after they had been psychologized into myths or illusions. Starting from Locke's fundamental error and carrying it to all its logical conclusions, later philosophers —first Berkeley and Hume, and then the phenomenalists and logical empiricists of the twentieth century—reached results that they or others had enough common sense to recognize as absurd; but though many have deplored the resulting puzzles and paradoxes, no one seems to have recognized that the only remedy for the effects thus produced lies in removing the cause, by correcting Locke's original error.

Locke's "way of ideas" still dominates British and American thought during the present century in the form of the "doctrine of sense-data." According to this doctrine, our own sense-data—or sense impressions—are the only things

---

[2] "I have used the word [idea]," Locke writes, "for whatsoever is meant by *phantasm, notion, species,* or whatever it is which the mind can be employed about in thinking" (*Essay Concerning Human Understanding,* Introduction, Section 8).

we know directly. Everything else is a "logical construction" out of them. The truth, I submit, is the other way
around. It is the sense-data which are the analytical constructions. They are items of experience only under very
special conditions; for the most part, they are special
experiences produced in psychological laboratories. They
are not elements of common experience.

Let me sum up this first major misfortune, which
philosophy suffered in modern times. The epistemologizing
and psychologizing tendencies that I have described are
twin aspects of one and the same misfortune—namely, that
the critical reaction to the dogmatic systems of the seventeenth century failed to recognize that it was tearing down
a straw man when it attacked the claims of philosophers
who had adopted the standards of *epistēmē* and when it
challenged their pretensions to be able to solve problems
beyond their competence (because they were still trans-
gressing the boundaries of their own limited domain to
forage in the domains of religion and of science). These two
tendencies worked to reinforce each other. It is not an
exaggeration to describe their combined effect as destructive of philosophy itself as well as of the straw man that was
being attacked.

(2)

I turn now to the second major disorder of philosophy in
modern times—the emulating of science and of mathematics. This begins in the seventeenth century. It can be
discerned in Francis Bacon and Thomas Hobbes, as well as
in Descartes, Spinoza, and Leibniz. Beginning then, it runs

through the following centuries right down to the present day.[3]

The philosophers of the seventeenth century, misled by their addiction to *epistēmē*, looked upon mathematics as the most perfect achievement of knowledge, and tried to "perfect" philosophy by mathematicizing it. This was done in different ways by Descartes, Spinoza, and Leibniz, but the effect upon philosophy was the same—the frustration of trying to achieve a precision of terminology and a rigor of demonstration that are appropriate in mathematics, because it deals exclusively with abstract entities, but inappropriate in philosophy as an attempt to answer first-order questions about that which is and happens in the world or about what ought to be done and sought.

The fact that science can be mathematicized to a certain extent—the achievements of mathematical physics in particular—accentuated the mistake on the part of those who failed to see that the application of mathematics to physics depends on the special data of measurement, which have no analogue in the non-investigative enterprise of philosophy.

This mistaken emulation of mathematics and the consequent effort to mathematicize philosophy reappear with unusual force in the twentieth century: in the "logical atomism" of Bertrand Russell, and in all the attempts to treat the language of mathematics as a model language, to be imitated in philosophical discourse. The effort to give philosophical terminology the simplicity of mathematical sym-

[3] "Philosophy," Whitehead remarks, "has been misled by the example of mathematics" (*Process and Reality*, New York, 1929, p. 12). "Under the influence of mathematics, deduction has been foisted onto philosophy as its standard method . . ." (*ibid.*, p. 16).

bolism and the univocity of mathematical terms, and the effort to give philosophical formulations the "analyticity" of mathematical statements, put philosophy into a strait-jacket from which it has but recently broken loose by a series of almost self-destructive convulsions.

Beginning also in the seventeenth century, philosophers began to be awed by the achievements of science and became more and more openly envious of certain features of science—the kind of progress which science makes, the kind of usefulness which it has, the kind of agreements and decisions which it can reach, and the kind of assent it wins from an ever widening public because its theories and conclusions can be tested empirically. Not recognizing that all these things can be achieved by philosophy in its own characteristic way, but only if it tries to achieve them in a manner appropriate to its own character as a non-investigative discipline, philosophers during the last three hundred years suffered and still suffer today from an unwarranted sense of inferiority to science.[4]

This sense of inferiority has, in turn, two further results. It has driven some philosophers to make all sorts of mistaken efforts to imitate science. It has led others, such as the positivists in our own century, to turn the whole domain of first-order inquiry over to science and to restrict philosophy to second-order questions, where it does not have to compete with science. Either result is unfortunate. Philosophy should neither ape science as a first-order discipline (in view of their basic difference in method), nor should it

[4] If there is any cause for envy of science on the part of philosophers, it should be based on the fact that, of the two, science has much the easier tasks and, therefore, can accomplish more, more quickly. See what is said on this point in Chapter 10, pp. 174–177.

be the second-order handmaiden of science conceived as the primary first-order discipline (in view of philosophy's rightful claim to its own first-order questions and, in addition, its superiority to science in rendering the world intelligible [5]).

(3)

The third major misfortune suffered by philosophy in modern times occurs by way of a reaction to a reaction. I am referring here to the counter-reactionary restoration of philosophical systems in post-Kantian thought—in Hegel, Schopenhauer, and Fichte on the Continent and in such British Hegelians as Bradley, Bosanquet, Caird, and Mc-Taggart and such American Hegelians as Josiah Royce.

The critical reaction to the philosophical systems of the seventeenth century reached its climax and, in a sense, spent itself in the Kantian critiques. Just as that critical reaction as a whole was justified by the dogmatic excesses of the seventeenth century, so the post-Kantian counter-reaction was justified by the excesses and mistakes of the critical movement from Locke to Kant—the epistemologizing and psychologizing tendencies described earlier. However, just as the dogmatic excesses of the seventeenth century could have been corrected without foisting these new misfortunes upon philosophy, so the psychologizing and epistemologiz-ing excesses of the critical movement could have been corrected without reinstating the very thing—the imposture of system building which the critical movement tried to get rid of.

That, unfortunately, is not the way things happened.

[5] On this last point, see Chapter 12, pp. 205–206.

Instead, what I shall call the "Hegelian misfortune" befell philosophy.[6] What we have here is the evil of system building carried to its furthest possible extreme—an extreme to which, it must in all fairness be said, Hegel's common-sense British followers did not go. The Hegelian system is much more dogmatic, much more rationalistic, and much more out of touch with common experience than the Cartesian, the Leibnizian, and the Spinozist systems of the seventeenth century. In addition, a fault intrinsic to the earlier systems becomes much more exacerbated in the Hegelian system. It offers those who come to it no alternatives except wholesale acceptance or rejection. It constitutes a world of its own, and has no commerce or conversation with anything outside itself. The conflict of systems of this sort (for example, that of Hegel and that of Schopenhauer) is totally beyond adjudication: each, like a sovereign state, acknowledges no superior jurisdiction and no impartial arbiter.

The plurification of systems in the nineteenth century, each a personal world view of great imaginative power and poetic scope, took philosophy further in the wrong direction than it had ever gone before—further away from the tendencies it had manifested in earlier epochs, tendencies to acquire the character of a cooperative venture and a public

[6] I think this appellation is justified by the fact that Hegel is the most powerful and most influential of the nineteenth-century system builders, as well as the focus of all the twentieth-century reactions to his type of philosophizing. See, for example, Karl Popper's now famous diatribe against Hegel, with the spirit of which I fully agree. See *The Open Society and Its Enemies,* Princeton, 1962, Chapter 12, especially pp. 252–273; and see also Section 17 of the Addendum which Popper added in 1961.

enterprise.[7] Last but not least, systems of the Hegelian type indulged in unrestrained cannibalism. They swallowed up both scientific and theological matters in an effort to deal in a thoroughly high-handed manner with all basic questions and to present, within the framework of the system, an all-embracing picture of the world. It should be added that these systems, particularly Hegel's own, became for some of their devotees a way of life and not merely a mode of thought or of inquiry. Hegel assumed the character of a secular prophet, announcing the coming of the kingdom of God in the earthly State, and arrogating to himself the gifts proper to a religious prophet and totally foreign to the talents of a philosopher.

(4)

The final misfortune of modern philosophy arose, as preceding ones did, by way of reaction to an existing state of affairs. This fourth and last disorder consists in three mistaken directions taken by twentieth century thought, having one central animus in common—namely, that they all spring from a deep revulsion to the Hegelian misfortune.

There is, first of all, the existentialist reaction to Hegel

[7] The fault of system building is, unfortunately, still in evidence in twentieth-century thought, especially in the work of certain phenomenologists and existentialists, and in the writings of those who still cherish the Hegelian ambition not only to encompass the whole universe in one's own system of thought, but also to engulf all other thinkers in it, by subsuming them in one's own categorical scheme. Even the work of Whitehead and Santayana shows some trace of system building, though they carefully avoid the dogmatism which usually attends the construction of a philosophical system.

and all forms of Hegelianism. I mention this first because, while it departs from Hegel in substance, it embodies two of the worst features of the Hegelian misfortune. The existentialist philosophers—Kierkegaard, Heidegger, Jaspers, Sartre, Merleau-Ponty, Marcel—all produce highly personal world views of their own, systems to be accepted or rejected as wholes, even if they are not rationalistically constructed, as Hegel's is. Like the Hegelian system, these, for the most part, offer themselves as pseudo-religions—that is, as philosophies to be adopted in the religious manner, by a kind of transcendental faith and as a way of life, never just as a set of arguable and testable opinions (which is all that philosophy, properly speaking, has to offer). The exceptions here, which really do prove the rule, are the Christian existentialists, who, leading religious lives as Christians, do not make the mistake of turning their philosophical creeds into pseudo-religions.

The other two reactions are alike in that they both move away from Hegel in procedure as well as in substance. Both, in despair about philosophy as first-order knowledge served up in the Hegelian manner, urge philosophy to retreat to the sanity and safety of an exclusively second-order discipline.

One of these reactions to Hegel is the retreat conducted by the positivists, Viennese, British, and American. When the members of the Vienna Circle referred to "metaphysics" and attacked it as an abomination which must be forever extirpated from the philosophical enterprise, they had Hegel, and only Hegel, in mind.

The other reaction is not to Hegel himself as much as to British Hegelianism. It is the retreat conducted by the British analysts and linguistic philosophers and their American followers.

The end result of both retreats is very much the same: philosophy is relegated to the plane of a second-order discipline. However, there is this difference between them: where the positivists were content to have philosophy serve as handmaiden to science in performing second-order functions of linguistic and logical clarification or commentary, the analysts and linguists took on other second-order tasks, among them the analysis of common-sense opinions as expressed in everyday speech, and the attempt to cure the puzzles and paradoxes which are of modern philosophy's own making, by virtue of its own epistemologizing and psychologizing tendencies, and especially the root substantive error in the "way of ideas" and the derivative "doctrine of sense-data."

At the expense of some repetition, I should like to offer three brief comments on these twentieth-century flights from the first order. (1) Like all the other reactions that we have surveyed, these are warranted by the disorders which provoked them, but they are misguided in the direction which they take. Instead of recommending a wholesale retreat to the second-order, they could have reacted to the excesses of Hegel and Hegelianism by trying to revive the mood and method of philosophy in an earlier day when, as in the ancient world, it dealt with first-order questions in an empirical and cooperative manner. (2) In different ways and to different degrees, both of these retreats to the second-order give free reign to the epistemologizing tendency which they inherit from the British empiricists of the eighteenth century. (3) What is perhaps even more unfortunate, therapeutic positivism and analysis try to cure philosophy of puzzles and paradoxes, all of which spring from "the way of ideas" and the consequent "doctrine of sense-data," while at the same time giving full sway to the psychologizing tendency that is the sole source of these puzzles and paradoxes.

(5)

So far I have had nothing good to say about the career of philosophy in modern times. However, just as, in treating the auspicious beginning which philosophy enjoyed in Greek antiquity, I also pointed out that its first epoch was not unattended by serious misfortunes, so now, in concluding an account of philosophy in modern times, I am going to point out two auspicious developments that relieve this long tale of disorders and misfortunes. More than that, they point, I believe, to the dawn of a new day.

The first of these is, perhaps, the more important of the two. It is the successive separation of all the positive sciences, both natural and social, from the parent stem of philosophy.

In the opening chapter of this book, I mentioned the suggestion sometimes advanced that philosophy is now bankrupt because it has now fully performed its historic function of giving birth to the particular positive sciences, from astronomy and physics to psychology and sociology.[8] I said there, and I say again, that if it were true that philosophy's only role in human culture is that of being the parent stem from which the particular sciences break off to lead lives of their own, then philosophy might very well be considered bankrupt—barren, dried up, finished. That, I

[8] See Chapter 1, pp. 4–5.

hope I have shown, is not true. While it is historically accurate to say that philosophy successively gave birth to the particular positive sciences, it is not philosophically correct to say that that is philosophy's sole or essential function; at least it is not correct to say that if the view of philosophy here being advanced is correct; for, on this view, philosophy is as much an autonomous first-order discipline as any of the sciences that have sprung from its womb. It seems to me quite conceivable that the investigative sciences might have developed first and that philosophy might have emerged later by staking out a separate domain through its appeal to common experience. However, it is understandable why things happened as they did: it was natural for investigation to have developed subsequently as a way of supplementing what was first known through common experience.

These considerations aside, the central fact of importance here is that it is only in modern times that the natural sciences have gradually separated themselves from what in the seventeenth century was still called "natural philosophy." Similarly, in the eighteenth and nineteenth centuries, the behavioral sciences gradually separated themselves from what was once called "moral philosophy." With these successive secessions, the scientific enterprise as a whole finally became clearly and plainly established as an autonomous branch of human knowledge and as a distinct mode of inquiry. At last, after twenty-five centuries, it becomes possible to draw a sharp line between the domains of science and philosophy; and philosophy is freed of the burden which, for lack of clarity on this point, it carried so long—the burden of treating, as philosophical, questions that belong to science and are outside philosophy's competence to treat.[9]

The second gain that has been made in modern times, almost as important as the first, is in one way only the restoration of an earlier condition beneficial to philosophy. However, it is not simply a return to an earlier condition, for it involves a much more consciously formulated policy and program for the conduct of philosophy as an intellectual enterprise.

What I have in mind here is the contribution to the development of philosophy that has been made in our own century by the British analysts and linguistic philosophers. As I pointed out in the first part of this book, their retreat to the plane of second-order questions has been accompanied by a way of doing philosophical work that is the very antithesis of personal system building, not only of the Hegelian type but of the Cartesian or Spinozist type as well.[10] It involves the tackling of philosophical problems, question by question; it involves cooperation among men working on the same problems; it involves the policing of their work by acknowledged standards or tests; it involves the adjudication of disputes and the settling of differences. Though this can be viewed as a return to the conception of philosophy as a cooperative enterprise, first enunciated by Aristotle, and also as a return to the spirit of the public disputations in the Middle Ages, it marks a great advance in

[9] This great cultural advance in the condition of philosophy is comparable to the advance made possible by the achievement of Aquinas in separating the domains of philosophy and dogmatic theology. It has taken many centuries for what Aquinas made possible to be realized; and it is not yet fully realized. Hence, more time may have to elapse before full advantage is taken of the sharp separation that is now possible between science and philosophy.

[10] See Chapter 3, pp. 62–63.

modern times. Since the interchanges in which Descartes, Leibniz, and Spinoza engaged with their critics or correspondents, it is really the only major effort in modern times to conduct philosophy as a public enterprise. If the spirit of this movement can be made to prevail at last against the central modern fault of system building, it may put philosophy back on the right track and keep it there.

In spite of all the regrettable vicissitudes through which philosophy has gone in modern times, the two gains that I have just described would, if sustained and combined with the advances in the right direction made in earlier epochs, promise philosophy a future much brighter than its past. It is to that hope which I turn in the next and last chapter of this book.

CHAPTER 17

Philosophy's Future

THERE IS LITTLE point in asking whether philosophy has a future, for that question hardly admits of a negative answer. The probability is great that in some sense there will always be philosophy—in the family of disciplines, in our education, in our culture.

Nor should we ask whether philosophy *will have* a future brighter than its past. That calls for a prediction which is too hazardous to make. Nothing that has been said in this book furnishes us with grounds for defending an optimistic prediction about philosophy's future. On the contrary, what we have seen of philosophy's past may lead us to think that the opposite prediction about its future is a more likely one.

This leaves the question to which I think an answer can be given with some confidence: *Can* philosophy have a future brighter than its past? The possibility of its having such a future can be argued for with some assurance. In the light of philosophy's past, as recounted in the preceding chapters, I can indicate why I think that philosophy *can have* a brighter future.

(1)

One way of doing this, of course, would be to remind the reader of the conditions laid down in this book as the requirements that philosophy must satisfy in order to deserve the respect now accorded history and science. To the extent that I have persuaded the reader that no intrinsic obstacles prevent philosophy from satisfying these conditions and realizing this possibility, the reader should also be persuaded that it is not unreasonable to be hopeful about philosophy's future.

I prefer, however, to take a slightly different course. I shall first list the misfortunes or disorders that philosophy has suffered in the past, which it should be possible to eliminate from its future. I shall then list the good starts, gains, or advances that philosophy has made, which it should be possible to preserve, consolidate, and enhance.

(i) *The negative features of philosophy's past which can be eliminated from its future:*

1. The illusion of *epistēmē*
2. Dogmatic systems and personal system building
3. Carrying a burden of problems beyond its competence, resulting from lack of sharp distinction of the domain of philosophy from the domain of science, on the one hand, and from the domain of religion and dogmatic theology, on the other
4. The emulation of science and mathematics in respects quite inappropriate to the conduct of the philosophical enterprise
5. Its assumption of quasi-religious status by offering itself as a way of life

6. The relinquishment of first-order inquiries to science, and the retreat to second-order questions exclusively

7. Suicidal epistemologizing with all its consequences

8. The psychologizing of experience, together with the destructive consequences of the "way of ideas" and the "doctrine of sense-data."

(ii) *The positive features of philosophy's past which can be preserved, consolidated, and enhanced:*

1. Plato's and Aristotle's exploration of first-order questions, both speculative and practical
   (This has been enhanced by the addition of questions posed and explored by philosophers in subsequent centuries.)

2. Aristotle's first approximation to philosophy's distinctive method, which involves common experience as a source and as a test of philosophical theories and conclusions
   (This, too, can be enhanced by our ability now to make a clearer distinction between special and common experience, in consequence of Point 3 below.)

3. The separation, in modern times, of the particular positive sciences from the parent stem of philosophy
   (As a result, science as an investigative mode of inquiry is at last quite distinct from philosophy as a non-investigative mode of inquiry, though both deal with first-order questions and deal with them empirically.)

4. The equally sharp separation, first seen as a possibility in the thirteenth century, of the domain of philosophy from the domain of religion or dogmatic theology
   (With the realization of that possibility, philosophy should be relieved of the burden of theological questions beyond its competence, just as the clear distinction between science and philosophy relieves

it of the burden of scientific questions beyond its competence.)

(2)

If the philosophical enterprise from now on took advantage of the four things just enumerated, that would give philosophy, for the first time in its history, a clearly defined domain of its own, a distinctive method of its own, and a sense of its own proper value, unembarrassed by comparisons with science, mathematics, or religion.

This is possible in the remainder of the twentieth century as never before. There are, in addition, hopeful indications that, in the years immediately ahead, philosophy can finally be exorcised of its bewitchment by the illusion of *epistēmē*, to be replaced by a sober respect for testable *doxa* as the only grade of organized knowledge that is achievable either in philosophy or science. I should like to add further, though this is less clear, that certain trends now current in analytic and linguistic philosophy indicate the possibility that philosophy may be cured of its suicidal epistemologizing and its suicidal psychologizing as well as cured of all the puzzles and paradoxes that were foisted on philosophy by these two tendencies.[1]

With this said, let me now mention two favorable aspects of philosophy's very recent past which I think can be not only preserved but also enhanced. I shall number these as following in sequence the four positive aspects of philosophy's past, enumerated in the preceding section.

---

[1] By itself, J. L. Austin's little book, *Sense and Sensibilia*, Oxford, 1963, goes a long way toward blowing up the "way of ideas" and the "doctrine of sense-data." But his critique does not stand alone. See above, Chapter 9, p. 156, fn. 9; p. 157, fn. 10.

5. *The conduct of philosophy as a public enterprise—as a collective, not an individual, pursuit.* The germ of this comes to us from two great moments in philosophy's distant past: first, from Aristotle's declaration of concern with the opinions of his predecessors and his sense that the pursuit of philosophical truth requires us to consider the opinions of all contributors to the discussion of philosophy's problems; and, second, from the mediaeval institution of the public debate of philosophical issues, together with the philosophical interchanges that occurred in the seventeenth century. The third significant moment belongs to the very recent past. The British analysts and linguistic philosophers, though restricting themselves to second-order questions, have conducted their inquiries and discussions in a fashion that totally eschews personal system building. They have also engaged in cooperative efforts to clarify and solve common problems.

6. *The establishment by the analytic and linguistic philosophers of a type of second-order work that aims at clarifying philosophical discourse.* If this were freed from the encumbrances of epistemologizing and psychologizing (which, as I pointed out above, at last seems possible); and if, in addition, this were accompanied by a return to first-order work in philosophy, the clarifying efforts might be directed fruitfully at the statement of first-order philosophical theories and conclusions, instead of being aimed exclusively at curing philosophy of the puzzles and paradoxes which are wholly the product of its own mistakes.

(3)

It is in connection with this sixth point that I am going to risk what looks like special pleading. I hope I may be pardoned for referring here to the program of the Institute for Philosophical Research and to the work that it has done in the last twelve years under my direction. The further prosecution of such work and the extension of it through similar undertakings in our universities would, in my judgment, advance the clarification of philosophical discourse about its own first-order theories or conclusions, and facilitate the conduct of philosophy as a public enterprise by helping philosophers to join issue and to debate disputed questions.

Briefly summarized, the work of the Institute involves (a) taking stock of the whole accumulation of philosophical opinions on a given subject, (b) treating all the relevant opinions *as if* they were contemporary efforts to solve a common problem, (c) clarifying that problem by *constructing* genuine issues about it, thus defining the agreements and disagreements that can be found in philosophical discourse about the subject in question, and (d) then *constructing*, from the recorded materials, some approximation to a rational debate of the issues, so far as that is possible.

The Institute refers to the method by which it carries out this program of second-order work in philosophy as "dialectical." The work of the dialectician thus conceived is an effort to clarify philosophical discourse itself. It makes no contribution to the substance of philosophical thought, nor does it impose upon philosophical thought any critical standards whereby the truth or falsity of philosophical theories is to be judged. Its only function, to borrow a word much in use by the analytic and linguistic philosophers, is therapeutic. However, where their therapeutic efforts are directed against the puzzles and paradoxes that arise from confusions and mistakes in the substance of philosophical thought, the dialectical effort attempts to remedy the deficiencies in philosophical thought which arise from a procedural rather than from a substantive failure on the part of philosophers—their failure to conduct philosophy as a public enterprise wherein they engage collectively and cooperatively in the pursuit of truth.

For a fuller statement of the objectives and methods of the dialectical projects undertaken by the Institute for Philosophical Research, the reader is referred to the General Introduction and Book I of my *The Idea of Freedom*.[2] The detailed results which emerge from the Institute's work cannot possibly be summarized briefly enough to be included here. The reader must be referred to the two volumes of *The Idea of Freedom* for the results obtained in the dialectical clarification of that idea, and to forthcoming volumes on the ideas of Love, Progress, Happiness, and Justice for the dialectical treatment of those ideas.[3]

However, I do think it useful, because of its striking relevance to the argument of this book to quote *in extenso* the evaluation of Western thought on the subject of freedom, which appears in the concluding pages of *The Idea of Freedom:*

. . . If the idea of rational debate is appropriate to the philosophical enterprise, as we think it is, then it would be hard to gainsay the fact that what has been accomplished in twenty-five centuries of Western thought about freedom is a very poor performance, indeed.

[2] New York, 1958. See especially pp. xvii–xxi, 4–6, 37–51, 57–68.
[3] Volume I of *The Idea of Freedom* was published in 1958; Volume II in 1961. The works on Love, Progress, Happiness, and Justice, now in the process of completion, are planned for publication in the immediate future.

Individual thinkers have presented us with elaborate theories and have told us, with clarity and cogency, the reasons for the conclusions they have reached about freedom. There has been no dearth of theoretical insights, no lack of originality or variety. Century after century, great intellectual resources have been lavished on the discussion of freedom. The signal contributions of individual genius have started new ways of thinking about the subject and enriched or deepened others. Yet the fact remains that the profound disagreements which have emerged from all this intellectual effort have not become well-disputed issues in a sustained and rationally conducted series of controversies about freedom.

What explanation can be given for this? For those who deny that philosophy is a rational process of inquiry competent to advance man's knowledge of the fundamental truths, no explanation is needed. In their view, the diversity of philosophical systems, like the diversity of great poetic works or other works of the imagination, should not be treated like conflicting hypotheses or formulations in the empirical sciences. It is an illusion to suppose that they can be so juxtaposed logically that they can be seen to disagree on this or that proposition wrenched from the systematic context in which it is embedded. That thinkers differ in their theories of freedom cannot be denied, but in all these differences of opinion there are no genuine disagreements which are capable of being resolved by any logical process. If, then, we should not look for real issues in the philosophical discussion of a subject like freedom, why should we be surprised to find that there is no debate?

Against this point of view, we offer these two volumes as overwhelming evidence to the contrary. We think that they establish beyond question the existence of genuine disagreements about freedom. Of these real issues, many are clearly disputable and some have in fact been disputed to a greater or less extent. Hence, we are justified in wondering why dispute has not taken place where it was possible and why, where it has taken place, it is less fully developed than it might have been. Some explanation is called for.

Perhaps the best explanation is that philosophers have been content to state their own theories of freedom, to present them as clearly as they could, to argue for their truth, and to deal with such objections as have occurred to them. This, it would appear, has been accepted as the philosophical task, and the best philosophers have discharged it admirably. But not even the best philosophers have thought it necessary to engage in controversy by disputing, point by point, the various issues on which they are opposed.

They have somehow assumed that their own position, in all its controversial bearings, would be understood and would ultimately be judged, *vis-à-vis* all competing theories, by some ideal board of review. Even if they had recognized the need to participate in full-scale debate, they might have been deterred by the difficulty of that undertaking. The time and effort required of them just to become acquainted with all the issues in which they were involved would have constituted too great a distraction from what they considered their primary or main task.

It was precisely for this reason that we proposed, in Book I, a division of labor in the philosophical enterprise as a whole. Creative philosophical thought is one kind of work; it is quite another task to review the whole discussion of a particular subject in order to discover the basic issues which have arisen and the extent to which they have been disputed. The latter task, we said, should be undertaken by the dialectician and specifically for the sake of helping the creative philosopher. But while the dialectician can provide the philosopher with a clarification of the agreements and disagreements that exist in a particular field of thought, and while he can show the extent to which issues have been disputed, either actually or implicitly, he cannot do more than this.

The dialectician cannot play successively the roles of opposed philosophers, jumping from one side of an issue to the other in order to create a debate where none has occurred, or to enrich one where it is poorly developed. In our judgment, no one but the philosopher himself can argue for his own point of view on a particular issue, or argue against the positions he rejects. He can be helped to do this by having the preparatory dialectical work done for him, so that he is as fully informed as possible about the state of the issue. He can then see clearly where he stands in opposition to others, who his opponents are, and what reasons have so far been given for any of the positions in conflict. With this information provided by the dialectician, it should then become a legitimate and feasible task for the philosopher to improve the state of the controversy by engaging in the dispute of issues to which he is a party by virtue of the theories he holds.

We are saying, in effect, that with this dialectical work on the idea of freedom completed, it is reasonable to expect the philosophers of subsequent generations to dispute the issues about this subject more explicitly and extensively than their predecessors have done. If the ideal of rational debate were, in consequence, more fully approximated in the various controversies about freedom, that might lead to the resolution of some age-old issues or at least enable us to see why they are irresolvable. In either case, an advance would have been made.

The dialectician's contribution to the pursuit of philosophical truth lies solely in the clarification of a field of thought for the sake of progress in that field. The progress itself must be made by the philosophers, not merely by the creative effort which adds new theories or insights but also by the equally creative effort to supply the arguments and counter-arguments that are called for by the issues which exist and either have not been disputed at all or have been inadequately debated.[4]

I am proposing that second-order work in philosophy, of the dialectical type represented by the Institute's efforts to clarify the state of philosophical opinion about Freedom, Love, Progress, Happiness, Justice, and the like, should be extended to cover the whole field of recorded philosophical thought, even though that is a project of gargantuan proportions. I am, further, proposing that dialectical work of this kind should be sustained as a continuing and essential

[4] Volume II, pp. 649–652.

part of the whole philosophical enterprise, subsidiary, as all second-order work should be, to the main philosophical effort on the plane of first-order questions.

If these things were done, the main effort could be much more effectively prosecuted in the future, for it would be carried on in the light of a much better understanding than philosophers now have of the contributions, both cumulative and conflicting, that have been made to the solution of their first-order problems. One might even hope that eventually there need be no division of labor between dialecticians working at their second-order tasks and philosophers trying to answer first-order questions. Philosophy might finally become the collective and cooperative pursuit that it should be—an enterprise in which the individual participants communicated effectively about their common problems, joined issue when their solutions were opposed, and engaged in rational debate for the sake of resolving their disagreements and reaching whatever measure of agreement is attainable in the field of debatable opinion.

(4)

I conclude with one last summary of the argument. *If* the negative features of philosophy's past are eliminated from its future, as they *can be;* and *if* the positive features that I have enumerated are preserved, consolidated, and enhanced, as they also *can be,* then it follows that philosophy *can have* a future brighter than its past.

The full realization of the possibility just indicated may require a future far beyond the present century. The twenty-five centuries of philosophy's Western past may be at the most the period of its infancy—its first uncertain steps

293

and stumblings. The gradual achievement of maturity in the philosophical enterprise may require a much longer span than the three hundred years—from the seventeenth century to the present—during which science appears to have outgrown its infancy and to have matured.

One reason for this delayed maturity may be that philosophical problems are more difficult than scientific problems, humanly speaking, if not intellectually. To conduct philosophical discussion fruitfully requires greater discipline of the passions than is needed to carry on scientific investigation in an efficient manner. It is easier to lift scientific research to the high plane of the perfect experiment than it is to lift philosophical discussion to the high plane of the ideal debate. In addition, the philosophical enterprise may be a much more complex form of intellectual life than the scientific endeavor is; and, like all higher organisms, therefore slower to mature.

Considering the biological origins of the rational animal, we should, perhaps, be filled with admiration that man took less than six thousand years after he emerged from the conditions of primitive life, to produce the civilization of the dialogue. Six thousand years is a short period in the span of human life on earth; and the twenty-five hundred years of the philosophical enterprise so far is shorter still. It should not tax our imaginations, therefore, to contemplate a much longer future in which the latent possibilities for philosophy's development are realized and philosophy gradually achieves intellectual maturity.